SCOOP

125 SPECIALTY ICE CREAMS
from the Nation's Best Creameries

By ELLEN BROWN

RUNNING PRESS
PHILADELPHIA · LONDON

Library of Congress Control Number: 2010925950

ISBN 978-0-7624-3798-6

Cover and interior design by Amanda Richmond
Edited by Kristen Green Wiewora
Typography: Archer, Brownstone, and Matrix

The publisher would like to offer warmest thanks to Bassetts of Philadelphia for generously providing their flavors for the book's photography. Additionally, the publisher would like to thank: Crate & Barrel, King of Prussia, PA; Scarlett Alley, Philadelphia, PA; Manor Home, Philadelphia, PA; Fante's, Philadelphia, PA; and Open House, Philadelphia, PA for loaning merchandise to be used in the photography.

Running Press Book Publishers
2300 Chestnut Street
Philadelphia, PA 19103-4371

Visit us on the web!
www.runningpresscooks.com

This book is dedicated to my wonderful family, especially my sister, Nancy Dubler, whose love and support sustain me like a luscious bowl of ice cream.

Table of Contents

Acknowledgments

While writing a book is a solitary task, it always takes a team to bring one to fruition.

My thanks go:

To all the wonderful people at ice cream shops around the country who were so generous with their time, as well as samples of their delicious flavors.

To Kristen Green Wiewora, editor extraordinaire at Running Press, for her guidance, patience, and help.

To Amanda Richmond of Running Press for her inspired art direction and design.

To Steve Legato for his fantastic photography, and his assistant, Andrea Monzo, for her help.

To Katrina Tekavec and her assistant, Sheila Magadentz, who accomplished the difficult task of food-styling ice cream with perfection and panache.

To Mariellen Melker for her creative foraging as prop stylist.

To Ed Claflin, my agent, for his constant support, encouragement, and great humor.

To many dear friends who tasted innumerable frozen treats, including Fox Wetle, Richard Besdine, Constance Brown, Kenn Speiser, Vicki Veh, Joe Chazan, Nick Brown, Bruce Tillinghast, Edye DeMaco, Tom Byrne, Karen Davidson, Beth and Ralph Kinder, and Kim Montour.

And to Tigger-Cat Brown and Patches-Kitten Brown, who kept me company from their perches in the office each day, and purred in anticipation every time another quart of cream was opened.

Preface

THE IDEA FOR THIS BOOK HAS been churning for more than forty years—since 1970, to be exact, when I moved to Cincinnati as a young reporter seeking scoops of the journalist genre. It was there, in a small ice cream shop in a tree-lined shopping district called Hyde Park Square, that the inner ice cream fanatic in me was awakened when I took my first bite of Graeter's chocolate chip ice cream. Studded with huge, irregular chunks of chocolate—you could pull them off your cone with your fingers if you cared to do so—this was not the chocolate chip that I had loved as a child in New York, when a stop at Howard Johnson's on the New York Thruway or the New Jersey Turnpike was a highlight of family vacations. While magical to me at the time, the "chips" in those childhood cones were tiny, akin to ground chocolate.

Graeter's put them to shame, and totally reset my personal standard for ice cream. Finding its equivalent in towns and cities around the nation became more than a hobby—it was a full-blown quest.

Fortunately, I got a job that facilitated this search. As the founding food editor of *USA Today* in the early 1980s I lived every foodie's dream—to go around the country and eat. While that job took me to some of the most exciting restaurants in the country, which were forging a style we now call New American Cuisine, it also took me to more down-to-earth events, such as pumpkin festivals and crawfish boils.

Along the way, I got the scoop on scoops. I discovered that artisanal ice cream wasn't unique to Graeter's; it was all across the country in big cities and small towns alike. And in the decades since, the number of small shops and dairies providing the highest-quality product has grown exponentially.

American ice cream production is both a big business and a small business. A few national companies control more than 40 percent of the market; these are the major brands, such as Häagen-Dazs, Ben & Jerry's, and Dreyer's, found in most supermarket freezer cases. These companies are to ice cream what Heineken is to beer; they represent an excellent product for the mass market.

A business like Moomers, a dairy in Traverse City, Michigan, which still bottles milk that must be shaken because it's not homogenized, is at the other end of the spectrum. It, along with individual shops like Sweet Republic in Scottsdale, Arizona, and Mitchell's in the Noe Valley section of San Francisco, is the microbrewery of ice creams, and it is the flavors and recipes from these kinds of ice cream shops and creameries that are featured in *Scoop*.

The twenty shops and dairies included generously shared samples of their signature ice creams and ingredient lists with me. From there, I adapted the recipes using ingredients and tools that are readily available to the home cook. (Most of us don't have easy access to pure fruit pastes or a commercial small-batch freezer.) In some cases, I've taken a few liberties with both foods and methods to achieve the closest copycat to the original.

Interspersed with the newly replicated recipes are a few ice creams that were inspired by ones I ate in restaurants and then replicated as additions to my own repertoire over the years. I take notes when I'm eating a dish so that I can try it at home—both savory dishes and desserts. I wanted you to enjoy these treats as well, and they're all from American restaurants.

Scoop is first and foremost a cookbook. The recipes are for sophisticated concepts and flavor combinations using only the best-quality ingredients. While most of the recipes qualify as super-premium ice creams (made with at least 16 percent milk fat), others are for leaner preparations, including fruit-only dairy-free sorbets, lowfat sherbets, and tangy frozen yogurts.

You'll find chapters in this book encompassing all-American favorites (think: top-selling vanilla, chocolate, and fruit flavors). But you'll also find recipes for new flavor combinations that I'm guessing will be vying for popularity with vanilla and chocolate in the decades to come.

This is by no means an exhaustive list of the wonderful artisanal dairies, creameries, and ice cream shops in this country. We have an abundance of riches when it comes to frozen treats, so if your personal favorite isn't included here, perhaps a sequel will list your special place or flavor.

I hope you enjoy making—not to mention eating!—all of these wonderful treats as much as I have. And learning a bit about the people behind them—that's the cherry on top. You'll have the whole scoop with *Scoop.*

Happy Churning!
Ellen Brown
Providence, Rhode Island

1 The Anatomy of Ice Cream

THE APPEAL OF ICE CREAM—AND its cousins sorbet, sherbet, and frozen yogurt—is pretty simple: It's cold and sweet. It's creamy and loaded with flavor. But the science underpinning why it's like that is actually rather complex.

This chapter provides you with an overview of what actually happens when you're making these frozen treats, and details each step of the process. You'll learn the role each ingredient plays in making ice cream, and you'll learn ways to change the formulation to suit your personal taste.

THE CHEMISTRY OF COLD

We're going to define ice creams, sherbets, and frozen yogurts as aerated frozen mixtures that contain dairy, sugar, and flavor. In the case of sorbet the dairy is removed from the formula, so sorbets will be discussed separately.

The key to the magic is the word *aerated*. If you simply put a dish of sweetened cream or a glass of orange juice in the freezer, you'll basically get flavored ice. Think of the fruit ices you buy on sticks to lick—that's what you get without aeration.

To produce ice cream's soft, creamy texture—something you can eat with a spoon—you need the stirring process that churns the chilled mix of ingredients, creating a microstructure of ice crystals, air bubbles, and small droplets of fat. These unlikely compatriots all live harmoniously, and gloriously, together in a thick solution created by the proteins in the dairy products you're using and the sugars you're adding to sweeten the confections.

In scientific terms, this formulation is known as a colloid, which means these very different materials that are usually separated stay together under certain conditions. We all know that water and fat don't mix; that's why vinaigrette dressings—called emulsions in the world of food chemistry—separate after a few minutes even when you have whisked them unmercifully.

In ice creams, you can have solids, liquids, and gasses all happily and deliciously mixed up. The condition that keeps them together is the low temperature. Ice molecules are held together in a pattern like a lattice trellis in the garden; it's solid but there are a lot of holes in it. As long as the temperature remains below 32°F (0°C), these molecules vibrate a bit but stay put. But if the temperature rises, they can escape from the lattice, which is why ice cream turns to liquid again when left on the kitchen table by that unruly child.

So the ice crystals are the solid part of ice cream, and it's the air bubbles formed by churning that create the soft texture. Ice cream is classified as a "foam," which means it contains air. Densely creamy super-premium ice creams like the ones featured in this book contain little air, while most supermarket brands beat lots of air in; in ice cream speak, it's referred to as "overrun." Just pick up a pint of specialty ice cream and compare it to a less expensive one. The super-premium pint can weigh up to fifty percent more. The air bubbles in ice cream foam are what fill the holes in the latticework trellis created by the ice crystals, and if they melt, the air bubbles escape and you have a dish of sweet and flavored liquid cream.

Ice cream is not the only genre of food that depends on a foam system to succeed. For breads and cakes to rise they need air bubbles, too; it's the yeast in bread dough that produces bubbles of carbon dioxide as it rises. The difference is that when these baked goods experience the heat of the oven the walls of these air bubbles harden, while in ice cream they dissipate. Then there are the properties of dairy products—sugars, salts, and proteins.

Both sugars and salts lower the freezing temperature of water. That's why you put salt on your driveway in the winter to keep ice from forming. There are natural calcium salts as well as lactose, a sugar, in milk. These salts and sugars play a bigger role in making ice cream than the granulated sugar or pinch of sodium chloride added to the base. The proteins in dairy products are also important because they trap some of the tiny air bubbles and keep the ice crystals from getting too big. Dairy products also contain natural emulsifiers that help keep the fat and liquid from separating.

There's one final category in the crucial components of ice cream, and that is fat. Cream has more of it and milk has less of it. That makes cream thicker, which means it coats the air bubbles more easily and keeps them from escaping. The higher fat content also keeps the ice crystals smaller. It's the fat that conveys that rich mouthfeel we know—and love—when eating ice cream.

FAMILIES OF ICE CREAM

There are basically two types of ice cream. One, sometimes referred to as French-style ice cream, starts with what is essentially a cooked custard base made with eggs. The others, which are made with only milk and/or cream, are known as Philadelphia-style or American-style mixtures. With rare exceptions, Italian *gelati* are American-style and made with more milk than cream. Even with less fat, gelato has a rich, creamy mouthfeel due to its density, because less air is beaten into the mixture.

When making an ice cream with eggs or egg yolks, it's the protein that helps to emulsify—there's that word again—the custard mixture. Let's go back to the oil and fat analogy for a minute: If you shake a salad dressing it will only stay together for a short period of time. But if you make a hollandaise sauce or mayonnaise it's the protein in the eggs that binds the sauce and holds it together.

So what performs the same function when no eggs are part of the mixture? One of these is the addition of more dairy solids, usually in the form of nonfat milk powder. These solids help to emulsify in a totally natural way. Small producers also include natural stabilizers such as guar gum and xanthan gum to create creaminess without eggs. They are both natural, gluten-free powders that create thickening and emulsification to give egg-free ice cream mixtures the same thickness as those made with eggs.

While both guar gum and xanthan gum are widely available in health food stores because they are used in gluten-free cooking, the role they play can also be filled with something you find for very little money on supermarket shelves and probably have in your pantry—cornstarch.

You use cornstarch to thicken gravies or Chinese stir-fries, and maybe you've made puddings with it, too. A few tablespoons added to a quart of liquid will make it thick. This viscosity creates the same creamy mouthfeel as when the custard is thickened with eggs, with fewer calories and far less cholesterol.

SHERBET-SAVVY

Sherbets are not synonymous with sorbets; the former contain some dairy products while the latter do not. Sherbets are usually made with milk rather than cream, which allows for the fruit flavors to be more pronounced, with little interruption from butterfat coating the taste buds.

Sherbet mixtures will not look homogenized and smooth the way ice cream bases do. They are likely to separate when chilled, but they will come together nicely once churned because the sugar content and dairy solids will control the size of the ice crystals and provide a creamy, smooth mouthfeel.

FLAVORED WATER WITH FLAIR

Sorbets and granitas are far easier to explain than ice cream, but there is some chemistry here, too. In both, what's crucial is the sugar concentration required to keep the ice crystals small. The real difference between the two is how they're processed. Sorbets are churned in the same fashion as ice creams and sherbets while granitas are only minimally stirred.

There are no granita recipes in this book; however, any of the sorbet recipes can be transformed into a granita. Freeze the base in a shallow pan in the freezer, stirring it about every fifteen minutes to keep it from separating and ensure that the flavor and sugar is evenly distributed. You can also do this by freezing the mixture in ice cube trays and unmolding the cubes when they are about fifty percent frozen. Stir again, and pack the "mush" back into the trays. The granita will then be done.

While the texture is the key difference

between a sorbet and a granita, you can create luscious sorbets by adding some stabilizers and thickeners to create a creamy and smooth texture without cream. One way to provide this viscosity is by including a small amount of unflavored gelatin. The gelatin is softened in water and then stirred into hot sugar syrup to dissolve it completely. While the resulting chilled mixture will hardly stand up on its own like a gelatin dessert, it will have enough body to form small ice crystals.

Through a combination of concentrating the sugar syrup and then adding cornstarch to it, sorbets can achieve the creaminess of ice cream. There are recipes utilizing this technique in many chapters of this book.

STEP BY STEP TO PERFECT PRODUCTS

You'll be thrilled to know there are very few techniques you need to learn to make ice cream, and they all can easily be mastered. As noted above, there are two basic bases—one made with eggs and one without. But one aspect common to both methods is the importance of heating the milk and cream to a temperature of about 175°F, which is essential to achieving a smooth texture. This temperature is just below the point of scalding; for a visual cue, it's when you see a film start to form on the surface of the milk.

Custard Creations

There is a very simple series of steps that goes into making the custard for an egg-enriched, or French-style, ice cream. The first is to heat your milk and cream along with any other flavorings or ingredients. If the recipe calls for dry ingredients such as nonfat dry milk powder or cocoa powder, they should be stirred into the milk and cream as it heats.

While the liquid is heating, it's time to whisk the egg yolks or eggs. I believe you get a better texture and flavor if the egg is beaten with some sugar, which is why I've divided the sugar in these recipes so that some dissolves in the hot liquid and the remainder is whisked along with the eggs. The mixture should have lightened in color from orange to pale yellow, and its texture should be as thick as a hollandaise sauce when you've finished whisking it.

Then comes the crucial step of "tempering" the eggs. This means that you beat about one-third of the heated milk into the beaten yolks. If you're pouring with one hand and stirring with the other, it's convenient to rest the mixing bowl on a damp kitchen towel to keep it from spinning. An alternative method is to put the pan of hot milk on a trivet on the counter near the mixing bowl and use a soup ladle to add the requisite amount of milk. Once you've added a third of the heated milk, pour the egg-and-milk mixture into the pan with the remaining hot milk.

For the next step, some split-second timing comes in. You want to keep the pan over medium heat so that it doesn't take all day to heat, and you want to keep stirring it constantly, reaching all over the bottom of the pan with the bowl of the spoon. At 160°F, the custard mixture will start to give off puffs of steam. When it reaches between 170°F and 175°F it will thicken and look like eggnog. To check, run your finger down the back of the wooden spoon; it's ready if it makes a clean line. That's what you're after; as soon as that happens remove the pan from the heat and keep stirring for thirty or forty seconds to start cooling it down. A common mistake is just to turn off the burner and leave the pan on it. The residual heat from the metal grate will keep cooking the custard.

I give a large range of time for this to happen because every cook defines medium heat in a slightly different way. It can take three minutes, or it might take you six minutes. But what's important is to keep stirring and not walk away.

You'll see that every custard recipe includes the caveat "do not allow it to boil." If it does, your eggs will scramble. It can begin to boil at about 185°F rather than 212°F, which is why I stress the need for a thermometer to simplify your cooking.

Concerning eggs and salmonella: You'll see that the only recipes in this book annotated with a note regarding eggs not fully cooked are a few meringues in Chapter 10. According to the U.S. Department of Agriculture as well as medical sources, eggs are fully cooked once they reach 165 F.

Other Thickening Strategies

Making a starch-thickened custard is the alternative to making an egg-based custard, and it's really almost impossible to mess it up, providing you watch the pot carefully so that the milk and cream don't boil over onto the stove. But, like making an egg mixture, there are a few key steps.

Cornstarch must first be dissolved in a cold liquid so it won't make lumps when it's blended into a hot liquid. And as long as you're blending the cornstarch, I added any nonfat dry milk powder to that step, too. So, rather than adding hot liquid to eggs you'll be adding the mixture of cold liquid and cornstarch powder to the almost simmering milk and cream. Once the cornstarch slurry is added, the liquid should simmer gently or until thickened.

Cooling It Down

These recipes employ a time-honored, effective technique for cooling liquids properly: time. The first step is to pour the ice cream custard into a container and press a sheet of plastic wrap directly onto the surface of the hot liquid. This prevents the dairy solids from coagulating and forming a thick "skin." When the custard reaches room temperature, you chill it to a temperature of between 38°F and 40°F by putting it on the top shelf of the refrigerator. And you preferably leave it overnight. This is called the "ripening" process in ice cream jargon.

But if you are in a hurry to get the machine going—it's 6 p.m. and you want to serve the ice cream for dessert at 8 p.m.—you can go through a rather laborious cooling process. But the goal is that it must not be any hotter than 40°F or the texture will not be smooth.

While the custard is heating, chill a metal mixing bowl in the freezer, and have a larger mixing bowl into which the chilled one will fit when the larger bowl is filled with ice. Then you're going to replicate the environment of an old-fashioned cranked ice cream maker by placing ice cubes and salt in the larger bowl, and stirring the custard in the smaller bowl set over the ice until it has chilled. You must be careful, however, as the ice melts, that you do not inadvertently get salty ice water into the custard.

EQUIPMENT LIST

You don't need a lot of special equipment to make great frozen desserts, and chances are you already have most of it. You'll need mixing bowls of different sizes, good knives, cutting boards, and whisks. In addition, here are some items that come in handy:

Rasp grater or Microplane: These look like a long, thin spatula but with grating holes on the blade. They are wonderful for grating citrus zests and fresh ginger.

Candy thermometer: I give a lot of visual clues as to when liquids are reaching the right temperature, but there's nothing like a candy thermometer clamped to the side of a pan to ensure success.

Instant-read thermometer: If you don't have one around to judge when meats are done you should buy it for that alone, but it's also useful for taking the temperature of custards.

Wooden spoons: The tried-and-true method of making egg custard detailed above really doesn't work with a plastic or metal spoon. You need a wooden spoon to see if the line stays cleanly drawn. And don't wash your wooden spoons in the dishwasher because they absorb the harsh detergent into the grain.

Strainers: Wire mesh strainers to solve lumpy-custard problems and remove coffee grounds or tea leaves from custards are essential.

Heavy-bottom saucepans: You'll notice that my recipes don't require the use of a double boiler. I think they take far too long to accomplish their goal of heating without boiling or scorching. But you do need a 1-quart and a 2-quart saucepan that has a thick metal bottom to evenly distribute the heat and not create "hot spots."

TYPES OF ICE CREAM MAKERS

You now have your mixture ready to go, and it's time to bring in the machines. There are basically three types of ice cream machines on the market, and the basic principle underlying them all is the same. The differences are how the machines are powered and how much they cost.

Ice cream machines haven't changed all that much since Nancy Johnson invented the first one in Philadelphia in the 1840s. The cold mixture is surrounded by a container that is colder than ice, and a dasher in the center is turned which scrapes the ice cream as it freezes from the sides of the tub and pushes it towards the center which beats in the air.

It may come as a shock—it did to me, at least—that old-fashioned hand-cranked ice cream makers that require lots of ice and salt are no less expensive than ones that are self-contained. If you think that using one is fun and it becomes a family event, then you have to think about the ratio of salt to ice. The salt lowers the temperature at which water freezes, making the brine so much colder than the custard that it makes ice cream. A good ratio to use is weight; use one part salt to eight parts ice. Other variations on this are one cup of rock salt to six pounds of crushed ice.

The other two types of ice cream makers don't require salt. They either have a drum that is frozen in the freezer and then makes the ice cream either by hand-cranking or electricity. The drums are made from metal and have two layers filled with a coolant. You freeze the drum in your freezer until it's solid and you can't hear liquid sloshing, and you pour the chilled custard into the drum. These machines work efficiently for even small batches, but you either have to make room in your freezer to give the drum a permanent home (you can fill it up with other food) or you have to plan at least a day ahead. Also, the drum will require a few hours to refreeze solid between churning batches.

While the mechanism is the same with spinning and churning, the top-of-the-line ice cream makers have their own built-in freezer. All you do is turn it on, and it does the rest. Many models even have automatic timers or sensors to turn off the motor once the mixture is properly churned.

So now you're ready to conquer the world of ice cream! You understand the how and why of this incomparable food, so go forth and churn away.

2 Vanilla with Verve

Even with the proliferation of flavors and fold-ins on the market, vanilla still captures the hearts of most Americans; it's the favorite of more than thirty percent of us.

But just like knowing the difference between the flavor of Kona and Colombian coffee beans or the varietal characteristics of Pinot Noir or Merlot wine grapes, vanilla connoisseurship is also on the rise. There are basically three different types of vanilla beans, and all are raised on plants that are part of the orchid family:

- *Bourbon vanilla* (sometimes called Bourbon-Madagascar vanilla) comes from islands in the Indian Ocean, and about seventy-five percent of the world's vanilla is in this category. The beans are long and thin, and they have a fruity sweetness.
- *Mexican vanilla* is the mother of the Bourbon vanilla beans; both are classified as vanilla planifolia. While the beans look very similar, Mexican vanilla has a spicier flavor and an almost woody note that balances the sweetness in the nose.
- *Tahitian vanilla beans,* botanically vanilla tahitiensis, are darker and thicker than the other two types, and the aroma is more floral and fruity and less spicy.

This chapter begins with a number of variations on basic vanilla and then moves on to recipes that are essentially vanilla ice cream but with some wonderful swirls and add-ins.

USING WHOLE BEANS

Vanilla beans should have a rich aroma when you buy them and they should be soft and a bit oily to the touch. Avoid beans that are brittle or have little scent.

To cut a bean open, place it on the counter and, holding one end in your hand, use a small, sharp paring knife to slice it open lengthwise. When you separate the halves, you'll see hundreds of tiny seeds. Scrape these out with the tip of your knife, but then add the pods to the liquids, too; you can strain them out later.

If your beans become dry, don't waste money and throw them out. They can be rehydrated in hot water and used as described above. Don't try to slice a dried-out bean, however, because your knife can slip.

VANILLA BEAN ICE CREAM

ADAPTED FROM LAPPERT'S,
RICHMOND, CA

*A bit of tanginess from buttermilk
powder balances the sweetness
of the custard and the
fragrance of the vanilla beans.*

MAKES ABOUT 1 QUART

1 1/2 cups heavy whipping cream
1 1/4 cups whole milk, divided
1/2 cup granulated sugar
1/4 cup light corn syrup
1/8 teaspoon kosher salt
2 vanilla beans
2 1/2 tablespoons cornstarch
2 tablespoons buttermilk powder
1/4 teaspoon pure vanilla extract

Buttermilk Powder

Made by Saco Foods, buttermilk powder is widely available in the baking aisle of many supermarkets. It's an easy way to achieve buttermilk flavor in both cooking and baking without ending up with half a quart of buttermilk going bad in the refrigerator.

Combine the cream, 1/2 cup milk, sugar, corn syrup, and salt in a saucepan. Split the vanilla beans in half lengthwise and scrape the seeds into the cream mixture. Add the pods to the pan.

Cook over medium heat, stirring frequently, until the mixture begins to steam; watch it carefully and make sure it does not come to a boil.

While the mixture heats, combine the remaining milk, cornstarch, buttermilk powder, and vanilla extract in a small bowl; stir until smooth and both of the powders have dissolved.

Add the cornstarch mixture to the pan, and bring to a boil over low heat, stirring constantly. Whisk the mixture until smooth, and simmer the mixture over very low heat, stirring constantly, for 2 minutes, or until thickened. Remove and discard the vanilla bean pods. If the mixture is lumpy, strain it through a sieve.

Transfer the hot liquid to a storage container, and press a sheet of plastic wrap directly onto the surface of the mixture to prevent a skin from forming. Refrigerate the mixture uncovered until it is completely chilled (below 40°F), or quick-cool it according to the method on page 14.

Freeze the mixture in an ice cream maker according to the manufacturer's instructions. Serve immediately for a soft ice cream, or transfer the mixture to an airtight storage container and freeze until hard. Allow the ice cream to sit at room temperature for 15 minutes before serving if frozen solid.

FRENCH VANILLA ICE CREAM

ADAPTED FROM McCONNELL'S,
SANTA BARBARA, CA

"French vanilla" doesn't refer to a particular bean, but rather to the high number of egg yolks in the custard that balance the aromatic and sweet vanilla with their richness. And that's what you'll find when making this ice cream.

MAKES ABOUT 1 QUART

$1^3/_4$ cups heavy whipping cream
$3/_4$ cup whole milk
$1/_2$ cup granulated sugar, divided
$1/_4$ cup nonfat dry milk powder
$1/_8$ teaspoon kosher salt
4 large egg yolks
2 teaspoons pure vanilla extract

Combine the cream, milk, $1/_4$ cup sugar, milk powder, and salt in a medium saucepan, and stir well to dissolve the milk powder. Bring the mixture just to a simmer over medium heat, stirring occasionally.

Beat the egg yolks, remaining $1/_4$ cup sugar, and vanilla extract in a mixing bowl with a whisk until thick and light yellow in color. Slowly beat about one third of the hot cream mixture into the eggs so they are gradually warmed up, and then return the contents of the mixing bowl to the saucepan. Place the pan over medium-low heat, and stir constantly, reaching all parts of the bottom of the pan, until the mixture reaches about 170°F on an instant-read thermometer; at this point it begins to emit steam, thicken slightly, and coat the back of a spoon. This takes 3 to 6 minutes. Do not allow the mixture to boil or the eggs will scramble. Strain the custard through a fine sieve, if desired.

Transfer the hot liquid to a storage container and press a sheet of plastic wrap directly onto the surface of the mixture to prevent a skin from forming. Refrigerate the mixture uncovered until it is completely chilled (below 40°F), or quick-cool it according to the method on page 14.

Freeze the mixture in an ice cream maker according to the manufacturer's instructions. Serve immediately for a soft ice cream, or transfer the mixture to an airtight storage container and freeze until hard. Allow the ice cream to sit at room temperature for 15 minutes before serving if frozen solid.

MEXICAN VANILLA GELATO

ADAPTED FROM GIOVANNA
GELATO, NEWTON, MA

*The aroma of spicy Mexican
vanilla really comes through in
this gelato, perhaps because it's
made with milk only and not with a
combination of milk and cream.*

MAKES ABOUT 1 QUART

3 cups whole milk, divided

$^1/_2$ cup granulated sugar

$^1/_4$ cup light corn syrup

2 tablespoons nonfat
dry milk powder

2 tablespoons cornstarch

Pinch of kosher salt

1 tablespoon pure Mexican
vanilla extract

Choosing Vanilla Extract

To meet the standards set by the
Food and Drug Administration, pure
vanilla extract must contain about 1
pound of vanilla beans per gallon;
that's why it's about twice as expensive as imitation extract. It's clearly
worth the money, considering how
little you use. Look at the labels carefully before you buy to make sure
you're getting pure extract.

Combine 2$^1/_2$ cups of the milk, sugar, and corn syrup in a
saucepan. Cook over medium heat, stirring frequently,
until the mixture begins to steam; watch it carefully and
make sure it does not come to a boil.

While the mixture heats, combine the remaining milk,
milk powder, cornstarch, salt, and vanilla extract in a
small bowl, and stir until smooth and both of the powders
have dissolved.

Add the cornstarch mixture to the pan and bring to a
boil over low heat, stirring constantly. Whisk the mixture
until smooth, and simmer the mixture over very low heat,
stirring constantly, for 2 minutes, or until thickened. If
the mixture is lumpy, strain it through a sieve.

Transfer the hot liquid to a storage container and
press a sheet of plastic wrap directly onto the surface of
the mixture to prevent a skin from forming. Refrigerate
the mixture uncovered until it is completely chilled
(below 40°F), or quick-cool it according to the method
on page 14.

Freeze the mixture in an ice cream maker according to
the manufacturer's instructions. Serve immediately for a
soft gelato, or transfer the mixture to an airtight storage
container and freeze until hard. Allow the gelato to sit at
room temperature for 15 minutes before serving if frozen
solid.

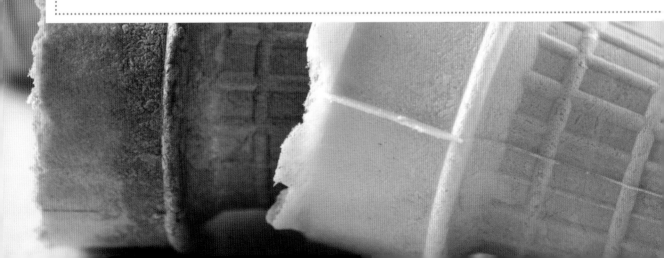

Giovanna Gelato, Newton, MA

EDUARDO KREINDEL WAS ACCUSTOMED TO DOING RENOVATIONS; THE BUENOS Aires native is a registered architect who had been designing buildings since 1980. But the result of his own basement renovation in 2008 wasn't the addition of a wide screen television or a wet bar. It was to transform the space into an ice cream factory with the addition of freezers, mixers, and sinks. Thus was the birth of Giovanna Gelato.

"In Argentina gelato, called *helado* in Spanish, was primarily made by Italian immigrants who would split their time between the two countries to take advantage of spring and summer in both hemispheres," he recalls. "When I moved to the United States I tried almost every brand of ice cream and never found a product that came even close, and this nostalgia led me to starting my business."

After studying with gelato masters in both Argentina and the United States and taking a production course in his native country, Giovanna was launched.

Kreindel produces very small batches, and now distributes his gelato and sorbets to supermarkets in both Massachusetts and Rhode Island as well as at farmers' markets near his suburban Boston home. Each container is hand-packed, and his flavor range grows as customers request additions.

While such flavors as Chocolate Hazelnut Gelato (page 52), called gianduja in Italian, and Mexican Vanilla Gelato (opposite) are traditional, Kreindel also gets creative with such products as Lemon Thyme Sorbet (page 184) and Lavender Gelato (page 185) as examples.

VANILLA GOAT MILK ICE CREAM

ADAPTED FROM LÁLOO'S,
PETALUMA, CA

The egg-thickened richness of this fragrant, award-winning ice cream, called Vanilla Snowflake by LaLoo's, is balanced by the slight sharpness of the goat cheese included in the creamy base.

MAKES ABOUT 1 QUART

3 cups goat milk

2 ounces fresh goat cheese, crumbled

$^1/_2$ cup granulated sugar, divided

2 tablespoons nonfat
dry milk powder

$^1/_8$ teaspoon kosher salt

4 large egg yolks

$1^1/_2$ teaspoons pure vanilla extract,
preferably from Madagascar

Combine the goat milk, goat cheese, $^1/_4$ cup sugar, milk powder, and salt in a medium saucepan, and stir well to dissolve the milk powder. Bring the mixture just to a simmer over medium heat, stirring occasionally.

Beat the egg yolks, remaining $^1/_4$ cup sugar, and vanilla extract in a mixing bowl with a whisk until thick and light yellow in color. Slowly beat about one third of the hot goat milk mixture into the eggs so they are gradually warmed up, and then return the contents of the mixing bowl to the saucepan. Place the pan over medium-low heat and stir constantly, reaching all parts of the bottom of the pan, until the mixture reaches about 170°F on an instant-read thermometer; at this point it begins to emit steam, thickens slightly, and coats the back of a spoon. This takes 3 to 6 minutes. Do not allow the mixture to boil or the eggs will scramble. Strain the custard through a fine sieve, if desired.

Transfer the hot liquid to a storage container, and press a sheet of plastic wrap directly onto the surface of the mixture to prevent a skin from forming. Refrigerate the mixture uncovered until it is completely chilled (below 40°F), or quick-cool it according to the method on page 14.

Freeze the mixture in an ice cream maker according to the manufacturer's instructions. Serve immediately for a soft ice cream, or transfer the mixture to an airtight storage container and freeze until hard. Allow the ice cream to sit at room temperature for 15 minutes before serving if frozen solid.

VANILLA ICE CREAM with GRAPE-NUTS

ADAPTED FROM THE DAILY
SCOOP, BARRINGTON, RI

Adding Grape-Nuts to vanilla ice cream is a New England tradition. The cereal adds textural interest as well as a slightly nutty flavor.

MAKES ABOUT 1 QUART

2 cups heavy whipping
cream, divided

$^3/_4$ cup whole milk

$^1/_2$ cup granulated sugar

$^1/_4$ cup light corn syrup

2 tablespoons nonfat
dry milk powder

2 tablespoons cornstarch

Pinch of kosher salt

$1^1/_4$ teaspoons pure vanilla extract

$^1/_2$ cup Grape-Nuts® cereal or
your favorite granola cereal

Keeping Fold–Ins Crunchy

Just as cereal gets soggy in milk, crunchy add-ins like cereal and cookie bits get soggy in ice cream. Never fold in something crunchy before the ice cream has churned, and if you're not going to be eating the ice cream within a few days, sprinkle the extras on top rather than incorporating them.

Combine 1½ cups of the cream, milk, sugar, and corn syrup in a saucepan. Cook over medium heat, stirring frequently, until the mixture begins to steam; watch it carefully and make sure it does not come to a boil.

While the mixture heats, combine the remaining cream, milk powder, cornstarch, salt, and vanilla extract in a small bowl, and stir until smooth and both of the powders have dissolved.

Add the cornstarch mixture to the pan, and bring to a boil over low heat, stirring constantly. Whisk the mixture until smooth, and simmer the mixture over very low heat, stirring constantly, for 2 minutes, or until thickened. If the mixture is lumpy, strain it through a sieve.

Transfer the hot liquid to a storage container, and press a sheet of plastic wrap directly onto the surface of the mixture to prevent a skin from forming. Refrigerate the mixture uncovered until it is completely chilled (below 40°F), or quick-cool it according to the method on page 14.

Freeze the mixture in an ice cream maker according to the manufacturer's instructions. Transfer the ice cream to a chilled mixing bowl, and fold in the cereal.

Serve immediately for a soft ice cream, or transfer the mixture to an airtight storage container and freeze until hard. Allow the ice cream to sit at room temperature for 15 minutes before serving if frozen solid.

MALTED VANILLA ICE CREAM

ADAPTED FROM HERRELL'S, NORTHAMPTON, MA

With the decline of soda fountains as part of American life, the famed malted, a milkshake made with malted powder, has also begun to disappear. The malted powder adds a great richness to this ice cream, which inherited the beloved flavor of the soda fountain.

MAKES ABOUT 1 QUART

2 teaspoons unflavored gelatin or powdered agar

2 cups whole milk, divided

$^1/_2$ cup malted milk powder

$1^1/_2$ cups heavy whipping cream

$^2/_3$ cup granulated sugar

$1^1/_2$ teaspoons pure vanilla extract

Pinch of kosher salt

Sprinkle the gelatin over $^1/_2$ cup cold water to soften.

Combine 1 cup of the milk and the malted milk powder in a blender, and blend until the powder dissolves. Pour the mixture into a saucepan.

Add the remaining milk, cream, sugar, vanilla extract, and salt to the saucepan, and cook over medium heat, stirring frequently, until the mixture begins to steam; watch it carefully and make sure it does not come to a boil. Add the gelatin, and stir to dissolve.

Transfer the hot liquid to a storage container, and press a sheet of plastic wrap directly onto the surface of the mixture to prevent a skin from forming. Refrigerate the mixture uncovered until it is completely chilled (below 40°F), or quick-cool it according to the method on page 14.

Freeze the mixture in an ice cream maker according to the manufacturer's instructions. Serve immediately for a soft ice cream, or transfer the mixture to an airtight storage container and freeze until hard. Allow the ice cream to sit at room temperature for 15 minutes before serving if frozen solid.

Herrell's, Northampton, MA

STEVE HERRELL SHOULD REALLY BE CONSIDERED THE GODFATHER OF ARTISANAL ice cream. His first shop, Steve's, in Somerville (near Boston), opened in 1973 and was the first company to grind up candies like Heath Bars and Reese's Cups to churn into ice cream. His term for this was "smoosh-ins®." Clearly, he was an ice cream visionary.

Herrell was born in Washington, D.C., in 1944, where he used to frequent ice cream shops on a regular basis and make hand-cranked ice cream in his backyard. After graduating from the University of Maryland he moved to Boston. Not long after that, he abandoned teaching high school English to enter the ice cream business.

Herrell sold Steve's in 1977, but his love affair with super-premium ice cream made with less air and more cream was not over. He moved to western Massachusetts and opened Herrell's in 1980. There are now four Herrell's locations in the state and his ice cream is even on the menu at Symphony Hall in Boston.

If Herrell's has one signature among its myriad flavors, it's Malted Vanilla, which tastes just like the vanilla malts he remembers from his youth.

VANILLA CHEESECAKE ICE CREAM

ADAPTED FROM THE LARK CREEK INN, LARKSPUR, CA

Here's a recipe I've been making for years after enjoying it at dinner. It really is reminiscent of the richest cheesecake you've ever eaten. Top it with Strawberry Sauce (page 216) or Caramel Sauce (page 213) for an even better treat.

MAKES ABOUT 1 QUART

1 (8-ounce) package cream cheese, at room temperature

$^3/_4$ cup whole milk

1 cup heavy whipping cream

$^3/_4$ cup sour cream

$^1/_2$ cup granulated sugar, divided

$1^1/_2$ teaspoons pure vanilla extract

$^1/_4$ teaspoon kosher salt

3 large egg yolks

Vanilla Plants

The actual vanilla orchid is native to Mexico where it was first cultivated by the Totonaco people in the area around what is now Veracruz. By the early eighteenth century vanilla orchid plants were introduced into the gardens and conservatories of British nobility.

Combine the cream cheese and milk in a food processor fitted with the steel blade or in a blender, and process until smooth. Transfer the mixture to a saucepan.

Add the cream, $^1/_4$ cup sugar, vanilla extract, and salt to the pan, and stir well. Bring the mixture just to a simmer, stirring occasionally.

Beat the eggs yolks and remaining $^1/_4$ cup sugar in a mixing bowl with a whisk until thick and light yellow in color. Slowly beat about one third of the hot cream mixture into the eggs so they are gradually warmed up, and then return the contents of the mixing bowl to the saucepan. Place the pan over medium-low heat and stir constantly, reaching all parts of the bottom of the pan, until the mixture reaches about 170°F on an instant-read thermometer; at this point it begins to emit steam, thicken slightly, and coat the back of a spoon. This takes 3 to 6 minutes. Do not allow the mixture to boil or the eggs will scramble. Strain the custard through a fine sieve, if desired. Whisk in the sour cream.

Transfer the hot liquid to a storage container, and press a sheet of plastic wrap directly onto the surface of the mixture to prevent a skin from forming. Refrigerate the mixture uncovered until it is completely chilled (below 40°F), or quick-cool it according to the method on page 14.

Freeze the mixture in an ice cream maker according to the manufacturer's instructions. Serve immediately for a soft ice cream, or transfer the mixture to an airtight storage container and freeze until hard. Allow the ice cream to sit at room temperature for 15 minutes before serving if frozen solid.

Variation: Use only $^1/_2$ teaspoon vanilla extract and add 2 teaspoons grated lemon or orange zest to the custard.

VANILLA ICE CREAM with SALTED BUTTER CARAMEL SWIRL

ADAPTED FROM SWEET
REPUBLIC, SCOTTSDALE, AZ

Adding a bit of salt to sweet caramel is becoming popular with chefs, and you'll find the slightly salty note a wonderful addition to this ice cream. It doesn't need embellishment, but some Hot Fudge Sauce (page 210) wouldn't be a bad thing.

MAKES ABOUT 1 QUART

Ice Cream
2 cups whole milk
1 cup heavy whipping cream
$1/2$ cup granulated sugar, divided
$1/4$ cup nonfat dry
milk powder
$1/8$ teaspoon kosher salt
3 large egg yolks
$1^1/2$ teaspoons pure vanilla extract

Caramel Swirl
$1/2$ cup granulated sugar
2 tablespoons unsalted butter
$1/4$ cup heavy whipping cream
1 teaspoon kosher salt
$1/4$ teaspoon pure vanilla extract

For the ice cream: Combine the milk, cream, $1/4$ cup sugar, milk powder, and salt in a medium saucepan, and stir well to dissolve the milk powder. Bring the mixture just to a simmer, stirring occasionally.

Beat the eggs yolks, remaining $1/4$ cup sugar, and vanilla in a mixing bowl with a whisk until thick and light yellow in color. Slowly beat about one third of the hot cream mixture into the eggs so they are gradually warmed up, and then return the contents of the mixing bowl to the saucepan. Place the pan over medium-low heat, and stir constantly, reaching all parts of the bottom of the pan, until the mixture reaches about 170°F on an instant-read thermometer; at this point it begins to emit steam, thicken slightly, and coat the back of a spoon. This takes 3 to 6 minutes. Do not allow the mixture to boil or the eggs will scramble. Strain the custard through a fine sieve, if desired.

Transfer the hot liquid to a storage container, and press a sheet of plastic wrap directly into the surface of the mixture to prevent a skin from forming. Refrigerate the mixture uncovered until it is completely chilled (below 40°F), or quick-cool it according to the method on page 14.

While the custard chills, make the swirl: Combine the sugar and $1/4$ cup water in a small saucepan, and bring to a boil over medium-high heat. Swirl the pan by the handle but do not stir. Raise the heat to high, and allow syrup to cook until it reaches a walnut brown color, swirling the pot by the handle frequently, about 3 to 4 minutes.

Remove the pan from the heat, and stir in the butter and cream using a long-handled spoon; the mixture will bubble furiously at first. Return the pan to low heat and stir until lumps melt and sauce is smooth. Stir in the salt and vanilla, and transfer the caramel to a small container. Allow it to cool to room temperature.

(continued)

Meanwhile, freeze the chilled ice cream custard in an ice cream maker according to the manufacturer's instructions.

After the ice cream has churned, add the swirl: Transfer one-sixth of the soft ice cream from the ice cream freezer to an airtight container. Top with a few spoonfuls of the caramel swirl, and then repeat with layers of ice cream and caramel until all the ice cream and caramel are layered.

Serve immediately for a soft ice cream, or freeze until hard. Allow the ice cream to sit at room temperature for 15 minutes before serving if frozen solid. When serving the ice cream, dig into the container vertically so each serving contains some of the swirl.

Variation: When layering the ice cream with the swirl, add ¹/₂ to ²/₃ cup chopped pecans or almonds, toasted in a 350°F oven for 5 to 7 minutes.

Sweet Republic, Scottsdale, AZ

LIKE MANY YOUNG AMERICANS WORKING ON WALL STREET, HELEN YUNG and Jan Wichayanuparp reassessed their personal and professional goals after the attacks on September 11. Seven years later, Sweet Republic, their vividly-colored ice cream shop in suburban Scottsdale, Arizona, was a reality.

"We love how ice cream is such a perfect blank canvas for expressing our taste and experiences from traveling and having lived all over the world," says Yung, a native of Hong Kong who graduated from Le Cordon Bleu in Sydney. She is the ice cream chef, while her partner, who grew up in Los Angeles but spent summers with family in Thailand, runs the business operation. Yung says that "contrast with balance is what makes food delicious" and this is reflected in the sweet-and-savory combinations, such as Roquefort blue cheese with Medjool dates. Her best-selling flavor is Salted Butter Caramel, which contrasts a salty caramel swirl with vanilla ice cream. While the shop only opened in 2008, Sweet Republic already has a devoted local following and has gained national attention in such publications as *Bon Appetit*.

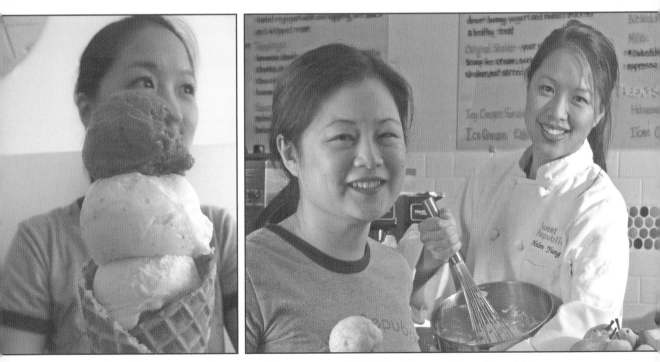

left: Helen Yung; *right*: Jan Wichayanuparp with Helen Yung at Sweet Republic

VANILLA ICE CREAM with BUTTERSCOTCH SWIRL

ADAPTED FROM BASSETTS,
PHILADELPHIA, PA

This is way more than a butterscotch swirl; it really gets equal billing with the ice cream. No sauce needed for this dish because it's built right in.

MAKES ABOUT 1 QUART

Ice Cream

1^1/$_2$ cups heavy whipping cream

1^1/$_4$ cups whole milk, divided

^{1}/$_2$ cup granulated sugar

^{1}/$_4$ cup light corn syrup

^{1}/$_8$ teaspoon kosher salt

2 vanilla beans

3 tablespoons nonfat
dry milk powder

2 tablespoons cornstarch

^{1}/$_4$ teaspoon pure vanilla extract

Butterscotch Swirl

^{3}/$_4$ cup firmly packed
light brown sugar

^{1}/$_4$ cup light corn syrup

3 tablespoons unsalted butter

Pinch of kosher salt

^{1}/$_3$ cup heavy whipping cream

^{1}/$_2$ teaspoon pure vanilla extract

For the ice cream: Combine the cream, ^{1}/$_2$ cup milk, sugar, corn syrup, and salt in a saucepan. Split the vanilla beans in half lengthwise and scrape the seeds into the cream mixture. Add the pods to the pan.

Cook over medium heat, stirring frequently, until the mixture begins to steam; watch it carefully and make sure it does not come to a boil.

While the mixture heats, combine the remaining milk, milk powder, cornstarch, and vanilla extract in a small bowl, and stir until smooth and both of the powders have dissolved.

Add the cornstarch mixture to the pan, and bring to a boil over low heat, stirring constantly. Whisk the mixture until smooth, and simmer the mixture over very low heat, stirring constantly, for 2 minutes, or until thickened. Remove and discard the vanilla bean pods. If the mixture is lumpy, strain it through a sieve.

Transfer the hot liquid to a storage container, and press a sheet of plastic wrap directly onto the surface of the mixture to prevent a skin from forming. Refrigerate the mixture uncovered until it is completely chilled (below 40°F), or quick-cool it according to the method on page 14.

While the custard chills, make the swirl: Combine the brown sugar, corn syrup, butter, and salt in a small saucepan. Bring to a boil over medium heat, stirring frequently. Increase the heat to high, and cook, stirring constantly, for 2 to 3 minutes, or until the bubbles are large and thick. Remove the pan from the heat, and carefully add the cream and vanilla, stirring with a long-handled spoon; the mixture will bubble furiously at first.

Return the pan to the stove and cook over low heat until the sauce is smooth. Remove from the heat and let the sauce cool to room temperature.

(continued)

Meanwhile, freeze the chilled ice cream custard in an ice cream maker according to the manufacturer's instructions.

After the ice cream has churned, add the swirl: Transfer the butterscotch to the bottom of a chilled mixing bowl. Pour the soft ice cream in a smooth layer atop the butterscotch and fold the two together gently using a wide rubber spatula.

Serve immediately for a soft ice cream, or freeze until hard. Allow the ice cream to sit at room temperature for 15 minutes before serving if frozen solid.

Variation: For a grown-up version, substitute 2 tablespoons brandy or rum for 2 tablespoons of the cream in the butterscotch sauce.

VANILLA ICE CREAM with CARAMEL and DATES

ADAPTED FROM LAPPERT'S, RICHMOND, CA

Chopped dates and caramel ribbons enliven the flavor of this ice cream, which is especially good in a Baked Alaska (page 228) or as a filling for Profiteroles (page 225).

MAKES ABOUT 1 QUART

$1^2/_3$ cups heavy whipping cream, divided

$1^1/_4$ cups whole milk, divided

$^1/_4$ cup granulated sugar

$^1/_4$ cup light corn syrup

$^1/_8$ teaspoon kosher salt

2 vanilla beans

2 tablespoons cornstarch

2 tablespoons buttermilk powder

$^1/_4$ teaspoon pure vanilla extract

16 caramel candies, unwrapped

$^1/_2$ cup chopped dates

Combine $1^1/_2$ cups of the cream, $^1/_2$ cup milk, sugar, corn syrup, and salt in a saucepan. Split the vanilla beans in half lengthwise and scrape the seeds into the cream mixture. Add the pods to the pan.

Cook over medium heat, stirring frequently, until the mixture begins to steam; watch it carefully and make sure it does not come to a boil.

While the mixture heats, combine the remaining milk, cornstarch, buttermilk powder, and vanilla extract in a small bowl and stir until smooth and both of the powders have dissolved.

Add the cornstarch mixture to the pan and bring to a boil over low heat, stirring constantly. Whisk the mixture until smooth, and simmer the mixture over very low heat, stirring constantly, for 2 minutes, or until thickened. Remove and discard the vanilla bean pods. If the mixture is lumpy, strain it through a sieve.

Transfer the hot liquid to a storage container and press a sheet of plastic wrap directly onto the surface of the mixture to prevent a skin from forming. Refrigerate the mixture uncovered until it is completely chilled (below 40°F), or quick-cool it according to the method on page 14.

While the ice cream custard chills, combine the caramel candies and remaining cream in a microwave-safe cup. Heat in the microwave on medium (50 percent) power for 30 seconds. Stir and repeat as necessary until the mixture is smooth. Set aside at room temperature.

Stir the dates into the chilled ice cream custard and freeze in an ice cream maker according to the manufacturer's instructions. After the ice cream has churned, add the caramel ribbons: Transfer one-

(continued)

sixth of the soft ice cream to an airtight container and top with a few spoonfuls of the caramel. Repeat until all ice cream and caramel are layered.

Serve immediately for a soft ice cream, or freeze until hard. Allow the ice cream to sit at room temperature for 15 minutes before serving if frozen solid. When serving the ice cream, dig into the container vertically so each serving contains some of the caramel.

Variation: Substitute chopped dried figs, chopped dried apricots, or even raisins for the dates.

Working with Dried Fruit

Dried fruit is hardly as hard as it was even a few decades ago, so plumping it is rarely necessary—especially if you're adding the fruit to a sauce that will simmer. That is not the case, however, when making ice cream because the fruit will not absorb hot liquid to soften. If you need to soften it, however, cover the fruit with boiling water for 15 minutes, then drain well before adding it to the custard.

CHERRY VANILLA ICE CREAM

ADAPTED FROM BASSETTS, PHILADELPHIA, PA

Cherry Vanilla is handily in the top dozen American favorites; the sweet fruit creates a great textural contrast.

MAKES ABOUT 1 QUART

1 1/2 cups heavy whipping cream
1 1/4 cups whole milk, divided
1/2 cup granulated sugar
1/4 cup light corn syrup
1/8 teaspoon kosher salt
2 vanilla beans
3 tablespoons nonfat dry milk powder
2 tablespoons cornstarch
1/4 teaspoon pure vanilla extract
3/4 cup chopped fresh black cherries

Combine the cream, 1/2 cup milk, sugar, corn syrup, and salt in a saucepan. Split the vanilla beans in half lengthwise and scrape the seeds into the cream mixture. Add the pods to the pan.

Cook over medium heat, stirring frequently, until the mixture begins to steam; watch it carefully and make sure it does not come to a boil.

While the mixture heats, combine the remaining milk, milk powder, cornstarch, and vanilla extract in a small bowl, and stir until smooth and both of the powders have dissolved.

Add the cornstarch mixture to the pan, and bring to a boil over low heat, stirring constantly. Whisk the mixture until smooth, and simmer the mixture over very low heat, stirring constantly, for 2 minutes, or until thickened. Remove and discard the vanilla bean pods. If the mixture is lumpy, strain it through a sieve.

Transfer the hot liquid to a storage container, and press a sheet of plastic wrap directly onto the surface of the mixture to prevent a skin from forming. Refrigerate the mixture uncovered until it is completely chilled (below 40°F), or quick-cool it according to the method on page 14.

Stir the chopped cherries into the chilled custard.

Freeze the mixture in an ice cream maker according to the manufacturer's instructions. Serve immediately for a soft ice cream, or transfer the mixture to an airtight storage container and freeze until hard. Allow the ice cream to sit at room temperature for 15 minutes before serving if frozen solid.

VANILLA ICE CREAM with RASPBERRY SWIRL and CHOCOLATE CHIPS

ADAPTED FROM BASSETTS,
PHILADELPHIA, PA

Bassetts's version of this ice cream contains miniature candies with a sweet raspberry center, but folding in chocolate chips creates the same wonderful combination of flavors.

MAKES ABOUT 1 QUART

Ice Cream
1¹/₂ cups heavy whipping cream

1¹/₄ cups whole milk, divided

¹/₂ cup granulated sugar

¹/₄ cup light corn syrup

¹/₈ teaspoon kosher salt

2 vanilla beans

3 tablespoons nonfat
dry milk powder

2 tablespoons cornstarch

¹/₄ teaspoon pure vanilla extract

³/₄ cup chocolate chips

Raspberry Swirl
1 cup fresh raspberries or
frozen raspberries, thawed

¹/₄ cup light corn syrup

1 teaspoon freshly
squeezed lemon juice

1 tablespoon cornstarch

Combine the cream, ¹/₂ cup milk, sugar, corn syrup, and salt in a saucepan. Split the vanilla beans in half lengthwise and scrape the seeds into the cream mixture. Add the pods to the pan.

Cook over medium heat, stirring frequently, until the mixture begins to steam; watch it carefully and make sure it does not come to a boil.

While the mixture heats, combine the remaining milk, milk powder, cornstarch, and vanilla extract in a small bowl and stir until smooth and both of the powders have dissolved.

Add the cornstarch mixture to the pan, and bring to a boil over low heat, stirring constantly. Whisk the mixture until smooth, and simmer the mixture over very low heat, stirring constantly, for 2 minutes, or until thickened. Remove and discard the vanilla beans. If the mixture is lumpy, strain it through a sieve.

Transfer the hot liquid to a storage container, and press a sheet of plastic wrap directly onto the surface of the mixture to prevent a skin from forming. Refrigerate the mixture uncovered until it is completely chilled (below 40°F), or quick-cool it according to the method on page 14.

While the custard chills, make the raspberry swirl: Combine the raspberries, corn syrup, and lemon juice in a small saucepan and bring to a boil over medium heat, stirring occasionally. Simmer the sauce for 5 minutes, stirring occasionally. Combine the cornstarch and 2 tablespoons of cold water in a small cup, and stir well. Add the mixture to the sauce and cook for 1 to 2 minutes, or until lightly thickened. Strain the sauce through a sieve to remove the seeds, if desired. Chill the sauce until cold.

Freeze the chilled custard in ice cream maker according to the manufacturer's instructions. Transfer the soft ice cream to a chilled mixing bowl and fold in the chocolate chips.

To make the swirl, spoon one-sixth of the ice cream into an airtight container. Top it with a few spoonfuls of the raspberry sauce and repeat until all the ice cream and raspberry sauce are layered.

Serve immediately for a soft ice cream, or freeze until hard. Allow the ice cream to sit at room temperature for 15 minutes before serving if frozen solid. When serving the ice cream, dig into the container vertically so each serving contains some of the swirl.

3 For the Love of Chocolate

While oenophiles may attest that the first duty of a wine is to be red, there are those of us who believe that the first duty of any dessert—including ice cream—is to have some serious chocolate in it.

This "food of the gods," like vanilla, is a gift from the Mexicans. Dark chocolate can also boast a health benefit; it contains catechins—some of the same antioxidants found in green tea. The catechins attack free radicals, which damage cells and are thought to lead to cancer and heart disease. So eating chocolate may help to prevent heart disease and cancer—as long as it's eaten in small quantities.

There's a range of recipes in this chapter, beginning with dishes that showcase chocolate and including some with additional ingredients that complement its flavor. While you'll find chocolate additions to ice creams and sorbets in other chapters, any recipe you find in this section has chocolate as the star.

A GUIDE TO CHOCOLATE

The key to all chocolate desserts is to use a high-quality product, and with the exceptions noted below, to use the type of chocolate specified in a recipe. The amount of additional sugar and other ingredients are calculated according to the sweetness level of the chocolate in a given recipe. Here is a guide to chocolate:

Unsweetened Chocolate: Also referred to as baking or bitter chocolate, this is the purest of all cooking chocolates. It is hardened chocolate liquor (which is the essence of the cocoa bean, not an alcohol) that contains no sugar. It is usually packaged in a bar of eight blocks weighing one ounce each. For a substitution, you can use three tablespoons of cocoa powder mixed with one tablespoon of vegetable oil for each ounce of unsweetened chocolate called for in a recipe.

Bittersweet Chocolate: This chocolate is slightly sweetened with sugar, the exact amounts of which varying by manufacturer. Bittersweet chocolate must contain 35 percent chocolate liquor, and it should be used when intense chocolate taste is desired. It can also be used interchangeably with semisweet chocolate in cooking and baking.

Semisweet Chocolate: This chocolate is sweetened with sugar, but unlike bittersweet, it also can have flavorings added to it, such as vanilla. It is sold in chips and pieces as well as in bars. You can substitute one ounce of unsweetened chocolate and four teaspoons of granulated sugar for each ounce of semisweet chocolate called for in a recipe.

Milk Chocolate: This is a mild-flavored chocolate which is used primarily for candy bars but rarely (except for milk chocolate chips) in cooking. It can have as little as 10 percent chocolate liquor, but must contain 12 percent milk solids.

Unsweetened Cocoa Powder: This is powdered chocolate that has had a portion of the cocoa butter removed. Cocoa keeps indefinitely in a cool place. Dutch process cocoa is formulated with reduced acidity, and it gives foods a mellower chocolate flavor. However, it also burns at a lower temperature than more common cocoa.

USING CHOCOLATE

Bittersweet, semisweet, and sweet chocolate can be used interchangeably in recipes, depending on personal taste, but since most chocolate desserts tend to be quite sweet, it's better to substitute a bittersweet chocolate for a semisweet one, rather than the other way around.

Chocolate chips and bits of broken chocolate should not be substituted for one another. Chocolate chips react differently in baking than chopped chocolate; they are formulated to retain their shape at high heat, and can form gritty granules in a cooled dessert.

Because chocolate can absorb aromas and flavors from other foods, it should always be wrapped tightly after being opened. Store chocolate in a cool, dry place, but avoid refrigerating or freezing it. If stored at a temperature high enough for the chocolate to begin to melt, the fat will rise to the surface and become a whitish powder called a "bloom." It will disappear, however, as soon as the chocolate is melted. Chocolates, like red wines, age and become more deeply flavored after six months, and can be kept for years if stored properly.

CHOCOLATE PUDDING ICE CREAM

ADAPTED FROM BOULDER ICE CREAM COMPANY, BOULDER, CO

This is such a wonderful, homey ice cream with great texture as well as flavor. It is the definition of comfort food in my mind.

MAKES ABOUT 1 QUART

$^1/_2$ cup granulated sugar, divided
2 tablespoons cornstarch
$^1/_3$ cup unsweetened cocoa powder
$1^1/_2$ cups heavy whipping cream
$^3/_4$ cup whole milk
4 ounces high-quality milk chocolate, chopped
2 tablespoons nonfat dry milk powder
$^1/_8$ teaspoon kosher salt
2 large eggs
1 large egg yolk
$^1/_2$ teaspoon pure vanilla extract

Combine $^1/_4$ cup of the sugar, cornstarch, cocoa powder, and cream in a saucepan, and whisk well. Bring to a boil over medium heat, whisking often. When the mixture begins to boil, reduce the heat to low, and whisk for 1 minute.

Add the milk, chopped chocolate, milk powder, and salt to the pan, and whisk well to melt the chocolate.

Beat the eggs, egg yolk, remaining $^1/_4$ cup sugar, and vanilla extract in a mixing bowl with a whisk until thick and light yellow in color. Slowly beat about one-third of the hot cream mixture into the eggs so they are gradually warmed up, and then return the contents of the mixing bowl to the saucepan. Place the pan over medium-low heat and stir constantly, reaching all parts of the bottom of the pan, until the mixture reaches about 170°F on an instant-read thermometer; at this point it begins to emit steam, thicken slightly, and coat the back of a spoon. This takes 3 to 6 minutes. Do not allow the mixture to boil or the eggs will scramble. Strain the custard through a fine sieve, if desired.

Transfer the hot liquid to a storage container, and press a sheet of plastic wrap directly onto the surface of the mixture to prevent a skin from forming. Refrigerate the mixture uncovered until it is completely chilled (below 40°F), or quick-cool it according to the method on page 14.

Freeze the mixture in an ice cream maker according to the manufacturer's instructions. Serve immediately for a soft ice cream, or transfer the mixture to an airtight storage container and freeze until hard. Allow the ice cream to sit at room temperature for 15 minutes before serving if frozen solid.

Variations: Add a few tablespoons of Kahlúa or rum to the custard for an adult treat, or add 1 or 2 tablespoons of instant coffee powder along with the cocoa powder for a mocha flavor.

DARK CHOCOLATE ICE CREAM

ADAPTED FROM BASSETTS, PHILADELPHIA, PA

The combination of a large amount of cocoa powder plus bittersweet chocolate gives this ice cream an incredible depth of flavor. Try it topped with Marshmallow Sauce (page 215) and Caramel Sauce (page 213).

MAKES ABOUT 1 QUART

$1^1/_2$ cups heavy whipping cream

$1^1/_4$ cups whole milk, divided

$3/_4$ cup unsweetened cocoa powder

$2/_3$ cup granulated sugar

$1/_4$ cup light corn syrup

$1/_8$ teaspoon kosher salt

3 tablespoons nonfat dry milk powder

2 tablespoons cornstarch

$1/_4$ teaspoon pure vanilla extract

$1/_4$ pound high-quality bittersweet chocolate, finely chopped

Combine the cream, $1/_2$ cup milk, cocoa powder, sugar, corn syrup, and salt in a saucepan. Cook over medium heat, stirring frequently, until the mixture begins to steam; watch it carefully and make sure it does not come to a boil.

While the mixture heats, combine the remaining milk, milk powder, cornstarch, and vanilla extract in a small bowl, and stir until smooth and both of the powders have dissolved.

Add the cornstarch mixture to the pan, and bring to a boil over low heat, stirring constantly. Whisk the mixture until smooth, and simmer the mixture over very low heat, stirring constantly, for 2 minutes, or until thickened. Remove from the heat. If the mixture is lumpy, strain it through a sieve.

Add the chopped chocolate to the custard, and allow it to sit for 2 minutes, or until melted. Whisk to blend.

Transfer the hot liquid to a storage container, and press a sheet of plastic wrap directly onto the surface of the mixture to prevent a skin from forming. Refrigerate the mixture uncovered until it is completely chilled (below 40°F), or quick-cool it according to the method on page 14.

Freeze the mixture in an ice cream maker according to the manufacturer's instructions. Serve immediately for a soft ice cream, or transfer the mixture to an airtight storage container and freeze until hard. Allow the ice cream to sit at room temperature for 15 minutes before serving if frozen solid.

Variation: Mocha Ice Cream

Add 2 tablespoons instant coffee powder to the recipe along with the cocoa powder, and increase the sugar by 2 tablespoons to balance the bitterness in the coffee.

BELGIAN CHOCOLATE GELATO

ADAPTED FROM COLD FUSION
GELATO, NEWPORT, RI

This intensely flavored gelato is totally elegant in flavor and texture. It makes a gorgeous filling for the Profiteroles (page 225).

MAKES ABOUT 1 QUART

$2^{1}/_{2}$ cups whole milk, divided

$^{3}/_{4}$ cup heavy whipping cream

$^{1}/_{2}$ cup granulated sugar

$^{1}/_{2}$ cup unsweetened cocoa powder

$^{1}/_{4}$ cup light corn syrup

$^{1}/_{8}$ teaspoon kosher salt

2 tablespoons nonfat dry milk powder

2 tablespoons cornstarch

$^{1}/_{4}$ teaspoon pure vanilla extract

$^{1}/_{4}$ pound high-quality Belgian bittersweet chocolate, finely chopped

Combine 2 cups of the milk, cream, sugar, cocoa powder, corn syrup, and salt in a saucepan. Cook over medium heat, stirring frequently, until the mixture begins to steam; watch it carefully and make sure it does not come to a boil.

While the mixture heats, combine the remaining milk, milk powder, cornstarch, and vanilla extract in a small bowl, and stir until smooth and both of the powders have dissolved.

Add the cornstarch mixture to the pan and bring to a boil over low heat, stirring constantly. Whisk the mixture until smooth, and simmer the mixture over very low heat, stirring constantly, for 2 minutes, or until thickened. Remove from the heat. If the mixture is lumpy, strain it through a sieve.

Add the chopped chocolate to the custard, and allow it to sit for 2 minutes, or until melted. Whisk to blend.

Transfer the hot liquid to a storage container, and press a sheet of plastic wrap directly onto the surface of the mixture to prevent a skin from forming. Refrigerate the mixture uncovered until it is completely chilled (below 40°F), or quick-cool it according to the method on page 14.

Freeze the mixture in an ice cream maker according to the manufacturer's instructions. Serve immediately for a soft gelato, or transfer the mixture to an airtight storage container and freeze until hard. Allow the gelato to sit at room temperature for 15 minutes before serving if frozen solid.

CHOCOLATE MALTED ICE CREAM

ADAPTED FROM BONNIE BRAE,
DENVER, CO

If you love chocolate malted milk balls, this is the recipe for you. The malt flavor of the candies is echoed by the malted milk powder in the ice cream.

MAKES ABOUT 1 QUART

1 1/4 cups heavy whipping cream
1 cup whole milk, divided
1/2 cup malted milk powder
1/3 cup granulated sugar
1/3 cup unsweetened cocoa powder
1/4 cup light corn syrup
1/8 teaspoon kosher salt
2 tablespoons nonfat
dry milk powder
2 tablespoons cornstarch
1/4 teaspoon pure vanilla extract
3/4 cup chopped malted milk balls

Combine the cream, 1/2 cup milk, malted milk powder, sugar, cocoa powder, corn syrup, and salt in a saucepan. Whisk well to dissolve the malt powder and cocoa.

Cook over medium heat, stirring frequently, until the mixture begins to steam; watch it carefully and make sure it does not come to a boil.

While the mixture heats, combine the remaining milk, milk powder, cornstarch, and vanilla extract in a small bowl, and stir until smooth and both of the powders have dissolved.

Add the cornstarch mixture to the pan, and bring to a boil over low heat, stirring constantly. Whisk the mixture until smooth and simmer over very low heat, stirring constantly, for 2 minutes, or until thickened. If the mixture is lumpy, strain it through a sieve.

Transfer the hot liquid to a storage container, and press a sheet of plastic wrap directly onto the surface of the mixture to prevent a skin from forming. Refrigerate the mixture uncovered until it is completely chilled (below 40°F), or quick-cool it according to the method on page 14.

Freeze the mixture in an ice cream maker according to the manufacturer's instructions. Transfer the soft ice cream to a chilled mixing bowl and fold in the chopped malted milk balls.

Serve immediately for a soft ice cream, or transfer the mixture to an airtight storage container and freeze until hard. Allow the ice cream to sit at room temperature for 15 minutes before serving if frozen solid.

Bonnie Brae, Denver, CO

THE STRIPED AWNING IN FRONT OF BONNIE BRAE ICE CREAM CONVEYS the message that has made this Denver shop a destination for more than twenty years; it reads "Yes! We Make It Here."

The shop was started in 1986 when two ice-cream enthusiast couples, Judy and Ken Simon and Cindy and Bob Pailet, saw a sweet opportunity when an ice cream parlor closed in the same space. Bonnie Brae, which means "pleasant hill" in Gaelic, is the name of the neighborhood in Denver in which it's located. While all four owners were avid ice cream makers as children, Judy Simon, who took courses in food science and ice cream production, oversees operations. She is assisted by Richard Brown, who has been the head chef at Bonnie Brae almost from the beginning.

The two concoct a wide range of flavors on a daily basis. Judy's favorite is the Apple Pie Ice Cream while Richard favors one of their grown-up flavors, Grand Marnier Chocolate Chip.

Richard says he loves to watch parents feed a child ice cream for the first time: "Suddenly there's this cold stuff, and then they taste it and it's sweet, and then there's a smile." And that's how the next generation of Bonnie Brae's customers is introduced.

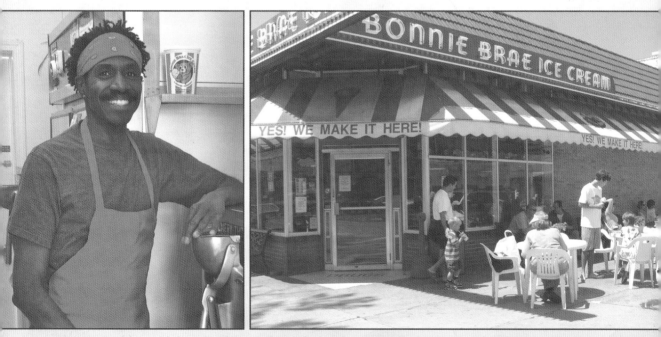

left: Richard Brown, head chef; *right*: Bonnie Brae ice cream shop

CHOCOLATE ORANGE ICE CREAM

ADAPTED FROM MOOMERS,
TRAVERSE CITY, MI

The citrus note from the orange is a classic contrast to the double chocolate hit from cocoa and bittersweet chocolate. It's one of those chocolate recipes that go nicely with fruit salad, too.

MAKES ABOUT 1 QUART

1¹/₂ cups whole milk, divided

1 cup heavy whipping cream

¹/₂ cup unsweetened cocoa powder

¹/₄ cup granulated sugar

¹/₄ cup light corn syrup

¹/₈ teaspoon kosher salt

¹/₄ cup frozen orange juice concentrate, thawed

3 tablespoons nonfat dry milk powder

2 tablespoons cornstarch

¹/₄ teaspoon pure vanilla extract

¹/₄ pound high-quality bittersweet chocolate, finely chopped

Combine 1 cup of the milk, cream, cocoa powder, sugar, corn syrup, and salt in a saucepan. Cook over medium heat, stirring frequently, until the mixture begins to steam; watch it carefully and make sure it does not come to a boil.

While the mixture heats, combine the remaining milk, orange juice concentrate, milk powder, cornstarch, and vanilla extract in a small bowl, and stir until smooth and both of the powders have dissolved.

Add the cornstarch mixture to the pan, and bring to a boil over low heat, stirring constantly. Whisk the mixture until smooth, and simmer the mixture over very low heat, stirring constantly, for 2 minutes, or until thickened. Remove from the heat. If the mixture is lumpy, strain it through a sieve.

Add the chopped chocolate to the custard, and allow it to sit for 2 minutes, or until melted. Whisk to blend.

Transfer the hot liquid to a storage container, and press a sheet of plastic wrap directly onto the surface of the mixture to prevent a skin from forming. Refrigerate the mixture uncovered until it is completely chilled (below 40°F), or quick-cool it according to the method on page 14.

Freeze the mixture in an ice cream maker according to the manufacturer's instructions. Serve immediately for a soft ice cream, or transfer the mixture to an airtight storage container and freeze until hard. Allow the ice cream to sit at room temperature for 15 minutes before serving if frozen solid.

CHOCOLATE-JALAPEÑO GELATO

ADAPTED FROM CIAO BELLA, FLORHAM PARK, NJ

The fresh chile in this richly flavored chocolate ice cream is a subtle aftertaste that enlivens the palate for the next bite.

MAKES ABOUT 1 QUART

$2\frac{1}{2}$ cups whole milk, divided

$\frac{3}{4}$ cup heavy whipping cream

$\frac{1}{2}$ cup granulated sugar

$\frac{1}{3}$ cup unsweetened cocoa powder

$\frac{1}{4}$ cup light corn syrup

1 medium jalapeño chile pepper, (seeds and ribs removed and discarded) and finely chopped

$\frac{1}{4}$ teaspoon kosher salt

2 tablespoons nonfat dry milk powder

2 tablespoons cornstarch

$\frac{1}{4}$ teaspoon pure vanilla extract

$\frac{1}{4}$ pound high-quality semisweet chocolate, finely chopped

Combine 2 cups of the milk, cream, sugar, cocoa powder, corn syrup, jalapeño, and salt in a saucepan. Cook over medium heat, stirring frequently, until the mixture begins to steam; watch it carefully and make sure it does not come to a boil.

While the mixture heats, combine the remaining milk, milk powder, cornstarch, and vanilla extract in a small bowl, and stir until smooth and both of the powders have dissolved.

Add the cornstarch mixture to the pan, and bring to a boil over low heat, stirring constantly. Whisk the mixture until smooth, and simmer the mixture over very low heat, stirring constantly, for 2 minutes, or until thickened. Remove from the heat. If the mixture is lumpy, strain it through a sieve.

Add the chopped chocolate to the custard, and allow it to sit for 2 minutes, or until melted. Whisk to blend.

Transfer the hot liquid to a storage container, and press a sheet of plastic wrap directly onto the surface of the mixture to prevent a skin from forming. Refrigerate the mixture uncovered until it is completely chilled (below 40°F), or quick-cool it according to the method on page 14.

Freeze the mixture in an ice cream maker according to the manufacturer's instructions. Serve immediately for a soft gelato, or transfer the mixture to an airtight storage container and freeze until hard. Allow the gelato to sit at room temperature for 15 minutes before serving if frozen solid.

Tip: Handling Hot Chiles

It's the seeds and ribs of chile peppers that contain the most of the heat. An easy way to make sure you've discarded them is to cut a pepper as if it were a relief sculpture. Cut off the tip, and then you'll be able to see the ribs. Cut the flesh between the ribs, and then discard the cage that remains.

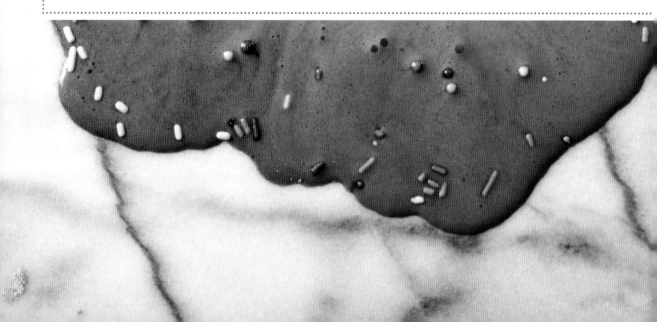

Ciao Bella, Florham Park, NJ

WHILE CIAO BELLA CAN BE CONSIDERED A NATIONAL COMPANY WITH A SECOND production facility in Eugene, Oregon, this book would not be complete without it. After all, Ciao Bella—which got started on the streets of New York's Little Italy in 1983—practically created the market for high-quality gelato that is flourishing today.

Ciao Bella's flavors, such as Chocolate Jalapeño Gelato (page 48) and Strawberry Sorbet (page 128) are all produced under the supervision of executive chef Danilo Zecchin. A native of Torino, Italy, Chef Zecchin graduated from restaurant school in his native city in 1978, and opened his first restaurant, called The White Buffalo. He moved to New York in 1984 and ended up as chef at the highly-acclaimed Queen Restaurant in Brooklyn before joining Ciao Bella in 1999.

While Ciao Bella is now carried in supermarkets, the company's success was based on placement with gourmet retailers. It has received more than a dozen awards from the National Association for the Specialty Food Trade. And the company hardly rests on its laurels; Ciao Bella is continually introducing both new flavors and new forms, such as its Key Lime Gelato featured in ice cream sandwiches made with graham crackers.

SWISS CHOCOLATE GELATO

ADAPTED FROM MORA
ICED CREAMERY,
BAINBRIDGE ISLAND, WA

This rich recipe combines various forms of chocolate with a hint of chocolate-flavored liqueur. Top it with some Maple Walnut Sauce (page 212) or Caramel Sauce (page 213).

MAKES ABOUT 1 QUART

1 1/2 cups whole milk

3/4 cup heavy whipping cream

2 tablespoons chocolate liqueur, such as Godiva

1/4 cup unsweetened cocoa powder

3 tablespoons nonfat dry milk powder

1/8 teaspoon kosher salt

4 ounces high-quality milk chocolate, chopped

2 large eggs

1 large egg yolk

1/4 cup granulated sugar

1/4 teaspoon pure vanilla extract

Combine the milk, cream, chocolate liqueur, cocoa powder, milk powder, and salt in a medium saucepan, and stir well to dissolve the milk powder. Bring the mixture just to a simmer, stirring occasionally. Remove from the heat.

Add the chopped chocolate, and allow it to sit for 2 minutes, or until melted. Whisk to blend.

Beat the eggs and yolk with the sugar and vanilla extract in a mixing bowl with a whisk until thick and light yellow in color. Slowly beat about one third of the hot cream mixture into the eggs so they are gradually warmed up, and then return the contents of the mixing bowl to the saucepan. Place the pan over medium-low heat and stir constantly, reaching all parts of the bottom of the pan, until the mixture reaches about 170°F on an instant-read thermometer; at this point it begins to emit steam, thicken slightly, and coat the back of a spoon. This takes 3 to 6 minutes. Do not allow the mixture to boil or the eggs will scramble. Strain the custard through a fine sieve, if desired.

Transfer the hot liquid to a storage container, and press a sheet of plastic wrap directly onto the surface of the mixture to prevent a skin from forming. Refrigerate the mixture uncovered until it is completely chilled (below 40°F), or quick-cool it according to the method on page 14.

Freeze the mixture in an ice cream maker according to the manufacturer's instructions. Serve immediately for a soft gelato, or transfer the mixture to an airtight storage container and freeze until hard. Allow the gelato to sit at room temperature for 15 minutes before serving if frozen solid.

CHOCOLATE MINT GELATO

ADAPTED FROM COLD FUSION
GELATO, NEWPORT, RI

*There are many recipes in this
book that pair chocolate and
mint; this heavenly gelato uses
mint oil as a refreshing foil to
the rich chocolate flavor.*

MAKES ABOUT 1 QUART

2$^1/_2$ cups whole milk, divided

$^3/_4$ cup heavy whipping cream

$^1/_2$ cup granulated sugar

$^1/_2$ cup unsweetened cocoa powder

$^1/_4$ cup light corn syrup

$^1/_8$ teaspoon kosher salt

2 tablespoons nonfat
dry milk powder

2 tablespoons cornstarch

$^3/_4$ to 1 teaspoon mint oil or
pure mint extract

$^1/_4$ pound high-quality bittersweet
chocolate, finely chopped

Combine 2 cups of the milk, cream, sugar, cocoa powder, corn syrup, and salt in a saucepan. Cook over medium heat, stirring frequently, until the mixture begins to steam; watch it carefully and make sure it does not come to a boil.

While the mixture heats, combine the remaining milk, milk powder, cornstarch, and mint oil in a small bowl and stir until smooth and both of the powders have dissolved.

Add the cornstarch mixture to the pan, and bring to a boil over low heat, stirring constantly. Whisk the mixture until smooth, and simmer the mixture over very low heat, stirring constantly, for 2 minutes, or until thickened. Remove from the heat. If the mixture is lumpy, strain it through a sieve.

Add the chopped chocolate to the custard, and allow it to sit for 2 minutes, or until melted. Whisk to blend.

Transfer the hot liquid to a storage container, and press a sheet of plastic wrap directly onto the surface of the mixture to prevent a skin from forming. Refrigerate the mixture uncovered until it is completely chilled (below 40°F), or quick-cool it according to the method on page 14.

Freeze the mixture in an ice cream maker according to the manufacturer's instructions. Serve immediately for a soft gelato, or transfer the mixture to an airtight storage container and freeze until hard. Allow the gelato to sit at room temperature for 15 minutes before serving if frozen solid.

Variation: Substitute 2 to 3 tablespoons of crème de menthe liqueur for the mint oil.

CHOCOLATE HAZELNUT GELATO

ADAPTED FROM GIOVANNA
GELATO, NEWTON, MA

*Called gianduja in Italian,
hazelnut-flavored chocolate is
a favorite of all generations.
While many recipes call for
straining out the nuts, I leave
them in to enhance the texture.*

MAKES ABOUT 1 QUART

$^3/_4$ cup skinned hazelnuts

$2^1/_2$ cups whole milk, divided

$^1/_2$ cup granulated sugar

$^1/_2$ cup unsweetened cocoa powder

$^1/_4$ cup light corn syrup

2 tablespoons nonfat
dry milk powder

2 tablespoons cornstarch

Pinch of kosher salt

$^1/_4$ teaspoon pure vanilla extract

Preheat the oven to 350°F. Line a baking sheet with heavy-duty aluminum foil.

Toast the hazelnuts for 5 to 7 minutes, or until browned. Combine the hazelnuts and 1 cup of the milk in a food processor fitted with the steel blade or in a blender, and purée until smooth; transfer to a saucepan.

Add 1 additional cup of the milk, sugar, cocoa powder, and corn syrup to the pan, and whisk well. Cook over medium heat, stirring frequently, until the mixture begins to steam; watch it carefully and make sure it does not come to a boil.

While the mixture heats, combine the remaining milk, milk powder, cornstarch, salt, and vanilla extract in a small bowl, and stir until smooth and both of the powders have dissolved.

Add the cornstarch mixture to the pan, and bring to a boil over low heat, stirring constantly. Whisk the mixture until smooth, and simmer the mixture over very low heat, stirring constantly, for 2 minutes, or until thickened. If the mixture is lumpy, strain it through a sieve.

Transfer the hot liquid to a storage container, and press a sheet of plastic wrap directly onto the surface of the mixture to prevent a skin from forming. Refrigerate the mixture uncovered until it is completely chilled (below 40°F), or quick-cool it according to the method on page 14.

Freeze the mixture in an ice cream maker according to the manufacturer's instructions. Serve immediately for a soft gelato, or transfer the mixture to an airtight storage container and freeze until hard. Allow the gelato to sit at room temperature for 15 minutes before serving if frozen solid.

CHOCOLATE-CABERNET ICE CREAM

ADAPTED FROM MOOMERS,
TRAVERSE CITY, MI

The alcohol in the wine boils away, but in the same way that many red wines are said to have notes of chocolate flavor, the acidity in the wine reduction cuts through some of the richness of the ice cream.

MAKES ABOUT 1 QUART

$^2/_3$ cup dry red wine,
preferably cabernet

$1^1/_2$ cups whole milk, divided

1 cup heavy whipping cream

$^1/_2$ cup unsweetened cocoa powder

$^1/_4$ cup granulated sugar

$^1/_4$ cup light corn syrup

$^1/_8$ teaspoon kosher salt

3 tablespoons nonfat
dry milk powder

2 tablespoons cornstarch

$^1/_4$ teaspoon pure vanilla extract

4 ounces high-quality bittersweet
chocolate, finely chopped

Place the wine in a saucepan and bring to a boil over medium-high heat, stirring occasionally. Reduce the heat to medium and cook until reduced by two-thirds.

Add 1 cup of the milk, cream, cocoa powder, sugar, corn syrup, and salt to the pan. Cook over medium heat, stirring frequently, until the mixture begins to steam; watch it carefully and make sure it does not come to a boil.

While the mixture heats, combine the remaining milk, milk powder, cornstarch, and vanilla extract in a small bowl, and stir until smooth and both of the powders have dissolved.

Add the cornstarch mixture to the pan, and bring to a boil over low heat, stirring constantly. Whisk the mixture until smooth, and simmer the mixture over very low heat, stirring constantly, for 2 minutes, or until thickened. Remove from the heat. If the mixture is lumpy, strain it through a sieve.

Add the chopped chocolate to the custard, and allow it to sit for 2 minutes, or until melted. Whisk to blend.

Transfer the hot liquid to a storage container, and press a sheet of plastic wrap directly onto the surface of the mixture to prevent a skin from forming. Refrigerate the mixture uncovered until it is completely chilled (below 40°F), or quick-cool it according to the method on page 14.

Freeze the mixture in an ice cream maker according to the manufacturer's instructions. Serve immediately for a soft ice cream, or transfer the mixture to an airtight storage container and freeze until hard. Allow the ice cream to sit at room temperature for 15 minutes before serving if frozen solid.

BRANDIED CHOCOLATE GELATO with WALNUTS

ADAPTED FROM MORA
ICED CREAMERY,
BAINBRIDGE ISLAND, WA

Crunchy walnuts stud this rich chocolate gelato laced with a bit of brandy. It's perfect topped with Butterscotch Sauce (page 213).

MAKES ABOUT 1 QUART

1 1/2 cups whole milk
3/4 cup heavy whipping cream
2 tablespoons brandy or Cognac
1/4 cup unsweetened cocoa powder
3 tablespoons nonfat
dry milk powder
1/8 teaspoon kosher salt
4 ounces high-quality milk
chocolate, chopped
2 large eggs
1 large egg yolk
1/4 cup granulated sugar
1/4 teaspoon pure vanilla extract
1/2 cup chopped walnuts

Combine the milk, cream, brandy, cocoa powder, milk powder, and salt in a medium saucepan, and stir well to dissolve the milk powder. Bring the mixture just to a simmer over medium heat, stirring occasionally. Remove from the heat.

Add the chopped chocolate, and allow it to sit for 2 minutes, or until melted. Whisk to blend.

Beat the eggs and yolk with the sugar and vanilla extract in a mixing bowl with a whisk until thick and light yellow in color. Slowly beat about one-third of the hot cream mixture into the eggs so they are gradually warmed up, and then return the contents of the mixing bowl to the saucepan. Place the pan over medium-low heat and stir constantly, reaching all parts of the bottom of the pan, until the mixture reaches about 170°F on an instant-read thermometer; at this point it begins to emit steam, thickens slightly, and coats the back of a spoon. This takes 3 to 6 minutes. Do not allow the mixture to boil or the eggs will scramble. Strain the custard through a fine sieve, if desired.

Transfer the hot liquid to a storage container, and press a sheet of plastic wrap directly onto the surface of the mixture to prevent a skin from forming. Refrigerate the mixture uncovered until it is completely chilled (below 40°F), or quick-cool it according to the method on page 14.

While the custard chills, prepare the nuts: Preheat the oven to 350°F. Line a baking sheet with aluminum foil.

Toast the walnuts for 5 to 7 minutes, or until browned. Stir the nuts into the chilled custard.

Freeze the mixture in an ice cream maker according to the manufacturer's instructions. Serve immediately for a soft gelato, or transfer the mixture to an airtight storage container and freeze until hard. Allow the gelato to sit at room temperature for 15 minutes before serving if frozen solid.

CHOCOLATE PEANUT BUTTER ICE CREAM

ADAPTED FROM MITCHELL'S,
SAN FRANCISCO, CA

*Imagine a frosty, creamy version
of a peanut butter cup candy—
this ice cream is it. Mitchell's special-
orders miniature versions of peanut
butter cups for this recipe, but
chopping up full-size candies works
just as well for this incredibly rich
ice cream that Mitchell's calls
Peanut Butter Indulgence.*

MAKES ABOUT 1 QUART

1$\frac{1}{4}$ cups heavy whipping cream

1 cup whole milk, divided

$\frac{1}{2}$ cup smooth commercial peanut
butter (not homemade or natural)

$\frac{1}{3}$ cup unsweetened cocoa powder

$\frac{1}{4}$ cup granulated sugar

$\frac{1}{4}$ cup light corn syrup

$\frac{1}{8}$ teaspoon kosher salt

2 tablespoons cornstarch

2 tablespoons nonfat
dry milk powder

$\frac{1}{4}$ teaspoon pure vanilla extract

1 (3.5-ounce) bar high-quality
bittersweet chocolate,
finely chopped

$\frac{1}{2}$ cup chopped peanut-butter-
filled candies, such as Reese's Cups

Combine the cream, $\frac{1}{2}$ cup milk, and peanut butter in a saucepan, and whisk until smooth. Add the cocoa powder, sugar, corn syrup, and salt to the pan. Cook over medium heat, stirring frequently, until the mixture begins to steam; watch it carefully and make sure it does not come to a boil.

While the mixture heats, combine the remaining milk, cornstarch, milk powder, and vanilla extract in a small bowl, and stir until smooth and both of the powders have dissolved.

Add the cornstarch mixture to the pan, and bring to a boil over low heat, stirring constantly. Whisk until smooth, and simmer the mixture for 2 minutes, or until thickened. Remove from the heat. If the mixture is lumpy, strain it through a sieve.

Add the chopped chocolate to the custard, and allow it to sit for 2 minutes, or until melted. Whisk to blend.

Transfer the hot liquid to a storage container, and press a sheet of plastic wrap directly onto the surface of the mixture to prevent a skin from forming. Refrigerate the mixture uncovered until it is completely chilled (below 40°F), or quick-cool it according to the method on page 14.

Freeze the mixture in an ice cream maker according to the manufacturer's instructions. Transfer the soft ice cream to a chilled mixing bowl and fold in the chopped candy.

Serve immediately for a soft ice cream, or transfer the mixture to an airtight storage container and freeze until hard. Allow the ice cream to sit at room temperature for 15 minutes before serving if frozen solid.

CHOCOLATE ICE CREAM with PEANUT BUTTER BROWNIES, CHOCOLATE CHUNKS, and CARAMEL SWIRL

ADAPTED FROM BASSETTS,
PHILADELPHIA, PA

Bassetts calls this flavor Gadzooks!, but it could also be called All but the Kitchen Sink. It's great as the filling for Baked Alaska (page 228).

MAKES ABOUT 1 QUART

Ice Cream
1 cup heavy whipping cream
3/4 cup whole milk, divided
1/3 cup granulated sugar
1/4 cup light corn syrup
1/8 teaspoon kosher salt
2 tablespoons nonfat
dry milk powder
1 1/2 tablespoons cornstarch
1/4 teaspoon pure vanilla extract
3/4 cup crumbled peanut butter
brownies or regular brownies
1/2 cup high-quality semisweet
chocolate chunks

Swirl
16 caramel candies, unwrapped
3 tablespoons
heavy whipping cream

For the ice cream: Combine the cream, 1/3 cup milk, sugar, corn syrup, and salt in a saucepan. Cook over medium heat, stirring frequently, until the mixture begins to steam; watch it carefully and make sure it does not come to a boil.

While the mixture heats, combine the remaining milk, milk powder, cornstarch, and vanilla extract in a small bowl, and stir until smooth and both of the powders have dissolved.

Add the cornstarch mixture to the pan, and bring to a boil over low heat, stirring constantly. Whisk the mixture until smooth, and simmer the mixture over very low heat, stirring constantly, for 2 minutes, or until thickened. If the mixture is lumpy, strain it through a sieve.

Transfer the hot liquid to a storage container, and press a sheet of plastic wrap directly onto the surface of the mixture to prevent a skin from forming. Refrigerate the mixture uncovered until it is completely chilled (below 40°F), or quick-cool it according to the method on page 14.

While the custard chills, make the swirl: Combine the caramel candies and cream in a microwave-safe cup. Heat in the microwave on medium (50 percent) power for 30 seconds. Stir, and repeat as necessary.

Freeze the chilled custard in an ice cream maker according to the manufacturer's instructions. Transfer the soft ice cream into a chilled mixing bowl and fold in the crumbled brownies and chocolate chunks.

To make the swirl, transfer one-sixth of the ice cream to an airtight container. Top it with a few spoonfuls of the caramel swirl and repeat until all the ice cream and swirl are layered.

Serve immediately for a soft ice cream, or freeze until hard. Allow the ice cream to sit at room temperature for 15 minutes before serving if frozen solid.

Bassetts, Philadelphia, PA

PHILADELPHIA HAS ALWAYS BEEN THE CENTER FOR AMERICAN ICE CREAM. It was there that Nancy Jackson invented the ice cream maker, and very shortly after that, in 1861, Lewis Dubois Bassett, a teacher at a Quaker school, starting churning ice cream in the backyard of his home in nearby Salem, New Jersey.

With its longevity of more than 150 years, Bassetts can boast being the oldest ice cream company in continuous operation in the country, and it's still run by folks named Bassett. The company has been nationally known as the standard-bearer of super-premium ice cream since before there was a name for it. You can still buy it today at Reading Terminal Market, where Bassetts has been sold since the building opened in 1893, and where the company hosts an annual ice cream festival each July.

Flavors such as the Dark Chocolate (page 42) have been available since almost the first day of operation, but new flavors are constantly being developed. A new addition is Green Tea Ice Cream (page 198), which is also being exported to China. Curiously, the Borscht Sorbet, made in 1959 for the visit of Soviet Premier Nikita Khrushchev, has not found its way onto the menu.

left: Louise Austin Basset, who ran the business from 1917 to 1925;
right: Bassetts at Reading Terminal Market, 1915

MINT CHOCOLATE CHIP ICE CREAM

ADAPTED FROM GRAETER'S, CINCINNATI, OH

The minty freshness of the ice cream almost comes as a surprise because there's no food coloring added; the ice cream is almost snowy white.

MAKES ABOUT 1 QUART

1$\frac{1}{2}$ cups heavy whipping cream

$\frac{3}{4}$ cup whole milk

$\frac{1}{2}$ cup granulated sugar, divided

2 tablespoons nonfat dry milk powder

$\frac{1}{8}$ teaspoon kosher salt

2 large eggs

$\frac{1}{2}$ to 1 teaspoon pure mint oil or mint extract

2 ounces bittersweet chocolate, chopped

2 tablespoons unsalted butter

Tip: Working with Extracts

With mint extract and mint oil a little bit goes a long way, and the intensity of flavor varies from brand to brand. It's best to start with just a few drops, adding more until you have the desired flavor.

Combine the cream, milk, $\frac{1}{4}$ cup sugar, milk powder, and salt in a medium saucepan, and stir well to dissolve the milk powder. Bring the mixture just to a simmer over medium heat, stirring occasionally.

Beat the eggs, remaining $\frac{1}{4}$ cup sugar, and mint extract in a mixing bowl with a whisk until thick and light yellow in color. Slowly beat about one third of the hot cream mixture into the eggs so they are gradually warmed up, and then return the contents of the mixing bowl to the saucepan. Place the pan over medium-low heat and stir constantly, reaching all parts of the bottom of the pan, until the mixture reaches about 170°F on an instant-read thermometer; at this point it begins to emit steam, thickens slightly, and coats the back of a spoon. This takes 3 to 6 minutes. Do not allow the mixture to boil or the eggs will scramble. Strain the custard through a fine sieve, if desired.

Transfer the hot liquid to a storage container, and press a sheet of plastic wrap directly onto the surface of the mixture to prevent a skin from forming. Refrigerate the mixture uncovered until it is completely chilled (below 40°F), or quick-cool it according to the method on page 14.

Combine the chocolate and butter in a small bowl, and heat in the microwave on medium power for 20 seconds. Stir, and repeat as necessary until the chocolate melts and the mixture is smooth. Allow it to cool slightly, but do not allow it to become hard.

Freeze the chilled custard in an ice cream maker according to the manufacturer's instructions. When the ice cream reaches a soft consistency, slowly pour the melted chocolate into the freezer, allowing it to churn with the ice cream.

Serve immediately for a soft ice cream, or transfer the mixture to an airtight storage container and freeze until hard. Allow the ice cream to sit at room temperature for 15 minutes before serving if frozen solid.

GRASSHOPPER PIE ICE CREAM

ADAPTED FROM MITCHELL'S,
SAN FRANCISCO, CA

*This minty, green ice cream is chock
full of chocolaty fold-ins. So you
might as well go all the way and top it
with Hot Fudge Sauce (page 210).*

MAKES ABOUT 1 QUART

1 cup heavy whipping cream

$^3/_4$ cup whole milk, divided

$^1/_4$ cup granulated sugar

$^1/_4$ cup light corn syrup

$^1/_8$ teaspoon kosher salt

2 tablespoons cornstarch

2 tablespoons nonfat dry milk powder

$^1/_4$ teaspoon pure vanilla extract

$^1/_2$ to 1 teaspoon pure
mint extract or mint oil

3 to 5 drops green food coloring
(optional)

$^3/_4$ cup chopped Fudge Brownies
(page 234) or purchased brownies

$^1/_2$ cup chocolate chips

Combine the cream, $^1/_2$ cup milk, sugar, corn syrup, and salt in a saucepan. Cook over medium heat, stirring frequently, until the mixture begins to steam; watch it carefully and make sure it does not come to a boil.

While the mixture heats, combine the remaining milk, cornstarch, milk powder, vanilla extract, mint extract, and food coloring in a small bowl, and stir until smooth and both of the powders have dissolved.

Add the cornstarch mixture to the pan, and bring to a boil over low heat, stirring constantly. Whisk until smooth, and simmer the mixture for 2 minutes, or until thickened. If the mixture is lumpy, strain it through a sieve.

Transfer the hot liquid to a storage container, and press a sheet of plastic wrap directly onto the surface of the mixture to prevent a skin from forming. Refrigerate the mixture uncovered until it is completely chilled (below 40°F), or quick-cool it according to the method on page 14.

Freeze the chilled custard in an ice cream maker according to the manufacturer's instructions. Transfer the soft ice cream to a chilled mixing bowl and fold in the brownie pieces and chocolate chips.

Serve immediately for a soft ice cream, or transfer the mixture to an airtight storage container and freeze until hard. Allow the ice cream to sit at room temperature for 15 minutes before serving if frozen solid.

CHOCOLATE ESPRESSO CRUNCH ICE CREAM

ADAPTED FROM THE DAILY SCOOP, BARRINGTON, RI

Chocolate-covered espresso beans are the elegant fold-ins in this richly flavored bittersweet chocolate ice cream.

MAKES ABOUT 1 QUART

2 cups heavy whipping cream, divided

$3/4$ cup whole milk

$1/2$ cup granulated sugar

$1/2$ cup unsweetened cocoa powder

$1/4$ cup light corn syrup

2 tablespoons nonfat dry milk powder

2 tablespoons cornstarch

Pinch of kosher salt

$1/4$ teaspoon pure vanilla extract

1 (3.5-ounce) bar high-quality bittersweet chocolate, chopped

$1/2$ cup crushed chocolate-covered espresso beans

Combine $1^1/2$ cups of the cream, milk, sugar, cocoa, and corn syrup in a saucepan. Cook over medium heat, stirring frequently, until the mixture begins to steam; watch it carefully and make sure it does not come to a boil.

While the mixture heats, combine the remaining cream, milk powder, cornstarch, salt, and vanilla extract in a small bowl and stir until smooth and both of the powders have dissolved.

Add the cornstarch mixture to the pan, and bring to a boil over low heat, stirring constantly. Whisk the mixture until smooth, and simmer the mixture over very low heat, stirring constantly, for 2 minutes, or until thickened. Remove from the heat. If the mixture is lumpy, strain it through a sieve.

Add the chopped chocolate to the custard, and allow it to sit for 2 minutes, or until melted. Whisk to blend.

Transfer the hot liquid to a storage container and press a sheet of plastic wrap directly onto the surface of the mixture to prevent a skin from forming. Refrigerate the mixture uncovered until it is completely chilled (below 40°F), or quick-cool it according to the method on page 14.

Stir the crushed espresso beans into the chilled custard and freeze in an ice cream maker according to the manufacturer's instructions. Serve immediately for a soft ice cream, or transfer the mixture to an airtight storage container and freeze until hard. Allow the ice cream to sit at room temperature for 15 minutes before serving if frozen solid.

4 For the Kick of Coffee

While I rarely drink hot coffee, I adore iced coffee with lots of cream and sugar added, so it's not surprising that coffee ice cream is also among my favorite ways to enjoy it. Of course, I'm not alone; coffee has been a popular ingredient in ice creams and desserts—frozen and otherwise—for years.

But until the past twenty years or so, there wasn't a lot of variety or attention to quality; most recipes simply called for brewed coffee, or occasionally, instant coffee powder. Today, however, ice cream makers are very specific about the varieties of beans used, and more often than not the beans are specified as freshly ground and are then steeped in the hot milk–and–cream mixture to extract their delicious aromatic oils as well as their flavor.

You can personalize any of these recipes merely by changing the type of bean used. Pick your favorite, and find even more reasons to love these ice creams.

ITALIAN ESPRESSO ICE CREAM

ADAPTED FROM BOULDER ICE
CREAM COMPANY, BOULDER, CO

This ice cream is as dark in color as it is rich in flavor. It's one of the few egg-thickened coffee ice creams in this book, and the custard adds to its overall appeal. Try topping it with Hot Fudge Sauce (page 210).

MAKES ABOUT 1 QUART

1 3/4 cups heavy whipping cream
3/4 cup whole milk
2/3 cup granulated sugar, divided
1/2 cup ground espresso coffee
2 tablespoons nonfat
dry milk powder
1/8 teaspoon kosher salt
2 large eggs
1 large egg yolk
1/2 teaspoon pure vanilla extract

Combine the cream, milk, 1/4 cup sugar, coffee, milk powder, and salt in a medium saucepan, and stir well to dissolve the milk powder. Bring the mixture just to a simmer over medium heat, stirring occasionally.

Cover the pan and remove the pan from the heat. Allow the mixture to steep for 30 minutes, then strain the mixture through a fine sieve, pressing with the back of a spoon to extract as much liquid as possible.

Beat the eggs, egg yolk, remaining sugar, and vanilla extract in a mixing bowl with a whisk until thick and light yellow in color. Slowly beat about one-third of the hot cream mixture into the eggs so they are gradually warmed up, and then return the contents of the mixing bowl to the saucepan. Place the pan over medium-low heat, and stir constantly, reaching all parts of the bottom of the pan, until the mixture reaches about 170°F on an instant-read thermometer; at this point it begins to emit steam, thickens slightly, and coats the back of a spoon. This takes 3 to 6 minutes. Do not allow the mixture to boil or the eggs will scramble. Strain the custard through a fine sieve, if desired.

Transfer the hot liquid to a storage container, and press a sheet of plastic wrap directly onto the surface of the mixture to prevent a skin from forming. Refrigerate the mixture uncovered until it is completely chilled (below 40°F), or quick-cool it according to the method on page 14.

Freeze the mixture in an ice cream maker according to the manufacturer's instructions. Serve immediately for a soft ice cream, or transfer the mixture to an airtight storage container and freeze until hard. Allow the ice cream to sit at room temperature for 15 minutes before serving if frozen solid.

CAPPUCCINO ICE CREAM

ADAPTED FROM McCONNELL'S,
SANTA BARBARA, CA

If you love a frothing cup of cappuccino scented with cinnamon, this is the ice cream for you! The inclusion of crushed coffee candies adds textural interest.

MAKES ABOUT 1 QUART

$1\frac{1}{4}$ cups heavy whipping cream
$\frac{3}{4}$ cup whole milk
$\frac{3}{4}$ cup strong brewed coffee
$\frac{1}{2}$ cup granulated sugar, divided
$\frac{1}{4}$ cup cocoa powder
$\frac{1}{4}$ cup nonfat dry milk powder
$\frac{1}{4}$ teaspoon pure vanilla extract
$\frac{1}{8}$ teaspoon ground cinnamon
$\frac{1}{8}$ teaspoon kosher salt
4 large egg yolks
$\frac{1}{2}$ cup crushed caramel coffee or cappuccino-flavored hard candies, like Werther's

Combine the cream, milk, coffee, $\frac{1}{4}$ cup sugar, cocoa powder, milk powder, vanilla extract, cinnamon, and salt in a medium saucepan, and stir well to dissolve the cocoa and milk powder. Bring the mixture just to a simmer over medium heat, stirring occasionally.

Beat the eggs yolks and remaining $\frac{1}{4}$ cup sugar in a mixing bowl with a whisk until thick and light yellow in color. Slowly beat about one-third of the hot cream mixture into the eggs so they are gradually warmed up, and then return the contents of the mixing bowl to the saucepan. Place the pan over medium-low heat and stir constantly, reaching all parts of the bottom of the pan, until the mixture reaches about 170°F on an instant-read thermometer; at this point it begins to emit steam, thickens slightly, and coats the back of a spoon. This takes 3 to 6 minutes. Do not allow the mixture to boil or the eggs will scramble. Strain the custard through a fine sieve, if desired.

Transfer the hot liquid to a storage container, and press a sheet of plastic wrap directly onto the surface of the mixture to prevent a skin from forming. Refrigerate the mixture uncovered until it is completely chilled (below 40°F), or quick-cool it according to the method on page 14.

Stir the crushed candies into the chilled custard.

Freeze the mixture in an ice cream maker according to the manufacturer's instructions. Serve immediately for a soft ice cream, or transfer the mixture to an airtight storage container and freeze until hard. Allow the ice cream to sit at room temperature for 15 minutes before serving if frozen solid.

CAPPUCCINO GOAT MILK ICE CREAM

ADAPTED FROM LÁLOO'S,
PETALUMA, CA

"Capraccino" is what LáLoo's calls this richly flavored ice cream because the word for goat in Italian is capra. The egg yolks add a buttery richness.

MAKES ABOUT 1 QUART

3 cups goat milk

2 ounces fresh goat cheese, crumbled

$1/2$ cup granulated sugar, divided

$1/3$ cup ground espresso coffee

$1/8$ teaspoon kosher salt

4 large egg yolks

$1/2$ teaspoon pure vanilla extract, preferably from Madagascar

Combine the goat milk, goat cheese, $1/4$ cup sugar, coffee, and salt in a medium saucepan, and stir well to dissolve the milk powder. Bring the mixture just to a simmer over medium heat, stirring occasionally.

Cover the pan and remove from the heat. Allow the mixture to steep for 30 minutes, then strain the mixture through a fine sieve, pressing with the back of a spoon to extract as much liquid as possible.

While the mixture steeps, beat the egg yolks, remaining $1/4$ cup sugar, and vanilla extract in a mixing bowl with a whisk until thick and light yellow in color. Slowly beat about one-third of the hot goat milk mixture into the eggs so they are gradually warmed up, and then return the contents of the mixing bowl to the saucepan. Place the pan over medium-low heat and stir constantly, reaching all parts of the bottom of the pan, until the mixture reaches about 170°F on an instant-read thermometer; at this point it begins to emit steam, thickens slightly, and coats the back of a spoon. This takes 3 to 6 minutes. Do not allow the mixture to boil or the eggs will scramble. Strain the custard through a fine sieve, if desired.

Transfer the hot liquid to a storage container and press a sheet of plastic wrap directly onto the surface of the mixture to prevent a skin from forming. Refrigerate the mixture uncovered until it is completely chilled (below 40°F), or quick-cool it according to the method on page 14.

Freeze the mixture in an ice cream maker according to the manufacturer's instructions. Serve immediately for a soft ice cream, or transfer the mixture to an airtight storage container and freeze until hard. Allow the ice cream to sit at room temperature for 15 minutes before serving if frozen solid.

LáLoo's, Petaluma, CA

LAURA HOWARD WAS AN ADMITTED ICE CREAM ADDICT, AND THEN HER YOGA instructor put her on a diet free of cow's milk. So she started making frozen concoctions with goat's milk, and the result is now LáLoo's, produced in sight of the lush vineyards of Sonoma County. Pronounced *lay-looz*, the firm began production in 2004, and the line now includes more than two dozen flavors.

Making ice cream is a radical departure for Howard. A graduate of the University of Miami, she was an advertising executive in Hollywood for fifteen years, managing a budget of more than a quarter-billion dollars in television commercials. Her circuitous route led her in 2000 to a life of studying yoga and Sanskrit. She then met photographer Douglas Gayeton while visiting Tuscany, and the two later married.

With their young daughter, the pair now lives on a goat farm in bucolic Sonoma County, where they also grow herbs like mint and basil included in some flavors. The company supports six family-owned goat farms where, she says, "the goats lead a good life." The resulting ice cream is low in both fat and lactose. Goat's milk also contains all the essential amino acids.

Both Laura and Douglas are also very involved in America's Slow Food movement founded by such culinary luminaries as Alice Waters. "The idea is to preserve tradition and quality in the cultivation, preparation, and consumption of food," she says. "Slow food equals culinary pleasure as well as good health." LáLoo's remains active with the Slow Food Nation and the Sonoma County Slow Food Convivium.

left: Buttercup, one of Laura's favorite goats; *right:* Laura Howard, co-founder of LáLoos

TURKISH COFFEE ICE CREAM

ADAPTED FROM McCONNELL'S,
SANTA BARBARA, CA

This ice cream could truly be an afternoon pick-me-up; the ground coffee included in the custard gives you a real caffeine jolt! This is for any coffee lover you know, and is even better topped with some Butterscotch Sauce (page 213).

MAKES ABOUT 1 QUART

1 1/4 cups heavy whipping cream
3/4 cup whole milk
1/2 cup granulated sugar, divided
1/3 cup ground espresso coffee, divided
1/4 cup nonfat dry milk powder
1/8 teaspoon kosher salt
4 large egg yolks
1/4 teaspoon pure vanilla extract

Combine the cream, milk, 1/4 cup sugar, 1/4 cup ground coffee, milk powder, and salt in a medium saucepan, and stir well to dissolve the milk powder. Bring the mixture just to a simmer over medium heat, stirring occasionally.

Cover the pan and remove from the heat. Allow the mixture to steep for 30 minutes, then strain the mixture through a fine sieve, pressing with the back of a spoon to extract as much liquid as possible. Reheat the coffee mixture until it is just simmering.

Beat the eggs yolks, remaining 1/4 cup sugar, and vanilla extract in a mixing bowl with a whisk until thick and light yellow in color. Slowly beat about one-third of the hot cream mixture into the eggs so they are gradually warmed up, and then return the contents of the mixing bowl to the saucepan. Place the pan over medium-low heat and stir constantly, reaching all parts of the bottom of the pan, until the mixture reaches about 170°F on an instant-read thermometer; at this point it begins to emit steam, thickens slightly, and coats the back of a spoon. This takes 3 to 6 minutes. Do not allow the mixture to boil or the eggs will scramble. Strain the custard through a fine sieve, if desired. Stir in the remaining ground coffee.

Transfer the hot liquid to a storage container, and press a sheet of plastic wrap directly onto the surface of the mixture to prevent a skin from forming. Refrigerate the mixture uncovered until it is completely chilled (below 40°F), or quick-cool it according to the method on page 14.

Freeze the mixture in an ice cream maker according to the manufacturer's instructions. Serve immediately for a soft ice cream, or transfer the mixture to an airtight storage container and freeze until hard. Allow the ice cream to sit at room temperature for 15 minutes before serving if frozen solid.

McConnell's, Santa Barbara, CA

WHEN GORDON F. "MAC" MCCONNELL WAS AN AIR FORCE PILOT in Europe during World War II he sampled many fantastic ice creams. After returning to his native Santa Barbara, he traded his wings for a whisk. With his wife, Ernestine, McConnell opened up an ice cream shop and factory on a site that once housed a silent film studio.

In addition to bringing European flavors to Santa Barbara, he also wanted to make ice creams with the same creamy texture, so he imported his equipment from France. McConnell's ice creams are French-style and include a large number of egg yolks to produce ice creams with a truly luxurious mouthfeel.

McConnell's was an instant hit, and such flavors as the French Vanilla remain on the menu today. Another popular favorite is Peppermint Stick (see Pink Peppermint Ice Cream, page 193), which is produced year-round, not just during the holiday season.

Longevity and consistency seem to go hand in hand at McConnell's. They've had the same master ice cream maker, Mike Vierra, for more than thirty years, and the organic cream has come from the same dairy since the day it opened. It's carted a few miles to the factory in what looks like a small gasoline truck dubbed the "iron udder."

left: The staff at McConnell's with their ice cream truck; *right*: "Mac" McConnell and Ernestine

KONA MOCHA CHIP

ADAPTED FROM LAPPERT'S,
RICHMOND, CA

*The fold-ins of hand-chopped
bittersweet chocolate add crunchy
texture and sweet chocolate flavor
to this creamy coffee ice cream.*

MAKES ABOUT 1 QUART

1^1/$_2$ cups heavy whipping cream

1^1/$_4$ cups whole milk, divided

^{1}/$_2$ cup ground Kona coffee

^{1}/$_3$ cup granulated sugar

^{1}/$_4$ cup light corn syrup

^{1}/$_8$ teaspoon kosher salt

2^1/$_2$ tablespoons cornstarch

2 tablespoons buttermilk powder

^{1}/$_4$ teaspoon pure vanilla extract

3 ounces bittersweet chocolate,
finely chopped

Combine the cream, ^{1}/$_2$ cup milk, coffee, sugar, corn syrup, and salt in a saucepan. Cook over medium heat, stirring frequently, until the mixture comes to a boil.

Cover the pan and remove from the heat. Allow the mixture to steep for 30 minutes, then strain the mixture through a fine sieve, pressing with the back of a spoon to extract as much liquid as possible.

While the mixture steeps, combine the remaining milk, cornstarch, buttermilk powder, and vanilla extract in a small bowl, and stir until smooth and both of the powders have dissolved.

Add the cornstarch mixture to the pan, and bring to a boil over low heat, stirring constantly. Whisk the mixture until smooth, and simmer the mixture over very low heat, stirring constantly, for 2 minutes, or until thickened. If the mixture is lumpy, strain it through a sieve.

Transfer the hot liquid to a storage container, and press a sheet of plastic wrap directly onto the surface of the mixture to prevent a skin from forming. Refrigerate the mixture uncovered until it is completely chilled (below 40°F), or quick-cool it according to the method on page 14. Refrigerate the chopped chocolate separately.

Stir the chopped chocolate into the chilled custard. Freeze the mixture in an ice cream maker according to the manufacturer's instructions. Serve immediately for a soft ice cream, or transfer the mixture to an airtight storage container and freeze until hard. Allow the ice cream to sit at room temperature for 15 minutes before serving if frozen solid.

CAPPUCCINO CHIP GELATO

ADAPTED FROM COLD FUSION
GELATO, NEWPORT, RI

*Miniature chocolate chips
are folded into this light,
espresso-spiked gelato.*

MAKES ABOUT 1 QUART

2 cups whole milk, divided

$^1/_4$ cup ground espresso coffee

$^3/_4$ cup heavy whipping cream

$^1/_2$ cup granulated sugar

$^1/_4$ cup light corn syrup

$^1/_8$ teaspoon kosher salt

2 tablespoons nonfat
dry milk powder

2 tablespoons cornstarch

$^1/_4$ teaspoon pure vanilla extract

$^1/_2$ cup miniature chocolate chips

Combine 1$^1/_2$ cups of the milk, coffee, cream, sugar, corn syrup, and salt in a saucepan. Cook over medium heat, stirring frequently, until the mixture begins to steam; watch it carefully and make sure it does not come to a boil.

Cover the pan and remove from the heat. Allow the mixture to steep for 30 minutes, then strain the mixture through a fine sieve, pressing with the back of a spoon to extract as much liquid as possible.

While the mixture steeps, combine the remaining milk, milk powder, cornstarch, and vanilla extract in a small bowl, and stir until smooth and both of the powders have dissolved.

Add the cornstarch mixture to the pan, and bring to a boil over low heat, stirring constantly. Whisk the mixture until smooth, and simmer the mixture over very low heat, stirring constantly, for 2 minutes, or until thickened. If the mixture is lumpy, strain it through a sieve.

Transfer the hot liquid to a storage container, and press a sheet of plastic wrap directly onto the surface of the mixture to prevent a skin from forming. Refrigerate the mixture uncovered until it is completely chilled (below 40°F), or quick-cool it according to the method on page 14.

Stir the chocolate chips into the chilled custard.

Freeze the mixture in an ice cream maker according to the manufacturer's instructions. Serve immediately for a soft gelato, or transfer the mixture to an airtight storage container and freeze until hard. Allow the gelato to sit at room temperature for 15 minutes before serving if frozen solid.

COFFEE FROZEN YOGURT with TOFFEE CRUNCH

ADAPTED FROM THE DAILY
SCOOP, BARRINGTON, RI

*The shop actually crushes
Heath Bars into the yogurt. While
the yogurt is light, the crushed
candy makes it seem indulgent.*

MAKES ABOUT 1 QUART

1 quart plain whole milk yogurt

2 tablespoons instant coffee powder

$^2/_3$ cup granulated sugar

$^1/_2$ teaspoon pure vanilla extract

$^1/_4$ teaspoon kosher salt

$^1/_2$ cup crushed chocolate-covered
toffee candy bar

Line a strainer with cheesecloth. Place the yogurt in the strainer, and set the strainer over a mixing bowl. Refrigerate the yogurt for 4 to 6 hours, or until it has lost about half of its volume. Discard the whey and place the yogurt in the mixing bowl.

While the yogurt drains, combine the instant coffee powder, sugar, vanilla extract, salt, and $^2/_3$ cup water in a small saucepan. Stir well, and heat over medium-high heat until the sugar and coffee powder dissolve. Transfer the mixture to a small bowl, and refrigerate until cold.

Beat the cold coffee mixture into the strained yogurt. Refrigerate the mixture uncovered until it is completely chilled (below 40°F), or quick-cool it according to the method on page 14. Stir in the crushed candies.

Freeze the mixture in an ice cream maker according to the manufacturer's instructions. Serve immediately for a soft frozen yogurt, or transfer the mixture to an airtight storage container and freeze until hard. Allow the frozen yogurt to sit at room temperature for 15 minutes before serving if frozen solid.

COFFEE, CHOCOLATE, and ALMOND ICE CREAM

ADAPTED FROM MITCHELL'S,
SAN FRANCISCO, CA

At Mitchell's, this ice cream is named Claire's Pie because it was created to replicate the owner's wife's famous ice cream pie, even including crushed graham crackers to represent the crust.

MAKES ABOUT 1 QUART

1 cup heavy whipping cream

$1/3$ cup ground coffee, preferably Colombian

$3/4$ cup whole milk, divided

$1/4$ cup granulated sugar

$1/4$ cup light corn syrup

$1/8$ teaspoon kosher salt

2 tablespoons cornstarch

2 tablespoons nonfat dry milk powder

$1/4$ teaspoon pure vanilla extract

$1/2$ cup coarsely chopped almonds

$1/3$ cup high-quality semisweet chocolate chips

2 graham crackers, crushed

Combine the cream, coffee, $1/2$ cup milk, sugar, corn syrup, and salt in a saucepan. Cook over medium heat, stirring frequently, until the mixture reaches a simmer.

Cover the pan and remove from the heat. Allow the mixture to steep for 30 minutes, then strain the mixture through a fine sieve, pressing with the back of a spoon to extract as much liquid as possible.

While the mixture steeps, combine the remaining milk, cornstarch, milk powder, and vanilla extract in a small bowl, and stir until smooth and both of the powders have dissolved.

Add the cornstarch mixture to the pan, and bring to a boil over low heat. Whisk until smooth, stirring constantly, and simmer the mixture for 2 minutes, or until thickened. If the mixture is lumpy, strain it through a sieve.

Transfer the hot liquid to a storage container, and press a sheet of plastic wrap directly onto the surface of the mixture to prevent a skin from forming. Refrigerate the mixture uncovered until it is completely chilled (below 40°F), or quick-cool it according to the method on page 14.

While the custard chills, toast the almonds: Preheat the oven to 350°F. Line a baking sheet with heavy-duty aluminum foil. Toast the almonds for 5 to 7 minutes, or until browned. Set aside.

Freeze the chilled custard in an ice cream maker according to the manufacturer's instructions. Transfer the soft ice cream to a chilled mixing bowl and fold in the toasted almonds, chocolate chips, and crushed graham crackers.

Serve immediately for a soft ice cream, or transfer the mixture to an airtight storage container and freeze until hard. Allow the ice cream to sit at room temperature for 15 minutes before serving if frozen solid.

COFFEE ICE CREAM with MACADAMIA NUTS, TOASTED COCONUT, and CHOCOLATE CHIPS

ADAPTED FROM LAPPERT'S,
RICHMOND, CA

Filled with Hawaiian ingredients, this ice cream is called Kauai Pie on Lappert's menu with good reason. The contrast of flavors and textures makes it irresistible both on its own and as the base for Baked Alaska (page 228).

MAKES ABOUT 1 QUART

1 $^1/_4$ cups heavy whipping cream

1 cup whole milk, divided

$^1/_2$ cup ground Kona coffee

$^1/_3$ cup granulated sugar

$^1/_4$ cup light corn syrup

$^1/_8$ teaspoon kosher salt

$^1/_2$ cup firmly packed sweetened shredded coconut

2 tablespoons cornstarch

2 tablespoons buttermilk powder

$^1/_4$ teaspoon pure vanilla extract

$^1/_2$ cup chopped macadamia nuts

$^1/_2$ cup miniature chocolate chips

Combine the cream, $^1/_2$ cup milk, coffee, sugar, corn syrup, and salt in a saucepan. Cook over medium heat, stirring frequently, until the mixture comes to a boil.

Cover the pan and remove from the heat. Allow the mixture to steep for 30 minutes, then strain the mixture through a fine sieve, pressing with the back of a spoon to extract as much liquid as possible.

Preheat the oven to 375°F. Line a baking sheet with heavy-duty aluminum foil.

Spread out the coconut on the baking sheet, and bake for 5 to 7 minutes, or until browned. Remove the pan from the oven, and transfer the coconut to a small container.

While the coconut toasts, combine the remaining milk, cornstarch, buttermilk powder, and vanilla extract in a small bowl, and stir until smooth and both of the powders have dissolved.

Add the cornstarch mixture to the pan, and bring to a boil over low heat, stirring constantly. Whisk the mixture until smooth, and simmer the mixture over very low heat, stirring constantly, for 2 minutes, or until thickened. If the mixture is lumpy, strain it through a sieve.

Transfer the hot liquid to a storage container, and press a sheet of plastic wrap directly onto the surface of the mixture to prevent a skin from forming. Refrigerate the mixture uncovered until it is completely chilled (below 40°F), or quick-cool it according to the method on page 14.

Stir the coconut, nuts, and chocolate chips into the chilled custard. Freeze the mixture in an ice cream maker according to the manufacturer's instructions. Serve immediately for a soft ice cream, or transfer the mixture to an airtight storage container and freeze until hard. Allow the ice cream to sit at room temperature for 15 minutes before serving if frozen solid.

Lappert's, Richmond, CA

TROPICAL FLAVORS PLAY A RECURRING ROLE IN MICHAEL LAPPERT'S LIFE—
and in his memories of ice cream. He spent his childhood in Venezuela, where he developed
a fondness for ice creams made with tropical fruits.

Then the tropics prompted his family's entrance into the ice cream business. In 1983,
Michael's father, Walter Lappert, decided that he wanted to retire to Hawaii and on a trip to
scout the exact location realized that what the islands were lacking was great ice cream. As
soon as the operation was up and running on Kauai, Michael opened his own Lappert's in
northern California, with shops in Marin County as his flagships.

While located in Northern California rather than in the islands, Lappert's maintains a tie
to the tropics in its list of flavors. One of his signature flavors is Kauai Pie, which blends high-
quality Kona coffee with other island treats like macadamia nuts and coconut (see Coffee Ice
Cream with Macadamia Nuts, Toasted Coconut, and Chocolate Chips, page 77).

In recent years, however, he has focused on fruit flavors and combining ice creams with sorbet
swirls. Mango Duo (page 104), which he calls Manila Mango, is an example of this technique.

left: Walter Lappert; *right*: Michael Lappert

5 Frozen from Fruits

There's no end to the fantastic combinations when you mix fruit and cream. The color can be vibrant or a pale pastel; the flavor can be succulent, sweet, or even a bit tart.

We're lucky that there basically isn't a fruit that hasn't been churned into an ice cream, and those are the recipes you'll find in this chapter. For something lighter, look ahead to Chapter 6 where you'll find all the sorbets and sherbets.

FRESH FROM THE FREEZER

While there's nothing like the flavor and aroma of a fresh fruit, it's better to use dry-packed frozen fruit rather than canned fruit or out-of-season or unripened fresh fruit for ice creams and sorbets. Dry-packed is the way fruits are described when they are frozen in individual pieces without any syrup or additional sugar. You'll find the fruits in plastic bags (not in tubs) in the freezer section. The frozen fruits are picked and frozen at the peak of ripeness, and for making frozen treats, they save time without sacrificing flavor.

But you do pay a premium price for the convenience of frozen fruit. While we can enjoy almost all fruits year-round, there are times when they are either in season locally or attractively priced. That's the time to stock up and freeze them yourself.

The best way to freeze fruits is to prepare them as noted in each individual recipe in this chapter (sliced or chopped, or for berries and other small fruits, just rinse them). Then arrange $1/2$- to 1-inch pieces on a baking sheet covered with plastic wrap, and freeze the whole tray. Once frozen, the fruit can be transferred to a heavy, resealable plastic bag. Mark the date on the bag, and use the fruit within two months.

Almost any fruit that can be frozen whole or in pieces can also be frozen as a purée, which then gives you a shortcut for making ice creams. Cut it into small chunks and place it in a food processor fitted with the steel blade or in a blender with $1/4$ cup of water for each cup of fruit. Freeze the purée in ice cube trays, and the cubes will melt quickly in the hot ice cream custard.

APPLE PIE
ICE CREAM

ADAPTED FROM BONNIE BRAE,
DENVER, CO

*Why serve ice cream on apple
pie when you can have ice cream
that tastes like apple pie? That's
what you're getting here, with a
sprinkling of aromatic spices.*

MAKES ABOUT 1 QUART

Ice Cream

2 tablespoons unsalted butter

2 Granny Smith apples, peeled,
cored, and chopped

$^1/_3$ cup granulated sugar

$^1/_4$ teaspoon ground cinnamon

$^1/_4$ teaspoon ground ginger

$^1/_8$ teaspoon freshly grated nutmeg

$1^1/_2$ cups heavy whipping
cream, divided

$^3/_4$ cup whole milk, divided

$^1/_4$ cup light corn syrup

$^1/_8$ teaspoon kosher salt

2 tablespoons nonfat
dry milk powder

2 tablespoons cornstarch

$^1/_4$ teaspoon pure vanilla extract

Streusel

$^1/_2$ cup graham cracker crumbs

3 tablespoons unsalted butter, melted

1 tablespoon granulated sugar

For the ice cream: Melt the butter in a skillet over medium-high heat. Add the apples, sugar, cinnamon, ginger, and nutmeg, and stir well. Reduce the heat to medium, and cook for 5 to 7 minutes, or until the apples are soft. Purée the apples and $^1/_4$ cup of the cream in a food processor fitted with the steel blade or in a blender. Transfer the mixture to a saucepan.

Add the remaining cream, $^1/_2$ cup milk, corn syrup, and salt to the saucepan. Cook over medium heat, stirring frequently, until the mixture begins to steam; watch it carefully and make sure it does not come to a boil.

While the mixture heats, combine the remaining milk, milk powder, cornstarch, and vanilla extract in a small bowl, and stir until smooth.

Add the cornstarch mixture to the pan, and bring to a boil over low heat, stirring constantly. Whisk the mixture until smooth, and simmer the mixture over very low heat, stirring constantly, for 2 minutes, or until thickened. If the mixture is lumpy, strain it through a sieve.

Transfer the hot liquid to a storage container, and press a sheet of plastic wrap directly onto the surface of the mixture to prevent a skin from forming. Refrigerate the mixture uncovered until it is completely chilled (below 40°F), or quick-cool it according to the method on page 14.

While the custard cools, make the streusel: Combine the graham cracker crumbs, butter, and sugar in a small bowl, and mix well. Set aside.

Freeze the chilled custard in an ice cream maker according to the manufacturer's instructions. Transfer the soft ice cream to a chilled mixing bowl and sprinkle the streusel over the top. Gently fold it in using a wide metal spatula.

Serve immediately for a soft ice cream, or transfer the mixture to an airtight storage container and freeze until hard. Allow the ice cream to sit at room temperature for 15 minutes before serving if frozen solid.

APRICOT ICE CREAM

ADAPTED FROM MOOMERS,
TRAVERSE CITY, MI

It's a mystery why more creameries don't make apricot ice cream! It's absolutely luscious, especially if you top it with Strawberry Sauce (page 216).

MAKES ABOUT 1 QUART

$2/3$ cup firmly packed dried apricots

$1/4$ cup apricot preserves

2 teaspoons freshly squeezed lemon juice

$1 1/2$ cups whole milk, divided

1 cup heavy whipping cream

$1/4$ cup granulated sugar

$1/4$ cup light corn syrup

$1/8$ teaspoon kosher salt

3 tablespoons nonfat dry milk powder

2 tablespoons cornstarch

$1/4$ teaspoon pure vanilla extract

Combine the dried apricots, apricot preserves, lemon juice, and $2/3$ cup water in a saucepan, and stir well. Bring to a boil over medium heat, stirring occasionally. Reduce the heat to low, and simmer for 3 minutes. Transfer the mixture to a food processor fitted with the steel blade or to a blender. Add 1 cup of the milk, and purée until smooth. Return the mixture to the saucepan.

Add the cream, sugar, corn syrup, and salt to the pan. Cook over medium heat, stirring frequently, until the mixture begins to steam; watch it carefully and make sure it does not come to a boil.

While the mixture heats, combine the remaining milk, milk powder, cornstarch, and vanilla extract in a small bowl, and stir until smooth and both of the powders have dissolved.

Add the cornstarch mixture to the pan, and bring to a boil over low heat, stirring constantly. Whisk the mixture until smooth, and simmer the mixture over very low heat, stirring constantly, for 2 minutes, or until thickened. If the mixture is lumpy, strain it through a sieve.

Transfer the hot liquid to a storage container and press a sheet of plastic wrap directly onto the surface of the mixture to prevent a skin from forming. Refrigerate the mixture uncovered until it is completely chilled (below 40°F), or quick-cool it according to the method on page 14.

Freeze the mixture in an ice cream maker according to the manufacturer's instructions. Serve immediately for a soft ice cream, or transfer the mixture to an airtight storage container and freeze until hard. Allow the ice cream to sit at room temperature for 15 minutes before serving if frozen solid.

BANANA BERRY FROZEN YOGURT

ADAPTED FROM THE DAILY
SCOOP, BARRINGTON, RI

*The combination of creamy banana
and succulent strawberry in this
refreshing frozen yogurt makes it
especially delicious with a fruit
salad—or all by itself.*

MAKES ABOUT 1 QUART

1 quart plain whole milk yogurt

$1/3$ cup granulated sugar

$1/2$ teaspoon pure vanilla extract

$1/4$ teaspoon kosher salt

1 medium-sized ripe banana,
thinly sliced

$1/4$ cup strawberry preserves

Tip: Freezing Bananas

It's a paradox that just when bananas look their worst—almost all black—they taste the best. If you have some in that condition, put them in the freezer right in their skins. They'll thaw rather quickly and can then be used in ice creams like this one, in smoothies, or in banana bread.

Line a strainer with cheesecloth. Place the yogurt in the strainer, and set the strainer over a mixing bowl. Refrigerate the yogurt for 4 to 6 hours, or until it has lost about half of its volume. Discard the whey and place the yogurt in the mixing bowl.

While the yogurt drains, combine the sugar, vanilla, salt, and $1/2$ cup water in a small saucepan. Stir well, and heat over medium-high heat until the sugar dissolves. Combine the sugar syrup, banana, and strawberry preserves in a food processor fitted with the steel blade or in a blender. Purée until smooth.

Beat the fruit mixture into the strained yogurt. Refrigerate the mixture uncovered until it is completely chilled (below 40°F), or quick-cool it according to the method on page 14.

Freeze the mixture in an ice cream maker according to the manufacturer's instructions. Serve immediately for a frozen yogurt, or transfer the mixture to an airtight storage container and freeze until hard. Allow the frozen yogurt to sit at room temperature for 15 minutes before serving if frozen solid.

BANANA CREAM PIE ICE CREAM

ADAPTED FROM BONNIE BRAE,
DENVER, CO

Sweet ripe bananas, cream cheese, and even a swirl of graham crackers are in every bite of this luscious ice cream.

MAKES ABOUT 1 QUART

Ice Cream
2 large ripe bananas, sliced

1 (3-ounce) package cream cheese, at room temperature

$^3/_4$ cup whole milk, divided

$1^1/_2$ cups heavy whipping cream

$^1/_3$ cup granulated sugar

$^1/_4$ cup light corn syrup

$^1/_8$ teaspoon kosher salt

2 tablespoons nonfat dry milk powder

2 tablespoons cornstarch

$^1/_2$ teaspoon pure vanilla extract

Streusel
$^1/_2$ cup graham cracker crumbs

3 tablespoons unsalted butter, melted

1 tablespoon granulated sugar

Combine the bananas, cream cheese, and $^1/_2$ cup milk in a food processor fitted with the steel blade or in a blender; purée until smooth. Transfer the purée to a saucepan.

Add the cream, sugar, corn syrup, and salt to the saucepan. Cook over medium heat, stirring frequently, until the mixture begins to steam; watch it carefully and make sure it does not come to a boil.

While the mixture heats, combine the remaining milk, milk powder, cornstarch, and vanilla extract in a small bowl, and stir until smooth and both of the powders have dissolved.

Add the cornstarch mixture to the pan, and bring to a boil over low heat, stirring constantly. Whisk the mixture until smooth, and simmer the mixture over very low heat, stirring constantly, for 2 minutes, or until thickened. If the mixture is lumpy, strain it through a sieve.

Transfer the hot liquid to a storage container, and press a sheet of plastic wrap directly onto the surface of the mixture to prevent a skin from forming. Refrigerate the mixture uncovered until it is completely chilled (below 40°F), or quick-cool it according to the method on page 14.

While the custard cools, make the streusel: Combine the graham cracker crumbs, butter, and sugar in a small bowl, and mix well. Set aside.

Freeze the chilled custard in an ice cream maker according to the manufacturer's instructions. Transfer the soft ice cream to a chilled mixing bowl and sprinkle the streusel over the top. Gently fold it in using a wide metal spatula.

Serve immediately for a soft ice cream, or transfer the mixture to an airtight storage container and freeze until hard. Allow the ice cream to sit at room temperature for 15 minutes before serving if frozen solid.

BLACK CHERRY ICE CREAM with FUDGE SWIRL and BROWNIES

ADAPTED FROM MOOMERS,
TRAVERSE CITY, MI

When Moomers was featured on Good Morning America, this was the ice cream sampled on the air.

MAKES ABOUT 1 QUART

Ice Cream

2 cups pitted black cherry halves, divided

$^1/_4$ cup granulated sugar

$1^1/_4$ cups whole milk, divided

$^3/_4$ cup heavy whipping cream

$^1/_4$ cup light corn syrup

$^1/_8$ teaspoon kosher salt

3 tablespoons nonfat dry milk powder

2 tablespoons cornstarch

2 teaspoons freshly squeezed lemon juice

$^1/_4$ teaspoon pure vanilla extract

$^2/_3$ cup chopped Fudge Brownies (page 234) or purchased brownies

Swirl

1 (3.5-ounce) bar bittersweet chocolate, chopped

2 tablespoons heavy whipping cream

2 tablespoons unsalted butter

Pinch of kosher salt

Combine 1$^1/_2$ cups of the cherries, sugar, and $^1/_3$ cup water in a saucepan, and stir well. Bring to a boil over medium-high heat, then reduce the heat to low and cook the cherries for 5 minutes. Transfer the cherry mixture to a food processor fitted with the steel blade or to a blender, and purée until smooth. Return the purée to the saucepan.

Add $^3/_4$ cup of the milk, cream, corn syrup, and salt to the pan. Cook over medium heat, stirring frequently, until the mixture begins to steam; watch it carefully and make sure it does not come to a boil.

While the mixture heats, combine the remaining milk, milk powder, cornstarch, lemon juice, and vanilla extract in a small bowl, and stir until smooth and both of the powders have dissolved.

Add the cornstarch mixture to the pan, and bring to a boil over low heat. Whisk until smooth, and simmer the mixture for 2 minutes, or until thickened. If the mixture is lumpy, strain it through a sieve.

Transfer the hot liquid to a storage container and press a sheet of plastic wrap directly onto the surface of the mixture to prevent a skin from forming. Refrigerate the mixture uncovered until it is completely chilled (below 40°F), or cool it according to the method on page 14.

While the custard chills, make the swirl: Combine the chocolate, cream, butter, and salt in a small microwave-safe bowl. Heat in the microwave on medium (50 percent) power for 30 seconds. Stir, and repeat as necessary, until the mixture is melted and smooth. Set aside at room temperature. Chop the remaining black cherries.

Stir the chopped cherries into the chilled custard and freeze in an ice cream maker according to the manufacturer's instructions. Transfer the soft ice cream to a chilled mixing bowl and fold in the brownie pieces.

(continued)

After the ice cream has churned, add the swirl: transfer one-sixth of the ice cream to an airtight container. Top it with a few spoonfuls of the fudge swirl, and repeat until all the ice cream and swirl is layered. When serving the ice cream, dig into the container vertically so each serving contains some of the swirl.

Serve immediately for a soft ice cream, or freeze until hard. Allow the ice cream to sit at room temperature for 15 minutes before serving if frozen solid.

Moomers Homemade Ice Cream, Traverse City, MI

MOOMERS IS TRULY A WORKING DAIRY FARM AND FAMILY BUSINESS. TWO generations of the Plummer family are involved with the operation of this business, founded in 1998.

Nancy Plummer grew up on the farm, which still delivers milk that needs to be shaken to integrate the cream into the milk below it. Her love of ice cream started at an early age; she recalls her grandmother serving it to her in pastel-toned tulip glasses. While teaching first grade at the local school, she worked for three years on flavor lists and drawings before her husband, Bob, started building the ice cream factory and shop.

Nancy now oversees the business along with her son Jon. While she can be found behind the cash register, she also helps decorate the myriad ice cream cakes that Moomers provides for weddings and parties.

But the shop means more to the Plummers and their community than ice cream. "We are a destination for locals to come and meet, and for tourists to visit for the 'Moomers Experience' during the summer months," says Nancy. Children get to take tours of the adjacent farm, and the neighbors were all on hand in 2008 when a Moomers ice cream was declared "The Best Scoop in America" on *Good Morning America.*

What was the winning flavor? Cherries MOObilee, which is called Black Cherry Ice Cream with Fudge Swirl and Brownies in this book (page 87). It highlights luscious regionally grown cherries, a fruit for which the area is justly proud. Moomers made a contest out of naming the ice cream—a winning customer came up with the name. Now that's local.

BLACK CHERRY ICE CREAM

ADAPTED FROM MOOMERS,
TRAVERSE CITY, MI

Michigan is the black cherry capital of the country, and Moomers utilizes this vivid fruit for many flavors. This makes a wonderful torte when separated by Meringue Layers (page 231).

MAKES ABOUT 1 QUART

2$\frac{1}{2}$ cups pitted black cherry halves, divided

$\frac{1}{3}$ cup granulated sugar

1$\frac{1}{2}$ cups whole milk, divided

1 cup heavy whipping cream

$\frac{1}{4}$ cup light corn syrup

$\frac{1}{8}$ teaspoon kosher salt

3 tablespoons nonfat dry milk powder

2 tablespoons cornstarch

1 tablespoon Kirsch (optional)

2 teaspoons freshly squeezed lemon juice

$\frac{1}{4}$ teaspoon pure vanilla extract

Combine 2 cups of the cherries, sugar, and $\frac{1}{2}$ cup water in a saucepan, and stir well. Bring to a boil over medium-high heat, then reduce the heat to low and cook the cherries for 5 minutes. Transfer the cherry mixture to a food processor fitted with the steel blade or to a blender, and purée until smooth. Return the purée to the pan.

Add 1 cup of the milk, cream, corn syrup, and salt to the pan. Cook over medium heat, stirring frequently, until the mixture begins to steam; watch it carefully and make sure it does not come to a boil.

While the mixture heats, combine the remaining milk, milk powder, cornstarch, Kirsch (if using), lemon juice, and vanilla extract in a small bowl, and stir until smooth and both of the powders have dissolved.

Add the cornstarch mixture to the pan, and bring to a boil over low heat. Whisk until smooth, and simmer the mixture for 2 minutes, or until thickened. If the mixture is lumpy, strain it through a sieve.

Transfer the hot liquid to a storage container and press a sheet of plastic wrap directly onto the surface of the mixture to prevent a skin from forming. Refrigerate the mixture uncovered until it is completely chilled (below 40°F), or quick-cool it according to the method on page 14.

While the custard chills, chop the remaining black cherries.

Stir the chopped cherries into the chilled custard and freeze in an ice cream maker according to the manufacturer's instructions. Serve immediately for a soft ice cream, or transfer the mixture to an airtight storage container and freeze until hard. Allow the ice cream to sit at room temperature for 15 minutes before serving if frozen solid.

BLACK CHERRY, CHOCOLATE CHIP, and WALNUT ICE CREAM

ADAPTED FROM BONNIE BRAE, DENVER, CO

This ice cream is the epitome of the ice cream sundae; it has a mixture of fruit, nuts, and chocolate built right in.

MAKES ABOUT 1 QUART

1$\frac{1}{2}$ cups fresh black cherry halves or 1 (12-ounce) package frozen black cherries, thawed, divided

$\frac{3}{4}$ cup whole milk, divided

1$\frac{1}{4}$ cups heavy whipping cream

$\frac{1}{3}$ cup granulated sugar

$\frac{1}{4}$ cup light corn syrup

$\frac{1}{8}$ teaspoon kosher salt

2 tablespoons nonfat dry milk powder

2 tablespoons cornstarch

$\frac{1}{4}$ teaspoon pure vanilla extract

$\frac{1}{2}$ cup chopped walnuts

$\frac{1}{2}$ cup chopped bittersweet chocolate or chocolate chips

Combine 1 cup of the cherries and $\frac{1}{2}$ cup milk in a food processor fitted with the steel blade or in a blender and purée until smooth. Transfer the purée to a saucepan.

Add the cream, sugar, corn syrup, and salt to the pan, and stir well. Cook over medium heat, stirring frequently, until the mixture begins to steam; watch it carefully and make sure it does not come to a boil.

While the mixture heats, combine the remaining milk, milk powder, cornstarch, and vanilla extract in a small bowl, and stir until smooth and both of the powders have dissolved.

Add the cornstarch mixture to the pan, and bring to a boil over low heat, stirring constantly. Whisk the mixture until smooth, and simmer the mixture over very low heat, stirring constantly, for 2 minutes, or until thickened. If the mixture is lumpy, strain it through a sieve.

Transfer the hot liquid to a storage container and press a sheet of plastic wrap directly onto the surface of the mixture to prevent a skin from forming. Refrigerate the mixture uncovered until it is completely chilled (below 40°F), or quick-cool it according to the method on page 14.

While the custard chills, toast the nuts: Preheat the oven to 350°F. Line a baking sheet with heavy-duty aluminum foil. Toast the nuts for 5 to 7 minutes, or until browned. Set aside.

Freeze the chilled custard in an ice cream maker according to the manufacturer's instructions. Transfer the soft ice cream to a chilled mixing bowl and fold in the remaining cherries, toasted walnuts, and chocolate chips.

Serve immediately for a soft ice cream, or transfer the mixture to an airtight storage container and freeze until hard. Allow the ice cream to sit at room temperature for 15 minutes before serving if frozen solid.

COCONUT ICE CREAM

ADAPTED FROM McCONNELL'S,
SANTA BARBARA, CA

This wonderful ice cream has been on McConnell's menu since the company was founded more than sixty years ago. There's a chewiness to it that's addictive, and it's even better topped with Hot Fudge Sauce (page 210).

MAKES ABOUT 1 QUART

1¼ cups heavy whipping cream
1 (14-ounce) can coconut milk
½ cup granulated sugar, divided
¼ cup nonfat dry milk powder
⅛ teaspoon kosher salt
2 large eggs
⅛ teaspoon pure vanilla extract
¾ cup firmly packed shredded sweetened coconut

Combine the cream, coconut milk, ¼ cup sugar, milk powder, and salt in a medium saucepan, and stir well to dissolve the milk powder. Bring the mixture just to a simmer, stirring occasionally.

Beat the eggs, remaining ¼ cup sugar, and vanilla extract in a mixing bowl with a whisk until thick and light yellow in color. Slowly beat about one-third of the hot cream mixture into the eggs so they are gradually warmed up, and then return the contents of the mixing bowl to the saucepan. Place the pan over medium-low heat and stir constantly, reaching all parts of the bottom of the pan, until the mixture reaches about 170°F on an instant-read thermometer; at this point it begins to emit steam, thickens slightly, and coats the back of a spoon. This takes 3 to 6 minutes. Do not allow the mixture to boil or the eggs will scramble. Strain the custard through a fine sieve, if desired. Stir in the coconut.

Transfer the hot liquid to a storage container and press a sheet of plastic wrap directly onto the surface of the mixture to prevent a skin from forming. Refrigerate the mixture uncovered until it is completely chilled (below 40°F), or quick-cool it according to the method on page 14.

Freeze the mixture in an ice cream maker according to the manufacturer's instructions. Serve immediately for a soft ice cream, or transfer the mixture to an airtight storage container and freeze until hard. Allow the ice cream to sit at room temperature for 15 minutes before serving if frozen solid.

BLACK RASPBERRY CHOCOLATE CHIP

ADAPTED FROM GRAETER'S, CINCINNATI, OH

The season for succulent black raspberries is very short, so freeze some when you see them at the market. A slice of Citrus Angel Food Cake (page 232) goes nicely with this treat.

MAKES ABOUT 1 QUART

1 (12-ounce) bag frozen black raspberries, thawed

$1^{1}/_{2}$ cups heavy whipping cream

$^{3}/_{4}$ cup whole milk

$^{3}/_{4}$ cup granulated sugar, divided

2 tablespoons nonfat dry milk powder

$^{1}/_{8}$ teaspoon kosher salt

2 large eggs

2 teaspoons freshly squeezed lemon juice

2 ounces bittersweet chocolate, chopped

2 tablespoons unsalted butter

Purée the raspberries in a food processor fitted with the steel blade or in a blender until smooth. Strain the purée through a sieve, if desired.

Combine the purée, cream, milk, $^{1}/_{2}$ cup sugar, milk powder, and salt in a medium saucepan, and stir well to dissolve the milk powder. Bring the mixture just to a simmer over medium heat, stirring occasionally.

Beat the eggs, remaining $^{1}/_{4}$ cup sugar, and lemon juice in a mixing bowl with a whisk until thick and light yellow in color. Slowly beat about one-third of the hot cream mixture into the eggs so they are gradually warmed up, and then return the contents of the mixing bowl to the saucepan. Place the pan over medium-low heat and stir constantly, reaching all parts of the bottom of the pan, until the mixture reaches about 170°F on an instant-read thermometer; at this point it begins to emit steam, thickens slightly, and coats the back of a spoon. This takes 3 to 6 minutes. Do not allow the mixture to boil or the eggs will scramble. Strain the custard through a fine sieve, if desired.

Transfer the hot liquid to a storage container, and press a sheet of plastic wrap directly into the surface of the mixture to prevent a skin from forming. Refrigerate the mixture uncovered until it is completely chilled (below 40°F), or quick-cool it according to the method on page 14.

Combine the chocolate and butter in a small microwave-safe cup, and heat in the microwave on medium (50 percent) power for 20 seconds. Stir, and repeat as necessary until the chocolate melts and the mixture is smooth. Allow it to cool slightly, but do not allow it to become hard.

Freeze the chilled custard in an ice cream maker according to the manufacturer's instructions. When the ice cream is a soft consistency, slowly pour the melted chocolate into the freezer, allowing it to churn with the ice cream.

Serve immediately for a soft ice cream, or transfer the mixture to an airtight storage container and freeze until hard. Allow the ice cream to sit at room temperature for 15 minutes before serving if frozen solid.

Graeter's, Cincinnati, OH

IN THE 1880S LOUIS CHARLES GRAETER IMMIGRATED FROM BAVARIA AND settled in Cincinnati, a town with a growing German population. In time, he married Regina Berger, the daughter of a prominent businessman, and they started the ice cream and confection business while raising a family. It's an old American success story: the Graeter family lived above the store.

After his death in 1919, his widow took over the business, expanded it with satellite stores in the city, and ran it until well past the end of World War II—while still living above the store. Now the fourth generation of the Graeter family runs the chain of more than a dozen shops in a region that now includes Lexington and Louisville, Kentucky, to the south, and Columbus and Dayton, Ohio, to the north.

Graeter's is known for the huge chocolate chips incorporated into many flavors. They are created in the same way they have been for more than a century. Near the end of the churning process in what is called a French Pot—used by only a few manufacturers today—chocolate is slowly poured in and the dasher creates the irregular lumps. They also feature a rotation of seasonal specialties that range from Watermelon Sorbet during the summer to Peppermint Eggnog for the holidays.

Celebrities who have visited Cincinnati have learned about Graeter's and spread the company's fame. Oprah Winfrey loves their Butter Pecan (page 132) and Sarah Jessica Parker and Marvin Hamlisch sing its praises.

Regina and Louis Graeter

BLUEBERRY PIE ICE CREAM

ADAPTED FROM GRAETER'S,
CINCINNATI, OH

This ice cream was developed as a fund raiser for a young girl in Cincinnati who had cancer; the flavor was so popular that it was added to the offerings permanently. There are bits of crust to add some crunch to the creaminess; freeze one slice when you make a blueberry pie or purchase a slice at a bakery.

MAKES ABOUT 1 QUART

1 1/2 cups fresh blueberries or frozen blueberries, thawed

1/2 cup granulated sugar, divided

1/4 cup freshly squeezed orange juice

1 1/2 cups heavy whipping cream

3/4 cup whole milk

2 tablespoons nonfat dry milk powder

1/8 teaspoon kosher salt

2 large eggs

3/4 cup chopped blueberry pie pieces

Combine the blueberries, 1/4 cup sugar, and orange juice in a saucepan and bring to a boil over low heat, stirring occasionally. Simmer the berries for 5 minutes, or until they thicken. Purée the berries in a food processor fitted with the steel blade or in a blender, and return the purée to the saucepan.

Add the cream, milk, milk powder, and salt to the saucepan, and stir well to dissolve the milk powder. Bring the mixture just to a simmer, stirring occasionally.

Beat the eggs and remaining 1/4 cup sugar in a mixing bowl with a whisk until thick and light yellow in color. Slowly beat about one-third of the hot cream mixture into the eggs so they are gradually warmed up, and then return the contents of the mixing bowl to the saucepan. Place the pan over medium-low heat and stir constantly, reaching all parts of the bottom of the pan, until the mixture reaches about 170°F on an instant-read thermometer; at this point it begins to emit steam, thickens slightly, and coats the back of a spoon. This takes 3 to 6 minutes. Do not allow the mixture to boil or the eggs will scramble. Strain the custard through a fine sieve, if desired.

Transfer the hot liquid to a storage container and press a sheet of plastic wrap directly onto the surface of the mixture to prevent a skin from forming. Refrigerate the mixture uncovered until it is completely chilled (below 40°F), or quick-cool it according to the method on page 14.

Freeze the mixture in an ice cream maker according to the manufacturer's instructions. Transfer the soft ice cream to a chilled mixing bowl and fold in the pie pieces.

Serve immediately for a soft ice cream, or transfer the mixture to an airtight storage container and freeze until hard. Allow the ice cream to sit at room temperature for 15 minutes before serving if frozen solid.

COCONUT ICE CREAM with CARAMEL SWIRL and FUDGE BROWNIE BITS

ADAPTED FROM BONNIE BRAE, DENVER, CO

At the creamery, this is called Bonnie Brae Bliss—try it and you'll understand why.

MAKES ABOUT 1 QUART

$1^2/_3$ cups heavy whipping cream, divided

1 (15-ounce) can cream of coconut, such as Coco Lopez, well-stirred

$^1/_4$ cup light corn syrup

$^1/_8$ teaspoon kosher salt

$^1/_4$ cup whole milk

2 tablespoons nonfat dry milk powder

2 tablespoons cornstarch

$^1/_4$ teaspoon pure vanilla extract

16 caramel candies, unwrapped

$^3/_4$ cup crumbled Fudge Brownies (page 234) or purchased brownies

Combine $1^1/_3$ cups of the cream, cream of coconut, corn syrup, and salt in a saucepan. Cook over medium heat, stirring frequently, until the mixture begins to steam; watch it carefully and make sure it does not come to a boil.

While the mixture heats, combine the milk, milk powder, cornstarch, and vanilla extract in a small bowl, and stir until smooth and both of the powders have dissolved.

Add the cornstarch mixture to the pan, and bring to a boil over low heat, stirring constantly. Whisk the mixture until smooth, and simmer the mixture over very low heat, stirring constantly, for 2 minutes, or until thickened. If the mixture is lumpy, strain it through a sieve.

Transfer the hot liquid to a storage container and press a sheet of plastic wrap directly onto the surface of the mixture to prevent a skin from forming. Refrigerate the mixture uncovered until it is completely chilled (below 40°F), or quick-cool it according to the method on page 14.

While the ice cream mixture chills, combine the caramel candies and remaining $^1/_3$ cup of cream in a microwave-safe cup. Heat in the microwave on medium power for 30 seconds. Stir, and repeat as necessary until the mixture is smooth. Set aside at room temperature.

Freeze the chilled custard in an ice cream maker according to the manufacturer's instructions. Transfer the ice cream to a bowl and fold in the brownie pieces.

To make the swirl, spoon one-sixth of the ice cream into an airtight container. Top it with a few spoonfuls of the caramel swirl, and then repeat until all ice cream and caramel are layered. When serving the ice cream, dig into the container vertically so each serving contains some of the swirl.

Serve immediately for a soft ice cream, or freeze until hard. Allow the ice cream to sit at room temperature for 15 minutes before serving if frozen solid.

COCONUT PINEAPPLE ICE CREAM

ADAPTED FROM MITCHELL'S,
SAN FRANCISCO, CA

This ice cream tastes like a piña colada without the rum. For a tropical dessert, serve it drizzled with a little rum.

MAKES ABOUT 1 QUART

1 cup heavy whipping cream

1 (15-ounce) can cream of coconut, such as Coco Lopez, well-stirred

$^1/_8$ teaspoon kosher salt

$^1/_4$ cup whole milk

2 tablespoons cornstarch

2 tablespoons nonfat dry milk powder

$^1/_4$ teaspoon pure vanilla extract

$^1/_2$ cup canned crushed pineapple, drained well

$^1/_4$ cup sweetened shredded coconut

Combine the cream, cream of coconut, and salt in a saucepan. Cook over medium heat, stirring frequently, until the mixture begins to steam; watch it carefully and makes sure it does not come to a boil.

While the mixture heats, combine the milk, cornstarch, milk powder, and vanilla extract in a small bowl, and stir until smooth and both of the powders have dissolved.

Add the cornstarch mixture to the pan, and bring to a boil over low heat. Whisk until smooth, and simmer the mixture for 2 minutes, or until thickened. If the mixture is lumpy, strain it through a sieve. Stir the pineapple and coconut into the custard.

Transfer the hot liquid to a storage container and press a sheet of plastic wrap directly onto the surface of the mixture to prevent a skin from forming. Refrigerate the mixture uncovered until it is completely chilled (below 40°F), or quick-cool it according to the method on page 14.

Freeze the mixture in an ice cream maker according to the manufacturer's instructions. Serve immediately for a soft ice cream, or transfer the mixture to an airtight storage container and freeze until hard. Allow the ice cream to sit at room temperature for 15 minutes before serving if frozen solid.

FIG GELATO

ADAPTED FROM GS GELATO,
FORT WALTON BEACH, FL

If I had to pick my favorite recipe in this book, it would be this one. I adore figs in every form—fresh or dried and in sweet or savory dishes. And it's almost impossible to find it in ice cream! Until now, that is.

MAKES ABOUT 1 QUART

$1/2$ pound dried Turkish figs, stemmed and diced

$1/2$ cup granulated sugar

2 cups whole milk, divided

$1/2$ cup heavy whipping cream

$1/4$ cup light corn syrup

$1/4$ teaspoon kosher salt

3 tablespoons nonfat dry milk powder

2 tablespoons cornstarch

$1/4$ teaspoon pure vanilla extract

Combine the figs, sugar, and 1 cup water in a small saucepan, and bring to a boil over medium heat, stirring occasionally. Reduce the heat to low and cook the figs, stirring frequently, for 15 to 17 minutes, or until very soft and the mixture is thick. Set aside.

Combine $1/2$ cups of the milk, cream, corn syrup, and salt in a saucepan. Cook over medium heat, stirring frequently, until the mixture begins to steam; watch it carefully and make sure it does not come to a boil.

While the mixture heats, combine the remaining milk, milk powder, cornstarch, and vanilla extract in a small bowl, and stir until smooth and both of the powders have dissolved.

Add the cornstarch mixture to the pan, and bring to a boil over low heat, stirring constantly. Whisk the mixture until smooth, and simmer the mixture over very low heat, stirring constantly, for 2 minutes, or until thickened. If the mixture is lumpy, strain it through a sieve.

Combine the figs and 1 cup of the hot custard in a food processor fitted with the steel blade or in a blender, and purée until smooth. Return the purée to the pan, and whisk to blend.

Transfer the hot liquid to a storage container and press a sheet of plastic wrap directly onto the surface of the mixture to prevent a skin from forming. Refrigerate the mixture uncovered until it is completely chilled (below 40°F), or quick-cool it according to the method on page 14.

Freeze the mixture in an ice cream maker according to the manufacturer's instructions. Serve immediately for a soft gelato, or transfer the mixture to an airtight storage container and freeze until hard. Allow the gelato to sit at room temperature for 15 minutes before serving if frozen solid.

LEMON POPPY SEED GELATO

ADAPTED FROM COLD FUSION
GELATO, NEWPORT, RI

Do you like the little bits of crunch in a lemon poppy seed muffin? If so, here's the frosty version. It's really nice served with fruit salad.

MAKES ABOUT 1 QUART

2$^1/_2$ cups whole milk, divided

$^3/_4$ cup heavy whipping cream

$^2/_3$ cup granulated sugar

$^1/_4$ cup light corn syrup

$^1/_4$ cup freshly squeezed lemon juice

2 teaspoons grated lemon zest

$^1/_8$ teaspoon kosher salt

2 tablespoons nonfat
dry milk powder

2 tablespoons cornstarch

1 tablespoon poppy seeds

Combine 2 cups of the milk, cream, sugar, corn syrup, lemon juice, lemon zest, and salt in a saucepan. Cook over medium heat, stirring frequently, until the mixture begins to steam; watch it carefully and make sure it does not come to a boil.

While the mixture heats, combine the remaining milk, milk powder, and cornstarch in a small bowl, and stir until smooth and both of the powders have dissolved.

Add the cornstarch mixture to the pan, and bring to a boil over low heat, stirring constantly. Whisk the mixture until smooth, and simmer the mixture over very low heat, stirring constantly, for 2 minutes, or until thickened. If the mixture is lumpy, strain it through a sieve. Stir in the poppy seeds.

Transfer the hot liquid to a storage container and press a sheet of plastic wrap directly onto the surface of the mixture to prevent a skin from forming. Refrigerate the mixture uncovered until it is completely chilled (below 40°F), or quick-cool it according to the method on page 14.

Freeze the mixture in an ice cream maker according to the manufacturer's instructions. Serve immediately for a soft gelato, or transfer the mixture to an airtight storage container and freeze until hard. Allow the gelato to sit at room temperature for 15 minutes before serving if frozen solid.

LYCHEE ICE CREAM

ADAPTED FROM MITCHELL'S,
SAN FRANCISCO, CA

There are few better desserts to end an Asian meal than this ice cream! Sweet lychee fruits are available fresh for only a short time each year, but canned ones work well for this light but luscious ice cream.

MAKES ABOUT 1 QUART

2 (15-ounce) cans lychee fruit, drained with syrup reserved

$1^1/_4$ cups heavy whipping cream

$1/_3$ cup light corn syrup

$1/_8$ teaspoon kosher salt

$1/_2$ cup whole milk

2 tablespoons cornstarch

2 tablespoons nonfat dry milk powder

2 teaspoons freshly squeezed lemon juice

$1/_4$ teaspoon pure vanilla extract

Pour the reserved syrup from the lychee fruits into a saucepan and bring to a boil over medium-high heat. Reduce the heat to low, and simmer the syrup until reduced by two-thirds.

Add the cream, corn syrup, and salt to the saucepan. Cook over medium heat, stirring frequently, until the mixture begins to steam; watch it carefully and make sure it does not come to a boil.

While the mixture heats, combine the milk, cornstarch, milk powder, lemon juice, and vanilla extract in a small bowl, and stir until smooth and both of the powders have dissolved.

Add the cornstarch mixture to the pan, and bring to a boil over low heat. Whisk until smooth, and simmer the mixture for 2 minutes, or until thickened. If the mixture is lumpy, strain it through a sieve.

Look over the lychee fruits carefully to make sure that all traces of the pits and tough shells have been discarded. Purée the lychee fruits with $3/_4$ of the custard in a food processor fitted with the steel blade or in a blender. Stir the purée back into the saucepan.

Transfer the hot liquid to a storage container and press a sheet of plastic wrap directly onto the surface of the mixture to prevent a skin from forming. Refrigerate the mixture uncovered until it is completely chilled (below 40°F), or quick-cool it according to the method on page 14.

Freeze the mixture in an ice cream maker according to the manufacturer's instructions. Serve immediately for a soft ice cream, or transfer the mixture to an airtight storage container and freeze until hard. Allow the ice cream to sit at room temperature for 15 minutes before serving if frozen solid.

Mitchell's, San Francisco, CA

THE MITCHELL FAMILY HAS SEEN THE CITY OF SAN FRANCISCO GROW UP around them. Back in the early 1890s, the Noe Valley area, now a bustling neighborhood, was still country, and the family operated a small commercial dairy on the site that is now Mitchell's Ice Cream. Larry and Jack Mitchell turned that space into an ice cream parlor in 1953, and that's where it remains.

Larry Mitchell, now in his 80s, has turned over the day-to-day operations to his children, Linda and Brian, but he still shows up almost every day to supervise the production, all of which takes place in the back of the store. While Larry Mitchell will always hold his Vanilla Ice Cream dear, Mitchell's is known nationally for their panoply of tropical flavors—including Lychee Ice Cream (page 101) and Mango Ice Cream (opposite). "We started importing mangos from the Philippines twenty years ago at the suggestion of a customer who was a fruit broker," says Mitchell. After that became an instant success, the store started importing other tropical treats, including ube, which is purple yam, and macapuno, a sweet coconut. In the past few years Mitchell's has expanded beyond the Asian tropics to South America with the introduction of an ice cream based on lúcuma, a Peruvian fruit with flavor similar to a sweet potato.

left: Larry Mitchell, left, and his brother Bob working the counter; *right*: Opening Day, 1953

MANGO ICE CREAM

ADAPTED FROM MITCHELL'S,
SAN FRANCISCO, CA

*The key to making this ice cream is
using a good-quality mango nectar,
which can usually be found in
the Hispanic food aisle of the
supermarket. Serve this with a slice
of Citrus Angel Food Cake (page 232).*

MAKES ABOUT 1 QUART

3 cups mango nectar

1 large mango, peeled, pitted,
and chopped

1 cup heavy whipping
cream, divided

$3/4$ cup whole milk, divided

$1/4$ cup granulated sugar

$1/4$ cup light corn syrup

$1/8$ teaspoon kosher salt

2 tablespoons cornstarch

2 tablespoons nonfat
dry milk powder

$1/4$ teaspoon pure
vanilla extract

Pour the mango nectar into a saucepan, and bring to a boil over medium-high heat. Reduce the heat to low, and simmer the nectar until it is reduced by two-thirds.

Combine the chopped fresh mango with $1/2$ cup of the cream in a food processor fitted with the steel blade or in a blender and purée.

Add the mango purée, remaining cream, $1/2$ cup milk, sugar, corn syrup, and salt to the saucepan with the reduced mango nectar, and stir well. Cook over medium heat, stirring frequently, until the mixture begins to steam; watch it carefully and make sure it does not come to a boil.

While the mixture heats, combine the remaining milk, cornstarch, milk powder, and vanilla extract in a small bowl, and stir until smooth and both of the powders have dissolved.

Add the cornstarch mixture to the pan, and bring to a boil over low heat. Whisk until smooth, and simmer the mixture for 2 minutes, or until thickened. If the mixture is lumpy, strain it through a sieve.

Transfer the hot liquid to a storage container and press a sheet of plastic wrap directly onto the surface of the mixture to prevent a skin from forming. Refrigerate the mixture uncovered until it is completely chilled (below 40°F), or quick-cool it according to the method on page 14.

Freeze the mixture in an ice cream maker according to the manufacturer's instructions. Serve immediately for a soft ice cream, or transfer the mixture to an airtight storage container and freeze until hard. Allow the ice cream to sit at room temperature for 15 minutes before serving if frozen solid.

MANGO DUO ICE CREAM

ADAPTED FROM LAPPERT'S,
RICHMOND, CA

There's a double dose of flavorful mango in Lappert's Manila Mango; it combines mango fruit gelées with brandy-spiked mango ice cream. Serve it on top of a fruit salad made with other tropical fruits such as pineapple and banana.

MAKES ABOUT 1 QUART

2 cups mango nectar

2 teaspoons unflavored gelatin
or powdered agar

$^3/_4$ cup heavy whipping cream

$^3/_4$ cup whole milk, divided

$^1/_4$ cup granulated sugar

$^1/_4$ cup light corn syrup

$^1/_8$ teaspoon kosher salt

2 tablespoons cornstarch

2 tablespoons buttermilk powder

2 cups puréed fresh mango
(2 or 3 mangoes,
depending on size)

$1^1/_2$ tablespoons brandy

Place the mango nectar in a small saucepan and bring to a boil over medium heat, stirring occasionally. Reduce the heat to low, and simmer the nectar until reduced by half. While the nectar simmers, sprinkle the gelatin over $^1/_2$ cup of cold water to soften. Stir the softened gelatin into the hot reduced nectar; transfer the mixture to a container, and chill until cold and solid.

Combine the cream, $^1/_4$ cup milk, sugar, corn syrup, and salt in a saucepan. Cook over medium heat, stirring frequently, until the mixture begins to steam; watch it carefully and make sure it does not come to a boil.

While the mixture heats, combine the remaining milk, cornstarch, and buttermilk powder in a small bowl, and stir until smooth and both of the powders have dissolved.

Add the cornstarch mixture to the pan, and bring to a boil over low heat, stirring constantly. Whisk the mixture until smooth, and simmer the mixture over very low heat, stirring constantly, for 2 minutes, or until thickened. If the mixture is lumpy, strain it through a sieve.

Stir the fresh mango purée and brandy into the custard, and whisk well.

Transfer the hot liquid to a storage container and press a sheet of plastic wrap directly onto the surface of the mixture to prevent a skin from forming. Refrigerate the mixture uncovered until it is completely chilled (below 40°F), or quick-cool it according to the method on page 14.

Freeze the chilled custard in an ice cream maker according to the manufacturer's instructions; transfer the soft ice cream into a chilled mixing bowl. Using the small end of a melon baller, add balls of the nectar jelly to the ice cream, and gently fold them in.

Serve immediately for a soft ice cream, or transfer the mixture to an airtight storage container and freeze until hard. Allow the ice cream to sit at room temperature for 15 minutes before serving if frozen solid.

PINEAPPLE COCONUT ICE CREAM with RASPBERRY SORBET SWIRL

ADAPTED FROM LAPPERT'S, RICHMOND, CA

Michael Lappert named this vivid pink-and-white combination after the small volcanic island of Nukuhiva in French Polynesia.

MAKES ABOUT 1 QUART

Sorbet

1 teaspoon unflavored gelatin or powdered agar

$^1/_2$ cup corn syrup

1 (12-ounce) bag frozen raspberries

$1^1/_2$ teaspoons freshly squeezed lemon juice

Ice Cream

$^3/_4$ cup heavy whipping cream

$^1/_2$ cup cream of coconut, such as Coco Lopez, well-stirred

$^1/_4$ cup light corn syrup

$^1/_8$ teaspoon kosher salt

$1^1/_2$ tablespoons cornstarch

2 tablespoons buttermilk powder

$^1/_4$ teaspoon pure vanilla extract

$^1/_2$ cup crushed canned pineapple, drained

For the sorbet: Sprinkle the gelatin over $^2/_3$ cup of cold water to soften. Combine the corn syrup and raspberries in a small saucepan, and bring to a boil over medium heat, stirring occasionally. Cook for 1 minute over low heat, and then stir in softened gelatin and lemon juice. Cook for 1 minute, or until the gelatin dissolves. Purée the mixture in a food processor fitted with the steel blade or in a blender. Strain it through a sieve to remove the seeds, if desired.

Transfer the hot liquid to a storage container and press a sheet of plastic wrap directly onto the surface of the mixture to prevent a skin from forming. Refrigerate the mixture uncovered until it is completely chilled (below 40°F), or quick-cool it according to the method on page 14.

Freeze the mixture in an ice cream maker according to the manufacturer's instructions. Place the sorbet in the freezer while making the ice cream.

For the ice cream: Combine the cream, cream of coconut, corn syrup, and salt in a saucepan. Cook over medium heat, stirring frequently, until the mixture begins to steam; watch it carefully and make sure it does not come to a boil.

While the mixture heats, combine the cornstarch, buttermilk powder, and vanilla extract with $^1/_2$ cup cold water in a small bowl, and stir until smooth and both of the powders have dissolved.

Add the cornstarch mixture to the pan, and bring to a boil over low heat. Whisk the mixture until smooth, and simmer the mixture for 2 minutes, or until thickened. Remove from the heat. If the mixture is lumpy, strain it through a sieve. Stir in the pineapple.

(continued)

Transfer the hot liquid to a storage container and press a sheet of plastic wrap directly onto the surface of the mixture to prevent a skin from forming. Refrigerate the mixture uncovered until it is completely chilled (below 40°F), or quick-cool it according to the method on page 14.

Freeze the mixture in an ice cream maker according to the manufacturer's instructions.

To add the sorbet swirl, allow the raspberry sorbet to sit at room temperature 15 minutes to soften. Transfer the sorbet to the bottom of a chilled mixing bowl and top with the soft ice cream in a smooth layer. Fold the two together gently with a wide rubber spatula.

Serve immediately for a soft ice cream, or transfer the mixture to an airtight storage container and freeze until hard. Allow the ice cream to sit at room temperature for 15 minutes before serving if frozen solid.

Substitutions for Gelatin

Since gelatin is made from animal tissue, many vegetarians substitute agar, a thickening agent made from seaweed used extensively in Japanese cooking. Powdered agar, found in many health food stores, can be used in the same amount as gelatin in any recipe.

STRAWBERRY ICE CREAM

ADAPTED FROM GRAETER'S,
CINCINNATI, OH

This recipe is the epitome of summer, and its vivid color is matched by its superb flavor. Why not top it with Strawberry Sauce (page 216) or serve it as an alternative to strawberry shortcake at a picnic?

MAKES ABOUT 1 QUART

$1^1/_2$ cups firmly packed sliced fresh strawberries or frozen strawberries, thawed

$^1/_2$ cup strawberry preserves

$1^1/_2$ cups heavy whipping cream

$^3/_4$ cup whole milk

2 tablespoons nonfat dry milk powder

$^1/_8$ teaspoon kosher salt

2 large eggs

$^1/_3$ cup granulated sugar

1 teaspoon freshly squeezed lemon juice

Combine the strawberries and preserves in a saucepan with $^1/_4$ cup water, and stir well. Bring the mixture to a simmer over low heat, stirring frequently. Simmer the berries for 5 minutes, or until they thicken. Purée the berries in a food processor fitted with the steel blade or in a blender, and return the purée to the saucepan.

Add the cream, milk, milk powder, and salt to the saucepan, and stir well to dissolve the milk powder. Bring the mixture just to a simmer, stirring occasionally.

Beat the eggs, sugar, and lemon juice in a mixing bowl with a whisk until thick and light yellow in color. Slowly beat about one-third of the hot cream mixture into the eggs so they are gradually warmed up, and then return the contents of the mixing bowl to the saucepan. Place the pan over medium-low heat and stir constantly, reaching all parts of the bottom of the pan, until the mixture reaches about 170°F on an instant-read thermometer; at this point it begins to emit steam, thickens slightly, and coats the back of a spoon. This takes 3 to 6 minutes. Do not allow the mixture to boil or the eggs will scramble.

Transfer the hot liquid to a storage container and press a sheet of plastic wrap directly onto the surface of the mixture to prevent a skin from forming. Refrigerate the mixture uncovered until it is completely chilled (below 40°F), or quick-cool it according to the method on page 14.

Freeze the mixture in an ice cream maker according to the manufacturer's instructions. Serve immediately for a soft ice cream, or transfer the mixture to an airtight storage container and freeze until hard. Allow the ice cream to sit at room temperature for 15 minutes before serving if frozen solid.

BORDEAUX STRAWBERRY ICE CREAM

ADAPTED FROM McCONNELL'S,
SANTA BARBARA, CA

*The reduced wine deepens
the fruit flavor in this
wonderful ice cream.*

MAKES ABOUT 1 QUART

$1/2$ cup dry red wine,
preferably Bordeaux

2 cups fresh strawberries,
rinsed, hulled, and sliced, or
frozen berries, thawed

$1/2$ cup granulated sugar, divided

$1^1/4$ cups heavy whipping cream

$1/4$ cup nonfat milk powder

$1/8$ teaspoon kosher salt

3 large egg yolks

$1/4$ teaspoon pure vanilla extract

Pour the wine into a small saucepan and bring to a boil over medium-high heat. Reduce the heat to low and simmer the wine until reduced by two-thirds. While the wine simmers, toss the strawberries with $1/4$ cup of sugar, and set aside.

Add the strawberries to the wine, and bring to a boil over medium-high heat. Reduce the heat to low, and simmer for 5 minutes. Purée the berry mixture in a food processor fitted with the steel blade or in a blender.

Combine the berry purée, cream, milk powder, and salt in a medium saucepan, and stir well to dissolve the milk powder. Bring the mixture just to a simmer, stirring occasionally.

Beat the egg yolks, remaining $1/4$ cup sugar, and vanilla extract in a mixing bowl with a whisk until thick and light yellow in color. Slowly beat about one-third of the hot cream mixture into the eggs so they are gradually warmed up, and then return the contents of the mixing bowl to the saucepan. Place the pan over medium-low heat and stir constantly, reaching all parts of the bottom of the pan, until the mixture reaches about 170°F on an instant-read thermometer; at this point it begins to emit steam, thickens slightly, and coats the back of a spoon. This takes 3 to 6 minutes. Do not allow the mixture to boil or the eggs will scramble. Strain the custard through a fine sieve, if desired.

Transfer the hot liquid to a storage container and press a sheet of plastic wrap directly onto the surface of the mixture to prevent a skin from forming. Refrigerate the mixture uncovered until it is completely chilled (below 40°F), or quick-cool it according to the method on page 14.

Freeze the mixture in an ice cream maker according to the manufacturer's instructions. Serve immediately for a soft ice cream, or transfer to an airtight storage container and freeze until hard. Allow the ice cream to sit at room temperature for 15 minutes before serving if frozen solid.

MIXED BERRY GELATO

ADAPTED FROM GS GELATO,
FORT WALTON BEACH, FL

The vivid color of the gelato matches the intensity of its flavor. The three popular berries when joined create an ice cream with complex and delicious flavor.

MAKES ABOUT 1 QUART

$^1/_2$ cup fresh raspberries or frozen raspberries, thawed

$^1/_2$ cup fresh sliced strawberries or frozen strawberries, thawed

$^1/_2$ cup fresh blueberries or frozen blueberries, thawed

$^1/_2$ cup granulated sugar

2 cups whole milk, divided

$^1/_2$ cup heavy whipping cream

$^1/_4$ cup light corn syrup

$^1/_4$ teaspoon kosher salt

3 tablespoons nonfat dry milk powder

2 tablespoons cornstarch

1 teaspoon freshly squeezed lemon juice

Combine the raspberries, strawberries, blueberries, sugar, and $^1/_2$ cup water in a saucepan and bring to a boil over medium-high heat, stirring frequently. Reduce the heat and simmer the berries for 3 minutes, then purée in a food processor fitted with the steel blade or in a blender. Transfer the mixture to a saucepan.

Add $1^1/_2$ cups of the milk, cream, corn syrup, and salt to the pan. Cook over medium heat, stirring frequently, until the mixture begins to steam; watch it carefully and make sure it does not come to a boil.

While the mixture heats, combine the remaining milk, milk powder, cornstarch, and lemon juice in a small bowl, and stir until smooth and both of the powders have dissolved.

Add the cornstarch mixture to the pan, and bring to a boil over low heat, stirring constantly. Whisk the mixture until smooth, and simmer the mixture over very low heat, stirring constantly, for 2 minutes, or until thickened. If the mixture is lumpy, strain it through a sieve.

Transfer the hot liquid to a storage container and press a sheet of plastic wrap directly onto the surface of the mixture to prevent a skin from forming. Refrigerate the mixture uncovered until it is completely chilled (below 40°F), or quick-cool it according to the method on page 14.

Freeze the mixture in an ice cream maker according to the manufacturer's instructions. Serve immediately for a soft gelato, or transfer the mixture to an airtight storage container and freeze until hard. Allow the gelato to sit at room temperature for 15 minutes before serving if frozen solid.

6 Lighter Fruity Freezes

I'm truly proud of this chapter. Not only because the flavors are delicious, and the sorbets and sherbets are refreshing and cooling on a summer day. But also because, after days of experimentation, I managed to recreate the luxurious mouthfeel of Italian *sorbettos*.

I've always been stymied because sorbets in Italy really taste as if they are made with cream, although there's no dairy in them. After trial and error—many more errors than successes—I discovered the secret recipe. I was finally able to produce that same creaminess through a combination of reducing the simple syrup to concentrate it, and then adding some thickening via a bit of cornstarch.

You'll find that formulation in many of the recipes in this chapter, and you'll also find more traditional French-style sorbet recipes made with gelatin to keep them soft. Feel free to use the two basic formulations interchangeably.

BLOOD ORANGE SORBET

ADAPTED FROM GS GELATO,
FORT WALTON BEACH, FL

*Americans have been warming
up to the vivid, reddish orange color
and bright flavor of blood oranges
only recently, and this sorbet
is a great way to enjoy it.*

MAKES ABOUT 1 QUART

$1/2$ cup granulated sugar

2 tablespoons cornstarch

Pinch of kosher salt

$2^{1}/_{2}$ cups freshly squeezed
blood orange juice

1 tablespoon blood orange zest

2 teaspoons freshly
squeezed lemon juice

Combine the sugar and $1/3$ cup water in a small saucepan. Bring to a boil over medium heat, swirling the pan to dissolve the sugar but not stirring the mixture. Increase the heat to high, and cook the syrup until the firm-ball stage and the temperature registers 245°F to 250°F on a candy thermometer; the bubbles will be very large and the mixture will be very thick.

While the syrup is cooking, combine the cornstarch and salt with $1/4$ cup cold water in a small cup, and stir well to dissolve the cornstarch.

Remove the pan from the heat, and stir the cornstarch mixture into the sugar syrup. Cook the mixture on low for 1 minute, or until it becomes translucent and very thick.

Add the blood orange juice, blood orange zest, and lemon juice to the saucepan, and cook over low heat, stirring constantly, until the mixture is smooth.

Transfer the hot liquid to a storage container, and refrigerate uncovered until it is completely chilled (below 40°F), or quick-cool it according to the method on page 14.

Freeze the mixture in an ice cream maker according to the manufacturer's instructions. Serve immediately for a soft sorbet, or transfer the mixture to an airtight storage container and freeze until hard. Allow the sorbet to sit at room temperature for 15 minutes before serving if frozen solid.

Variation: Tangerine Sorbet

If it is difficult to get blood oranges where you live, substitute tangerine juice and zest for the orange, and add 2 tablespoons freshly squeezed lemon juice: blood oranges are a bit tarter than tangerines.

CANTALOUPE SORBET

ADAPTED FROM COLD FUSION
GELATO, NEWPORT, RI

*Cantaloupe is mostly water,
so you don't need much more to
make a cantaloupe sorbet. In
addition to enjoying it for dessert,
use a scoop to top off a glass of
lemonade or a wine spritzer.*

MAKES ABOUT 1 QUART

$1/2$ cup granulated sugar

2 tablespoons cornstarch

Pinch of kosher salt

1 small ripe cantaloupe,
peeled, seeded, and diced

1 tablespoon freshly
squeezed lemon juice

Combine the sugar and $1/3$ cup water in a small saucepan. Bring to a boil over medium heat, swirling the pan to dissolve the sugar but not stirring the mixture. Increase the heat to high, and cook the syrup until the firm-ball stage and the temperature registers 245°F to 250°F on a candy thermometer; the bubbles will be very large and the mixture will be very thick.

While the syrup is cooking, combine the cornstarch and salt with $1/4$ cup cold water in a small cup, and stir well to dissolve the cornstarch.

Remove the pan from the heat, and stir the cornstarch mixture into the sugar syrup. Cook the mixture on low for 1 minute, or until it becomes translucent and very thick. Set aside.

Purée the cantaloupe in a food processor fitted with the steel blade or in a blender. Add the cantaloupe purée and lemon juice to the pan with the cornstarch mixture, and whisk until smooth.

Transfer the hot liquid to a storage container, and refrigerate uncovered until it is completely chilled (below 40°F), or quick-cool it according to the method on page 14.

Freeze the mixture in an ice cream maker according to the manufacturer's instructions. Serve immediately for a soft sorbet, or transfer the mixture to an airtight storage container and freeze until hard. Allow the sorbet to sit at room temperature for 15 minutes before serving if frozen solid.

Cold Fusion Gelato, Newport, RI

NEWPORT IS THE MECCA OF SAILING IN THE U.S., AND THE MAIN DRAG through town is named America's Cup Avenue. During the summer, this village of Gilded Age mansions and yachts is the state's primary tourist destination, and the Cold Fusion Gelato shop is now part of the town's appeal.

Torrance Kopfer was a Wall Street banker until 2001, when he decided it was "clearly more fun to make gelato and sorbet that make people smile." You can find him in the kitchen peeling melons for Cantaloupe Sorbet (page 117) or grinding coffee for Cappuccino Chip Gelato (page 73).

While many of Cold Fusion's flavors are drawn from the authentic Italian tradition, and more than sixty on a given day are offered seasonally at his shop as well as at a Whole Foods Market about thirty miles away, Kopfer also enjoys working with local chefs and devising more exotic flavors. His Blueberry Pomegranate Sorbet (page 126) is the result of such collaboration.

While the business now includes distribution to some area supermarkets as well as restaurants, Kopfer wants it to remain an artisan product. "Our product is handmade, and each batch is taste-tested to ensure the highest possible quality. We also try to source ingredients locally whenever possible to support farmers and dairies," he says.

Gelato is not Kopfer's first artistic endeavor; he was trained as a classical violinist before his Wall Street years. But now that he's a professional gelato maker, surfing and flying have become his pastimes.

LEMON SHERBET

ADAPTED FROM GAGA'S,
WARWICK, RI

*Here is the way lemon sherbet
was meant to be eaten! It's tart
but has enough sugar to balance it,
and it's creamy but doesn't coat the
palate to tone down the lemon.
A slice of Citrus Angel Food Cake
(page 232) on the side is heaven.*

MAKES ABOUT 1 QUART

$3/4$ cup freshly squeezed
lemon juice

$1^1/4$ cups granulated sugar

$1^1/4$ cups whole milk, divided

1 cup heavy whipping cream

1 tablespoon grated lemon zest

$1/8$ teaspoon kosher salt

1 tablespoon cornstarch

$1/4$ teaspoon pure lemon
oil (optional)

Combine the lemon juice and sugar in a saucepan. Cook over low heat, stirring occasionally, until the sugar dissolves. Add $3/4$ cup of the milk, cream, lemon zest, and salt and cook over low heat, stirring occasionally, until the mixture begins to steam; watch it carefully and make sure it does not come to a boil.

While the mixture heats, combine the remaining milk and cornstarch in a small cup, and stir well. Add the cornstarch mixture to the pan, and bring to a boil over low heat. Whisk until smooth, and simmer the mixture for 2 minutes, or until lightly thickened. Stir in lemon oil, if using. If the mixture is lumpy, strain it through a sieve.

Transfer the hot liquid to a storage container, and press a sheet of plastic wrap directly onto the surface of the mixture to prevent a skin from forming. Refrigerate the mixture uncovered until it is completely chilled (below 40°F), or quick-cool it according to the method on page 14.

Freeze the mixture in an ice cream maker according to the manufacturer's instructions. Serve immediately for a soft sherbet, or transfer the mixture to an airtight storage container and freeze until hard. Allow the sherbet to sit at room temperature for 15 minutes before serving if frozen solid.

ORANGE SHERBET

ADAPTED FROM GAGA'S,
WARWICK, RI

*Most orange sherbet has just
a hint of orange flavor, but this
one is full of sunny citrus flavor.
It's rich enough to use in a
Baked Alaska (page 228) too.*

MAKES ABOUT 1 QUART

$1^1/_2$ cups whole milk, divided

1 cup heavy whipping cream

$^1/_3$ cup granulated sugar

$^1/_3$ cup frozen orange juice
concentrate, thawed

$^1/_8$ teaspoon kosher salt

1 navel orange, washed lightly

1 tablespoon cornstarch

$^1/_4$ teaspoon pure orange oil (optional)

Combine 1 cup of the milk, cream, sugar, orange juice concentrate, and salt in a saucepan. Grate the orange zest from the navel orange directly into the liquid, then squeeze the juice from the orange and add it to the pan.

Cook over medium heat, stirring frequently, until the mixture begins to steam; watch it carefully and make sure it does not come to a boil.

While the mixture heats, combine remaining milk and cornstarch in a small cup, and stir well.

Add the cornstarch mixture to the pan, and bring to a boil over low heat. Whisk until smooth, and simmer the mixture for 2 minutes, or until lightly thickened. Stir in orange oil, if using. If the mixture is lumpy, strain it through a sieve.

Transfer the hot liquid to a storage container, and press a sheet of plastic wrap directly onto the surface of the mixture to prevent a skin from forming. Refrigerate the mixture uncovered until it is completely chilled (below 40°F), or quick-cool it according to the method on page 14.

Freeze the mixture in an ice cream maker according to the manufacturer's instructions. Serve immediately for a soft sherbet, or transfer the mixture to an airtight storage container and freeze until hard. Allow the sherbet to sit at room temperature for 15 minutes before serving if frozen solid.

GaGa's, Warwick, RI

DECADES BEFORE LADY GAGA EMERGED IN THE WORLD OF POP CULTURE THERE was a beloved lady who was called "Gaga" by her toddler grandson. Jessie McRae King, who passed away in 1993, was one of those grandmothers of whom legends are made. Whenever young Jim King arrived at her house, there would be a frosty dish of homemade lemon or raspberry and orange sherbet awaiting him.

Her recipes, saved on well-worn 3-by-5-inch recipe cards, became the foundation for GaGa's, which was founded in 2001 by her grandson. Technically, GaGa's products (with 3.5 percent butterfat) fall into an icy void between the legal definitions of sherbet, which has less than 2 percent butterfat, and ice cream, which must contain at least 10 percent butterfat. That's why King, a former broadcaster, calls his products SherBetter. Customers in New England and upstate New York seem to agree; they rave about the creamy mouthfeel with vibrant, fresh fruit taste of the ice creams.

GaGa's is a small family operation, with King's children affixing labels to pint containers after school and his wife, Michelle, handling the public relations. And his father, Jack King (Gaga's son), helps out, too.

King says, "The dictionary describes 'gaga' as crazy, infatuated, marked by wild enthusiasm. That pretty much sums up the personality of the GaGa brand and what it means to me!"

Jessie McRae King, called Gaga by her grandchildren

PEACH SORBET

ADAPTED FROM SWEET
REPUBLIC, SCOTTSDALE, AZ

*While a sorbet and not an ice cream,
this is rich enough because of its
smooth texture to become a torte
with Meringue Layers (page 231).*

MAKES ABOUT 1 QUART

5 ripe peaches or 2 (12-ounce) bags
frozen peach slices, thawed

$^1/_3$ cup granulated sugar

2 tablespoons cornstarch

Pinch of kosher salt

$^1/_4$ cup corn syrup

1 tablespoon freshly squeezed
lemon juice

If using fresh peaches, bring a large saucepan of water to a boil over high heat. Add the whole peaches and blanch them for 40 seconds. Remove the peaches from the pan with a slotted spoon, and run them under cold water. When cool enough to handle, slip off the skins, discard the pits, and cut the peaches into 1-inch cubes. Using either fresh or frozen peaches, purée them in a food processor fitted with the steel blade or in a blender. Set aside.

Combine the sugar and $^1/_3$ cup water in a small saucepan. Bring to a boil over medium heat, swirling the pan to dissolve the sugar but not stirring the mixture. Increase the heat to high, and cook the syrup until the firm-ball stage and the temperature registers 245°F to 250°F on a candy thermometer; the bubbles will be very large and the mixture will be very thick.

While the syrup is cooking combine the cornstarch and salt with $^1/_4$ cup cold water in a small cup, and stir well to dissolve the cornstarch.

Remove from the heat, and stir the cornstarch mixture into the sugar syrup. Cook the mixture on low for 1 minute, or until it becomes translucent and very thick. Add the peach purée, corn syrup, and lemon juice to the pan with the cornstarch mixture, and whisk until smooth.

Transfer the hot liquid to a storage container, and refrigerate uncovered until it is completely chilled (below 40°F), or quick-cool it according to the method on page 14.

Freeze the mixture in an ice cream maker according to the manufacturer's instructions. Serve immediately for a soft sorbet, or transfer the mixture to an airtight storage container and freeze until hard. Allow the sorbet to sit at room temperature for 15 minutes before serving if frozen solid.

PEACH MELBA SORBET

ADAPTED FROM BLUE MOON
SORBET, QUECHEE, VT

Peach Melba is the famed dessert named for a famous opera singer, Dame Nellie Melba, in the late nineteenth century. It always contains both peaches and raspberries, as does this blushing pink sorbet.

MAKES ABOUT 1 QUART

2 teaspoons unflavored gelatin or powdered agar

3 ripe peaches or 1 (16-ounce) bag frozen peach slices

$^3/_4$ cup fresh raspberries or frozen raspberries, thawed

$^1/_2$ cup granulated sugar

$^1/_8$ teaspoon kosher salt

1 tablespoon freshly squeezed lemon juice

Sprinkle the gelatin over $^1/_2$ cup of cold water to soften.

If using fresh peaches, bring a saucepan of water to a boil over high heat. Add the peaches and blanch them for 40 seconds. Remove the peaches from the pan with a slotted spoon, and run them under cold water. When cool enough to handle, slip off the skins, discard the pits, and cut the peaches into 1-inch cubes.

Using either fresh or frozen peaches, purée the peaches and raspberries in a food processor fitted with the steel blade or in a blender.

Transfer the purée to a saucepan and stir in the sugar, salt, and 1 cup of water. Heat the mixture to dissolve the sugar. Stir in the softened gelatin and cook for 1 minute, or until the gelatin dissolves. Stir in the lemon juice.

Transfer the hot liquid to a storage container, and refrigerate uncovered until it is completely chilled (below 40°F), or quick-cool it according to the method on page 14.

Freeze the mixture in an ice cream maker according to the manufacturer's instructions. Serve immediately for a soft sorbet, or transfer the mixture to an airtight storage container and freeze until hard. Allow the sorbet to sit at room temperature for 15 minutes before serving if frozen solid.

PINK GRAPEFRUIT SORBET

ADAPTED FROM MORA
ICED CREAMERY,
BAINBRIDGE ISLAND, WA

Pink grapefruits are so much sweeter than their white counterparts, and this pale pink sorbet conveys a wonderful balance of tart and sweet. If you can't find pink grapefruits, increase the sugar by a few tablespoons.

MAKES ABOUT 1 QUART

$1/2$ cup granulated sugar

2 tablespoons cornstarch

Pinch of kosher salt

$3^1/2$ cups freshly squeezed pink grapefruit juice

Combine the sugar and $1/3$ cup water in a small saucepan. Bring to a boil over medium heat, swirling the pan to dissolve the sugar but not stirring the mixture. Increase the heat to high, and cook the syrup until the firm-ball stage and the temperature registers 245°F to 250°F on a candy thermometer; the bubbles will be very large and the mixture will be very thick.

While the syrup is cooking, combine the cornstarch and salt with $1/4$ cup cold water in a small cup, and stir well to dissolve the cornstarch.

Remove the syrup from the heat, and stir the cornstarch mixture into the sugar syrup. Cook the mixture on low for 1 minute, or until it becomes translucent and very thick. Add the grapefruit juice to the pan with the cornstarch mixture, and whisk until smooth.

Transfer the hot liquid to a storage container, and refrigerate uncovered until it is completely chilled (below 40°F), or quick-cool it according to the method on page 14.

Freeze the mixture in an ice cream maker according to the manufacturer's instructions. Serve immediately for a soft sorbet, or transfer the mixture to an airtight storage container and freeze until hard. Allow the sorbet to sit at room temperature for 15 minutes before serving if frozen solid.

PEAR GINGER SORBET

ADAPTED FROM BLUE MOON
SORBET, QUECHEE, VT

*Like bananas, pears ripen well
off the tree, so wait until they're
buttery and sweet before
making this easy sorbet.*

MAKES ABOUT 1 QUART

2 teaspoons unflavored gelatin
or powdered agar

5 ripe pears (about $2^3/_4$ pounds),
peeled, cored, and diced

$^1/_2$ cup granulated sugar

1 tablespoon freshly squeezed
lemon juice

2 teaspoons grated
fresh ginger

Sprinkle the gelatin over $^1/_2$ cup cold water to soften.

Combine the pears, sugar, lemon juice, ginger, and $^1/_2$ cup water in a saucepan, and stir well. Bring to a boil, then cover the pan, reduce the heat to low, and cook the pears for 10 to 12 minutes, stirring occasionally, or until the pears are very tender when pierced with the tip of a knife. Stir in the softened gelatin and cook for 1 minute, or until the gelatin dissolves. Set aside to cool for 5 minutes.

Purée the mixture in a food processor fitted with the steel blade or in a blender.

Transfer the hot liquid to a storage container, and refrigerate uncovered until it is completely chilled (below 40°F), or quick-cool it according to the method on page 14.

Freeze the mixture in an ice cream maker according to the manufacturer's instructions. Serve immediately for a soft sorbet, or transfer the mixture to an airtight storage container and freeze until hard. Allow the sorbet to sit at room temperature for 15 minutes before serving if frozen solid.

POMEGRANATE BLUEBERRY SORBET

ADAPTED FROM COLD FUSION
GELATO, NEWPORT, RI

Sweet-tart pomegranate juice is the liquid in which succulent blueberries are simmered to release their intoxicating flavor. Serve this on biscuits as a shortcake or with a slice of Citrus Angel Food Cake (page 232).

MAKES ABOUT 1 QUART

$3/4$ cup pomegranate juice

3 cups fresh blueberries or frozen
   blueberries, thawed

$1/2$ cup granulated sugar

2 tablespoons cornstarch

Pinch of kosher salt

Tip: Measuring Frozen Berries

When frozen berries thaw they deflate like tiny balloons, so always measure them when still rock-hard, and then allow them to melt.

Place the pomegranate juice in a saucepan and bring to a boil over high heat. Reduce the heat to medium, and cook until reduced by one-fourth. Add the blueberries, and cook for 5 minutes. Purée the mixture in a food processor fitted with the steel blade or in a blender, and set aside.

Combine the sugar and $1/3$ cup water in a small saucepan. Bring to a boil over medium heat, swirling the pan to dissolve the sugar but not stirring the mixture. Increase the heat to high, and cook the syrup until the firm-ball stage and the temperature registers 245°F to 250°F on a candy thermometer; the bubbles will be very large and the mixture will be very thick.

While the syrup is cooking, combine the cornstarch and salt with $1/4$ cup cold water in a small cup, and stir well to dissolve the cornstarch.

Remove the syrup from the heat, and stir the cornstarch mixture into the sugar syrup. Cook the mixture on low for 1 minute, or until it becomes translucent and very thick. Add the blueberry purée to the pan with the cornstarch mixture, and whisk until smooth.

Transfer the hot liquid to a storage container, and refrigerate uncovered until it is completely chilled (below 40°F), or quick-cool it according to the method on page 14.

Freeze the mixture in an ice cream maker according to the manufacturer's instructions. Serve immediately for a soft sorbet, or transfer the mixture to an airtight storage container and freeze until hard. Allow the sorbet to sit at room temperature for 15 minutes before serving if frozen solid.

RASPBERRY SHERBET

ADAPTED FROM GAGA'S,
WARWICK, RI

*I happen to not be bothered by
raspberry seeds, so I never strain
them out. But if they will interfere
with your enjoyment of this vibrantly
flavored, creamy sherbet, feel free to
strain away. This is too ethereal a
dessert to have anything mar it.*

MAKES ABOUT 1 QUART

1 (12-ounce) package frozen
raspberries, thawed

$1/4$ cup raspberry preserves

$1^1/_2$ cups whole milk, divided

1 cup heavy whipping cream

$1/_3$ cup granulated sugar

$1/_8$ teaspoon kosher salt

1 tablespoon cornstarch

Combine the raspberries and raspberry preserves in a food processor fitted with the steel blade or in a blender. Purée until smooth. Strain the purée through a sieve, if desired. Set aside.

Combine the purée, 1 cup milk, cream, sugar, and salt in a saucepan. Cook the mixture over low heat, stirring occasionally, until the mixture begins to steam. While the mixture heats, combine remaining milk and cornstarch in a small cup, and stir well.

Add the cornstarch mixture to the pan, and bring to a boil over low heat. Whisk until smooth, and simmer the mixture for 2 minutes, or until lightly thickened. If the mixture is lumpy, strain it through a sieve.

Transfer the hot liquid to a storage container and press a sheet of plastic wrap directly onto the surface of the mixture to prevent a skin from forming. Refrigerate the mixture uncovered until it is completely chilled (below 40°F), or quick-cool it according to the method on page 14.

Freeze the mixture in an ice cream maker according to the manufacturer's instructions. Serve immediately for a soft sherbet, or transfer the mixture to an airtight storage container and freeze until hard. Allow the sherbet to sit at room temperature for 15 minutes before serving if frozen solid.

STRAWBERRY SORBET

ADAPTED FROM CIAO BELLA,
FLORHAM PARK, NJ

*Light and refreshing, this sorbet
is primarily strawberries churned
until frozen. Freeze some fresh
strawberries when they're in
season so you can enjoy it
throughout the summer.*

MAKES ABOUT 1 QUART

2 teaspoons unflavored gelatin
or powdered agar

$^3/_4$ cup granulated sugar

2 tablespoons freshly squeezed
lemon juice

$1^1/_2$ pounds fresh strawberries,
hulled and sliced

Sprinkle the gelatin over $^1/_2$ cup of cold water to soften.

Combine the sugar, lemon juice, and 1 cup water in a saucepan, and cook over medium heat, stirring occasionally, until the sugar dissolves. Stir in the softened gelatin and cook for 1 minute, or until the gelatin dissolves. Set aside to cool for 5 minutes.

Purée the strawberries and $^3/_4$ cup of the syrup in a food processor fitted with the steel blade or in a blender. Stir in the remaining syrup.

Transfer the hot liquid to a storage container, and refrigerate uncovered until it is completely chilled (below 40°F), or quick-cool it according to the method on page 14.

Freeze the mixture in an ice cream maker according to the manufacturer's instructions. Serve immediately for a soft sorbet, or transfer the mixture to an airtight storage container and freeze until hard. Allow the sorbet to sit at room temperature for 15 minutes before serving if frozen solid.

WILD BLUEBERRY SORBET

ADAPTED FROM BLUE MOON
SORBET, QUECHEE, VT

*It only seems fair that after
enduring harsh winters the people
of New England are rewarded with
intensely sweet and succulent
wild blueberries in the summer.
One of the best ways to enjoy
them is in this sorbet.*

MAKES ABOUT 1 QUART

2 teaspoons unflavored gelatin
or powdered agar

3 cups wild blueberries

$1/2$ cup granulated sugar

2 tablespoons freshly
squeezed lemon juice

Sprinkle the gelatin over $1/2$ cup of cold water to soften.

Combine the blueberries, sugar, lemon juice, and $1/2$ cup water in a saucepan, and bring to a boil over medium-high heat, stirring occasionally. Cook for 3 minutes, stirring occasionally. Stir in the softened gelatin and cook for 1 minute, or until the gelatin dissolves. Set aside to cool for 5 minutes.

Purée the mixture in a food processor fitted with the steel blade or in a blender.

Transfer the hot liquid to a storage container, and refrigerate uncovered until it is completely chilled (below 40°F), or quick-cool it according to the method on page 14.

Freeze the mixture in an ice cream maker according to the manufacturer's instructions. Serve immediately for a soft sorbet, or transfer the mixture to an airtight storage container and freeze until hard. Allow the sorbet to sit at room temperature for 15 minutes before serving if frozen solid.

Tip: Substitutions for Wild Blueberries

Unless you're lucky enough to live in a state like Maine or Michigan where they grow wild, it's really difficult to find the tiny, intensely flavored berries used for this sorbet. But everyone can find larger blueberries—even if they're frozen. Feel free to substitute them, and then substitute $1/3$ cup blueberry preserves for $1/3$ cup of the water. The flavor will be similar.

7 | Starring Nuts and Seeds

Butter pecan is right up there in the top ten list of ice cream flavors, and if you're a fan of crunchy nuts dotting your creamy frozen treats then don't stop there. Not only does this chapter contain recipes for even more sophisticated flavor combinations (though not necessarily more perfect ones!), there are also lots of recipes using other nuts—from almonds to pistachios to walnuts.

While nuts are the large seeds of fruits that have a hard external husk, tiny sesame seeds have an equally rich aroma once the oils are toasted. You'll find a few recipes that use them, too.

CARING FOR CRUNCHIES

While we think of nuts as hard and indestructible—as anyone cracking the shell of a walnut will verify—those hard coverings are beneficial because in reality nuts are rather delicate and are susceptible to oxidation once shelled and the crunchy meats are exposed to light and air.

I am a realist. I'm not going to shell nuts for cooking, other than the occasional round of pistachios that are almost impossible to find already shelled. And I'm assuming that you're not going to shell them yourself, either.

But do store them in the freezer to prevent the oils from going rancid, and sniff nuts if you're buying them from a bulk bin. Old nuts will have an off aroma. The freezer is also dark, which helps preserve nuts' freshness.

It's also better to buy whole nuts and chop them yourself rather than buying pre-chopped nuts because the more surface area of the nut meat that is exposed to the air, the faster the oils will be harmed.

BUTTER PECAN ICE CREAM

ADAPTED FROM GRAETER'S, CINCINNATI, OH

Oprah Winfrey raved about this ice cream on her show, and you'll taste why. It's loaded with toasted pecans; tossing them with melted butter and salt before adding them to the ice cream infuses those delicious flavors into every bite.

MAKES ABOUT 1 QUART

1$\frac{1}{2}$ cups chopped pecans
3 tablespoons unsalted butter, melted
$\frac{3}{4}$ teaspoon kosher salt
1$\frac{1}{2}$ cups heavy whipping cream
$\frac{3}{4}$ cup whole milk
$\frac{1}{2}$ cup granulated sugar, divided
2 tablespoons nonfat
dry milk powder
2 large eggs
$\frac{1}{2}$ teaspoon pure vanilla extract

Preheat the oven to 350°F. Line a baking sheet with heavy-duty aluminum foil.

Toast the nuts for 5 to 7 minutes, or until they are brown and fragrant. Remove the pan from the oven, and stir in the melted butter and salt. Set aside.

Combine the cream, milk, $\frac{1}{4}$ cup sugar, and milk powder in a medium saucepan, and stir well to dissolve the milk powder. Bring the mixture just to a simmer, stirring occasionally.

Beat the eggs, remaining $\frac{1}{4}$ cup sugar, and vanilla extract in a mixing bowl with a whisk until thick and light yellow in color. Slowly beat about one-third of the hot cream mixture into the eggs so they are gradually warmed up, and then return the contents of the mixing bowl to the saucepan. Place the pan over medium-low heat and stir constantly, reaching all parts of the bottom of the pan, until the mixture reaches about 170°F on an instant-read thermometer; at this point it begins to emit steam, thickens slightly, and coats the back of a spoon. This takes 3 to 6 minutes. Do not allow the mixture to boil or the eggs will scramble. Strain the custard through a fine sieve, if desired. Stir in the chopped pecans.

Transfer the hot liquid to a storage container, and press a sheet of plastic wrap directly onto the surface of the mixture to prevent a skin from forming. Refrigerate the mixture uncovered until it is completely chilled (below 40°F), or quick-cool it according to the method on page 14.

Freeze the mixture in an ice cream maker according to the manufacturer's instructions. Serve immediately for a soft ice cream, or transfer the mixture to an airtight storage container and freeze until hard. Allow the ice cream to sit at room temperature for 15 minutes before serving if frozen solid.

HONEY TOASTED PECAN GELATO

ADAPTED FROM CIAO BELLA, FLORHAM PARK, NJ

The mild flavor of honey is a wonderful foil to the nuttiness of the pecans in this light ice cream. Try it as part of a Baked Alaska (page 228).

MAKES ABOUT 1 QUART

2 cups whole milk, divided
$^3/_4$ cup heavy whipping cream
$^2/_3$ cup honey
$^1/_8$ teaspoon kosher salt
2 tablespoons nonfat dry milk powder
2 tablespoons cornstarch
$^1/_2$ teaspoon pure vanilla extract
$^3/_4$ cup chopped pecans

Combine 1$^1/_2$ cups of the milk, cream, honey, and salt in a saucepan. Cook over medium heat, stirring frequently, until the mixture begins to steam; watch it carefully and make sure it does not come to a boil.

While the mixture heats, combine the remaining milk, milk powder, cornstarch, and vanilla in a small bowl, and stir until smooth and both of the powders have dissolved.

Add the cornstarch mixture to the pan, and bring to a boil over low heat, stirring constantly. Whisk the mixture until smooth, and simmer the mixture over very low heat, stirring constantly, for 2 minutes, or until thickened. If the mixture is lumpy, strain it through a sieve.

Transfer the hot liquid to a storage container, and press a sheet of plastic wrap directly onto the surface of the mixture to prevent a skin from forming. Refrigerate the mixture uncovered until it is completely chilled (below 40°F), or cool it according to the method on page 14.

While the custard chills, toast the pecans: Preheat the oven to 350°F. Line a baking sheet with heavy-duty aluminum foil. Toast the pecans for 5 to 7 minutes, or until browned. Set aside to cool, then cover and chill in the refrigerator.

Freeze the chilled custard in an ice cream maker according to the manufacturer's instructions. Transfer the soft ice cream to a chilled mixing bowl and fold in the pecans.

Serve immediately for a soft gelato, or transfer the mixture to an airtight storage container and freeze until hard. Allow the gelato to sit at room temperature for 15 minutes before serving if frozen solid.

CARAMEL PECAN ICE CREAM

ADAPTED FROM BOULDER ICE CREAM, BOULDER, CO

The pecans in this are extra crunchy because they're caramelized before being added to the caramel ice cream. Topped with Hot Fudge Sauce (page 210), you have a world-class sundae.

MAKES ABOUT 1 QUART

Ice Cream

$3/4$ cup granulated sugar

4 tablespoons ($1/2$ stick) unsalted butter, cut into small pieces

$1 3/4$ cups heavy whipping cream

$3/4$ cup whole milk

2 tablespoons nonfat dry milk powder

$1/8$ teaspoon kosher salt

2 large eggs

1 large egg yolk

1 teaspoon pure vanilla extract

Pecans

$2/3$ cup chopped pecans

3 tablespoons firmly packed light brown sugar

1 tablespoon light corn syrup

Pinch of kosher salt

For the ice cream, combine the sugar and $1/2$ cup water in a saucepan, and bring to a boil over medium-high heat. Swirl the pan by the handle but do not stir. Raise the heat to high, and allow syrup to cook until it reaches a walnut brown color, swirling the pot by the handle frequently.

Remove the pan from the heat, and stir in the butter and 1 cup of the cream with a long-handled spoon; the mixture will bubble furiously at first. Return the pan to low heat and stir until lumps melt and mixture is smooth.

Add the remaining cream, milk, milk powder, and salt to the pan, and stir well to dissolve the milk powder. Bring the mixture just to a simmer, stirring occasionally.

Beat the eggs and egg yolk in a mixing bowl with a whisk until thick and light yellow in color. Slowly beat about one-third of the hot cream mixture into the eggs so they are gradually warmed up, and then return the contents of the mixing bowl to the saucepan. Place the pan over medium-low heat and stir constantly, reaching all parts of the bottom of the pan, until the mixture reaches about 170°F on an instant-read thermometer; at this point it begins to emit steam, thickens slightly, and coats the back of a spoon. This takes 3 to 6 minutes. Do not allow the mixture to boil or the eggs will scramble. Strain the custard through a fine sieve, if desired.

Transfer the hot liquid to a storage container, and press a sheet of plastic wrap directly onto the surface of the mixture to prevent a skin from forming. Refrigerate the mixture uncovered until it is completely chilled (below 40°F), or quick-cool it according to the method on page 14.

While the custard chills, caramelize the pecans: Preheat the oven to 350°F. Line a baking sheet with heavy-duty aluminum foil.

Toast the nuts for 5 to 7 minutes, until brown and

fragrant. Remove the pan from the oven, and set aside. Maintain the oven temperature.

Combine the brown sugar, corn syrup, $1/4$ cup of water, and salt in a small saucepan, and bring to a boil over medium heat, stirring occasionally. Cook for 3 minutes. Add the toasted nuts to the syrup, and stir to coat well. Remove the nuts from the pan with a slotted spoon, and spread them out on the foil-lined baking sheet. Bake the nuts for 10 to 12 minutes, or until golden brown. Allow the nuts to cool to room temperature.

Freeze the chilled custard in an ice cream maker according to the manufacturer's instructions. Transfer the soft ice cream to a chilled mixing bowl and fold in the caramelized pecans.

Serve immediately for a soft ice cream, or transfer the mixture to an airtight storage container and freeze until hard. Allow the ice cream to sit at room temperature for 15 minutes before serving if frozen solid.

Boulder Ice Cream Company, Boulder, CO

PURITY AND QUALITY ARE SO IMPORTANT TO THIS TWENTY-YEAR-OLD FIRM: The milk is sourced from dairies no more than a forty-five minute drive from the plant in the Rocky Mountains near Boulder, and those dairies have to be ones that use no Bovine Growth Hormone (BGH) or other hormones on their cows.

And that's the way owner Scott Roy plans to keep it.

Roy, a native of nearby Colorado Springs, entered the business more by serendipity than design. He bought Boulder Ice Cream in 1997, five years after its founding, because, he says, "I liked the product so much I bought the business." In addition to his shop, his ice cream is sold in nine states in the West.

Next to purity, sustainability is paramount to Roy. His first coupon for the store was to have his customers bring in his recyclable containers for a discount on their next pint. The factory is now housed in a building that is heated from a heat exchanger system with the freezer compressors; it is lit with skylights, uses one hundred percent wind power, and diverts eighty percent of solid waste away from landfills through recycling and composting.

But none of these environmental concerns is at the expense of flavor! Which is why his customers keep growing in number.

HAZELNUT GELATO

ADAPTED FROM COLD FUSION
GELATO, NEWPORT, RI

*This hazelnut gelato is drawn
directly from the repertoire
of classic Italian recipes.*

MAKES ABOUT 1 QUART

$1/2$ pound skinned hazelnuts

$1/2$ cup granulated sugar

2 cups whole milk, divided

$3/4$ cup heavy whipping cream

$1/4$ cup light corn syrup

$1/8$ teaspoon kosher salt

2 tablespoons nonfat
dry milk powder

2 tablespoons cornstarch

$1/4$ teaspoon pure vanilla extract

Preheat the oven to 350°F. Line a baking sheet with heavy-duty aluminum foil.

Toast the hazelnuts for 5 to 7 minutes, or until browned. Combine the hazelnuts and sugar in a food processor fitted with the steel blade and chop very finely using on-and-off pulsing. Transfer the mixture to a saucepan.

Add $1/2$ cups of the milk, cream, corn syrup, and salt to the pan. Cook over medium heat, stirring frequently, until the mixture begins to steam; watch it carefully and make sure it does not come to a boil.

While the mixture heats, combine the remaining milk, milk powder, cornstarch, and vanilla extract in a small bowl, and stir until smooth and both of the powders have dissolved.

Add the cornstarch mixture to the pan, and bring to a boil over low heat, stirring constantly. Whisk the mixture until smooth, and simmer the mixture over very low heat, stirring constantly, for 2 minutes, or until thickened. If the mixture is lumpy, strain it through a sieve.

Transfer the hot liquid to a storage container, and press a sheet of plastic wrap directly into the surface of the mixture to prevent a skin from forming. Refrigerate the mixture uncovered until it is completely chilled (below 40°F), or quick-cool it according to the method on page 14.

Freeze the mixture in an ice cream maker according to the manufacturer's instructions. Serve immediately for a soft gelato, or transfer the mixture to an airtight storage container and freeze until hard. Allow the gelato to sit at room temperature for 15 minutes before serving if frozen solid.

PISTACHIO HALVAH ICE CREAM

ADAPTED FROM ZEYTIN,
NEW YORK, NY

Middle Eastern food is becoming more popular, and so are desserts made with halvah, which is a sesame paste candy; it's found in many Jewish delicatessens as well as in Middle Eastern groceries. This dish uses both pistachios and pistachio halvah for a nutty sensation.

MAKES ABOUT 1 QUART

1 cup shelled pistachio nuts

$1/4$ cup granulated sugar

2 cups whole milk, divided

1 cup heavy whipping cream

$1/4$ teaspoon kosher salt

2 tablespoons nonfat
dry milk powder

2 tablespoons cornstarch

$1/2$ teaspoon pure almond extract

$1/4$ teaspoon pure vanilla extract

$1/4$ pound pistachio halvah,
finely chopped

Combine the pistachios and the sugar in a food processor fitted with the steel blade. Grind them finely using on-and-off pulsing, but do not purée them into a paste.

Combine the nut mixture, $1^1/_2$ cups of the milk, cream, and salt in a saucepan. Cook over medium heat, stirring frequently, until the mixture begins to steam; watch it carefully and make sure it does not come to a boil.

Cover the pan and remove the pan from the heat. Allow the mixture to steep for 30 minutes, then strain the mixture through a fine sieve, pressing with the back of a spoon to extract as much liquid as possible. Return the mixture to the pan.

While the mixture steeps, combine the remaining milk, milk powder, cornstarch, almond extract, and vanilla extract in a small bowl, and stir until smooth and both of the powders have dissolved.

Add the cornstarch mixture to the pan, and bring to a boil over low heat, stirring constantly. Whisk the mixture until smooth, and simmer the mixture over very low heat, stirring constantly, for 2 minutes, or until thickened. If the mixture is lumpy, strain it through a sieve.

Transfer the hot liquid to a storage container, and press a sheet of plastic wrap directly onto the surface of the mixture to prevent a skin from forming. Refrigerate the mixture uncovered until it completely chilled (below 40°F), or quick-cool it according to the method on page 14.

Stir the pistachio halvah into the chilled custard and freeze in an ice cream maker according to the manufacturer's instructions.

Serve immediately for a soft ice cream, or transfer the mixture to an airtight storage container and freeze until hard. Allow the ice cream to sit at room temperature for 15 minutes before serving if frozen solid.

PISTACHIO GELATO

ADAPTED FROM GS GELATO,
FORT WALTON BEACH, FL

*GS Gelato imports pistachio
nuts from Sicily to make this
creamy, light green creation.
The nuts steep in the milk to add
even more aromatic flavor.*

MAKES ABOUT 1 QUART

2 cups shelled and roasted
pistachio nuts, divided

$^1/_2$ cup granulated sugar

$2^1/_2$ cups whole milk, divided

$^1/_2$ cup heavy whipping cream

$^1/_4$ cup light corn syrup

$^1/_4$ teaspoon kosher salt

3 tablespoons nonfat
dry milk powder

2 tablespoons cornstarch

$^1/_2$ teaspoon pure almond extract

$^1/_4$ teaspoon pure vanilla extract

Combine 1$^1/_2$ cups of the pistachios and the sugar in a food processor fitted with the steel blade. Grind them finely using on-and-off pulsing, but do not purée them into a paste.

Combine the nut mixture, 2 cups of the milk, cream, corn syrup, and salt in a saucepan. Cook over medium heat, stirring frequently, until the mixture begins to steam; watch it carefully and make sure it does not come to a boil.

Cover the pan and remove from the heat. Allow the mixture to steep for 30 minutes, then strain the mixture through a fine sieve, pressing with the back of a spoon to extract as much liquid as possible. Return the mixture to the pan.

While the mixture steeps, combine the remaining milk, milk powder, cornstarch, almond extract, and vanilla extract in a small bowl, and stir until smooth and both of the powders have dissolved.

Add the cornstarch mixture to the pan, and bring to a boil over low heat, stirring constantly. Whisk the mixture until smooth, and simmer the mixture over very low heat, stirring constantly, for 2 minutes, or until thickened. If the mixture is lumpy, strain it through a sieve.

Transfer the hot liquid to a storage container, and press a sheet of plastic wrap directly onto the surface of the mixture to prevent a skin from forming. Refrigerate the mixture uncovered until it is completely chilled (below 40°F), or quick-cool it according to the method on page 14.

Freeze the mixture in an ice cream maker according to the manufacturer's instructions. While the gelato churns, coarsely chop the remaining pistachio nuts. Transfer the soft ice cream to a bowl and fold in the pistachio nuts.

Serve immediately for a soft gelato, or transfer the mixture to an airtight storage container and freeze until hard. Allow the gelato to sit at room temperature for 15 minutes before serving if frozen solid.

GS Gelato, Fort Walton Beach, FL

GUIDO TREMOLINI AND SIMONA FARONI—THE G AND S OF GS GELATO—BELIEVE that a love of food is built into their DNA; after all, they're Italian!

The couple, both working in the restaurant business, married in Italy in the early 1990s; they moved to Florida in 1996 after Tremolini visited family in the panhandle area of the state and fell in love with the region. The two also share a love of authentic Italian gelato and wanted to recreate it in their adopted home.

"True Italian gelato, what we knew and what we loved, didn't exist in that part of the country," says Faroni, who has cherished childhood memories of sitting on the curb of the local *gelateria*, "savoring every lick of strawberry sorbetto or coconut gelato," she says.

Some of the most popular flavors they make today are Blood Orange Sorbet (page 114) with oranges imported from Sicily and Pistachio Gelato (page 138) made with nuts from the same region. They have been delighted that their customers enjoy some of their more unusual flavors, too, such as a Rosemary Olive Oil Gelato (page 188) made with extra-virgin olive oil and scented with aromatic Mexican vanilla.

"We put love and passion into every flavor we produce, because gelato is not just a flavorful treat, it is the result of centuries of Italian tradition," says Faroni. And the people of Florida seem to agree.

Guido Tremolini and Simona Faroni

BUTTERY MIXED NUT ICE CREAM

ADAPTED FROM MOOMERS,
TRAVERSE CITY, MI

The Plummer family calls this ice cream Nuts to You. And if you're a nut lover, then this is a recipe not to be missed.

MAKES ABOUT 1 QUART

$^1/_2$ cup raw peanuts

$^1/_3$ cup chopped pecans

$^1/_3$ cup chopped almonds

$^1/_4$ cup chopped walnuts

$^1/_4$ cup shelled pistachio nuts

3 tablespoons unsalted
butter, melted

$^1/_2$ teaspoon kosher salt

$1^1/_2$ cups whole milk, divided

1 cup heavy whipping cream

$^1/_3$ cup granulated sugar

$^1/_4$ cup light corn syrup

3 tablespoons nonfat
dry milk powder

2 tablespoons cornstarch

$^1/_4$ teaspoon pure vanilla extract

Preheat the oven to 350°F. Line a baking sheet with heavy-duty aluminum foil.

Place the peanuts, pecans, almonds, and walnuts on the baking sheet. Toast the almonds for 5 to 7 minutes, or until browned. Add the pistachio nuts, melted butter, and salt to the baking sheet; toss to coat.

Reserve $^1/_3$ of the nut mixture, and transfer the remainder to a food processor fitted with the steel blade or to a blender. Add 1 cup of the milk, and purée until smooth. Transfer the purée to a saucepan.

Add the cream, sugar, and corn syrup to the pan. Cook over medium heat, stirring frequently, until the mixture begins to steam; watch it carefully and make sure it does not come to a boil.

While the mixture heats, combine the remaining milk, milk powder, cornstarch, and vanilla extract in a small bowl, and stir until smooth and both of the powders have dissolved.

Add the cornstarch mixture to the pan, and bring to a boil over low heat, stirring constantly. Whisk the mixture until smooth, and simmer the mixture over very low heat, stirring constantly, for 2 minutes, or until thickened. If the mixture is lumpy, strain it through a sieve.

Transfer the hot liquid to a storage container and press a sheet of plastic wrap directly onto the surface of the mixture to prevent a skin from forming. Refrigerate the mixture uncovered until it is completely chilled (below 40°F), or quick-cool it according to the method on page 14.

Stir the reserved nuts into the chilled custard and freeze in an ice cream maker according to the manufacturer's instructions. Serve immediately for a soft ice cream, or transfer the mixture to an airtight storage container and freeze until hard. Allow the ice cream to sit at room temperature for 15 minutes before serving if frozen solid.

MAPLE WALNUT ICE CREAM

ADAPTED FROM THE DAILY
SCOOP, BARRINGTON, RI

*Here is a New England classic.
Walnuts—even when toasted—are
essentially bitter, and the maple
smoothes off those rough edges.*

MAKES ABOUT 1 QUART

$^3/_4$ cup coarsely chopped walnuts

2 cups heavy whipping
cream, divided

$^3/_4$ cup whole milk

$^3/_4$ cup pure maple syrup

2 tablespoons nonfat
dry milk powder

2 tablespoons cornstarch

Pinch of kosher salt

$^1/_4$ teaspoon pure vanilla extract

Preheat the oven to 350°F. Line a baking sheet with heavy-duty aluminum foil.

Toast the nuts for 5 to 7 minutes, or until browned and fragrant. Remove the nuts from the oven and set aside.

Combine $1^1/_2$ cups of the cream, milk, and maple syrup in a saucepan. Cook over medium heat, stirring frequently, until the mixture begins to steam; watch it carefully and make sure it does not come to a boil.

While the mixture heats, combine the remaining cream, milk powder, cornstarch, salt, and vanilla extract in a small bowl, and stir until smooth and both of the powders have dissolved.

Add the cornstarch mixture to the pan, and bring to a boil over low heat, stirring constantly. Whisk the mixture until smooth, and simmer the mixture over very low heat, stirring constantly, for 2 minutes, or until thickened. If the mixture is lumpy, strain it through a sieve.

Transfer the hot liquid to a storage container and press a sheet of plastic wrap directly onto the surface of the mixture to prevent a skin from forming. Refrigerate the mixture uncovered until it is completely chilled (below 40°F), or quick-cool it according to the method on page 14.

Freeze the mixture in an ice cream maker according to the manufacturer's instructions. Transfer the soft ice cream to a chilled mixing bowl and fold in the walnuts.

Serve immediately for a soft ice cream, or transfer the mixture to an airtight storage container and freeze until hard. Allow the ice cream to sit at room temperature for 15 minutes before serving if frozen solid.

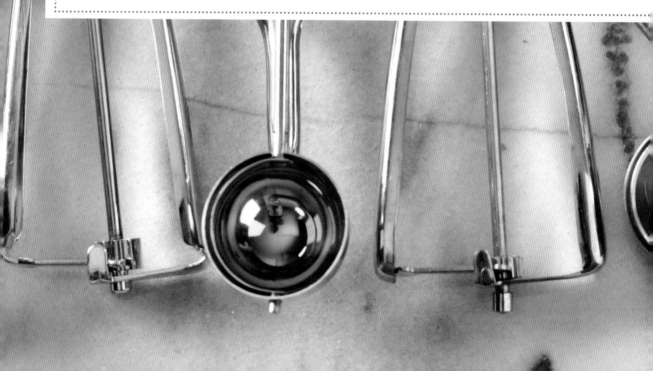

The Daily Scoop, Barrington, RI

THE LOVE OF ICE CREAM WAS A FACTOR LEADING TO LOVE AND MARRIAGE FOR Deb and Bob Saunders. The couple, both natives of Barrington, a village near Providence, began dating when Deb was only in high school. So when the two avid boaters would pull into a port, instead of stopping for a beer, they would begin a quest for the best local ice cream the town had to offer.

Deb later went on to attend law school and now works for the Supreme Court of the state of Rhode Island, and Bob owned a few gas stations. But in 2003 they decided to fulfill the dream of opening their own ice cream shop.

The Daily Scoop now sells to a few area supermarkets, but is a destination for ice cream lovers all around Rhode Island and nearby towns in Massachusetts. One of their signature flavors is a New England-only classic—Vanilla Ice Cream with Grape Nuts (page 23). Another regional specialty is Maple Walnut (this page), which is chock full of walnuts. They are also known for some of their frozen yogurts, including Banana Berry (page 84), which gives equal billing to bananas and strawberries.

While Deb is certainly old enough to drink when the two travel these days, they still like to seek out a great ice cream shop at every destination.

CHESTNUT ICE CREAM

ADAPTED FROM NEW RIVERS,
PROVIDENCE, RI

New Rivers is my favorite restaurant in my adopted hometown of Providence. Chef Bruce Tillinghast makes this fabulous ice cream in the fall, when fresh chestnuts are in season, but vacuum-packed chestnuts make it far easier to make at home.

MAKES ABOUT 1 QUART

1 (12- to 14-ounce) jar unsweetened cooked chestnuts, divided

$^3/_4$ cup whole milk

$1^1/_2$ cups heavy whipping cream

$^2/_3$ cup firmly packed light brown sugar

$^1/_2$ teaspoon kosher salt

2 large eggs

2 large egg yolks

$^1/_3$ cup granulated sugar

$^1/_4$ teaspoon pure vanilla extract

Combine 1 cup of the chestnuts and milk in a food processor fitted with the steel blade or in a blender. Purée until smooth. Pour the mixture into a medium saucepan.

Add the cream, brown sugar, and salt to the pan, and stir well. Bring the mixture just to a simmer, stirring occasionally.

Beat the eggs, egg yolks, granulated sugar, and vanilla extract in a mixing bowl with a whisk until thick and light yellow in color. Slowly beat about one-third of the hot cream mixture into the eggs so they are gradually warmed up, and then return the contents of the mixing bowl to the saucepan. Place the pan over medium-low heat and stir constantly, reaching all parts of the bottom of the pan, until the mixture reaches about 170°F on an instant-read thermometer; at this point it begins to emit steam, thickens slightly, and coats the back of a spoon. This takes 3 to 6 minutes. Do not allow the mixture to boil or the eggs will scramble. Strain the custard through a fine sieve, if desired.

Transfer the hot liquid to a storage container and press a sheet of plastic wrap directly onto the surface of the mixture to prevent a skin from forming. Refrigerate the mixture uncovered until it is completely chilled (below 40°F), or quick-cool it according to the method on page 14.

While the custard chills, chop the remaining chestnuts.

Stir the chopped chestnuts into the chilled custard and freeze in an ice cream maker according to the manufacturer's instructions. Serve immediately for a soft ice cream, or transfer the mixture to an airtight storage container and freeze until hard. Allow the ice cream to sit at room temperature for 15 minutes before serving if frozen solid.

PEANUT BUTTER CHOCOLATE CHIP ICE CREAM

ADAPTED FROM GRAETER'S, CINCINNATI, OH

Peanut butter ice cream— especially when it's punctuated with big, chunky chocolate chips— is delicious reminder of a the best parts of childhood.

MAKES ABOUT 1 QUART

$^3/_4$ cup smooth commercial peanut butter (not natural or homemade)

$^3/_4$ cup whole milk

$1^1/_2$ cups heavy whipping cream

$^1/_3$ cup granulated sugar

2 tablespoons nonfat dry milk powder

$^1/_8$ teaspoon kosher salt

2 large eggs

$^1/_4$ teaspoon pure vanilla extract

2 ounces bittersweet chocolate, chopped

2 tablespoons unsalted butter

Combine the peanut butter and milk in a food processor fitted with the steel blade or in a blender. Purée until smooth. Pour the mixture into a medium saucepan.

Add the cream, sugar, milk powder, and salt to the pan, and stir well to dissolve the milk powder. Bring the mixture just to a simmer over medium heat, stirring occasionally.

Beat the eggs and vanilla in a mixing bowl with a whisk until thick and light yellow in color. Slowly beat about one-third of the hot cream mixture into the eggs so they are gradually warmed up, and then return the contents of the mixing bowl to the saucepan. Place the pan over medium-low heat and stir constantly, reaching all parts of the bottom of the pan, until the mixture reaches about 170°F on an instant-read thermometer; at this point it begins to emit steam, thickens slightly, and coats the back of a spoon. This takes 3 to 6 minutes. Do not allow the mixture to boil. Strain the custard through a fine sieve, if desired.

Transfer the hot liquid to a storage container, and press a sheet of plastic wrap directly onto the surface of the mixture to prevent a skin from forming. Refrigerate the mixture uncovered until it is completely chilled (below 40°F), or quick-cool it according to the method on page 14.

Combine the chocolate and butter in a small microwave-safe cup, and heat in the microwave on medium power for 20 seconds. Stir, and repeat as necessary until the mixture is smooth. Allow it to cool slightly.

Freeze the chilled custard in an ice cream maker according to the manufacturer's instructions. When the ice cream is a soft consistency, slowly pour the melted chocolate into the freezer, allowing it to churn with the ice cream.

Serve immediately for a soft ice cream, or transfer the mixture to an airtight storage container and freeze until hard. Allow the ice cream to sit at room temperature for 15 minutes before serving if frozen solid.

PEANUT BUTTER BANANA ICE CREAM

ADAPTED FROM THE DAILY
SCOOP, BARRINGTON, RI

*You'll be hard pressed to
find two foods creamier
than ripe, sweet bananas and
peanut butter; when they're
combined in this ice cream it's
sensational. Serve it topped with
Strawberry Sauce (page 216)
for a PB&J experience.*

MAKES ABOUT 1 QUART

2 tablespoons unsalted butter

2 ripe bananas, cut into
$^1/_2$-inch slices

$^1/_4$ cup granulated sugar

$^3/_4$ cup whole milk

$^1/_2$ cup commercial peanut butter
(not homemade or natural)

$1^1/_4$ cups heavy whipping
cream, divided

2 tablespoons nonfat
dry milk powder

2 tablespoons cornstarch

$^1/_4$ teaspoon kosher salt

$^1/_2$ teaspoon pure vanilla extract

Heat the butter in a skillet over medium heat. Add the bananas, and sprinkle the bananas with the sugar. Cook over medium heat, stirring frequently, for 3 to 5 minutes, or until the bananas are soft.

Combine the bananas, milk, and peanut butter in a food processor fitted with the steel blade or in a blender, and purée until smooth.

Transfer the mixture to a saucepan and stir in $^3/_4$ cup of the cream. Cook over medium heat, stirring frequently, until the mixture begins to steam; watch it carefully and make sure it does not come to a boil.

While the mixture heats, combine the remaining cream, milk powder, cornstarch, salt, and vanilla in a small bowl, and stir until smooth and both of the powders have dissolved.

Add the cornstarch mixture to the pan, and bring to a boil over low heat, stirring constantly. Whisk the mixture until smooth, and simmer the mixture over very low heat, stirring constantly, for 2 minutes, or until thickened. If the mixture is lumpy, strain it through a sieve.

Transfer the hot liquid to a storage container and press a sheet of plastic wrap directly onto the surface of the mixture to prevent a skin from forming. Refrigerate the mixture uncovered until it is completely chilled (below 40°F), or quick-cool it according to the method on page 14.

Freeze the mixture in an ice cream maker according to the manufacturer's instructions. Serve immediately for a soft ice cream, or transfer the mixture to an airtight storage container and freeze until hard. Allow the ice cream to sit at room temperature for 15 minutes before serving if frozen solid.

ALMOND, COCONUT, and CHOCOLATE CHIP ICE CREAM

ADAPTED FROM THE DAILY
SCOOP, BARRINGTON, RI

*If you're a fan of Almond Joy®
candy bars, then this ice cream
will be a sure hit. But it's even better
than a candy bar because it has big
pieces of crunchy almonds all
through it, not just on top.*

MAKES ABOUT 1 QUART

1$\frac{1}{3}$ cups heavy whipping
cream, divided

1 (15-ounce) can cream of coconut,
such as Coco Lopez, well-stirred

2 tablespoons nonfat
dry milk powder

2 tablespoons cornstarch

Pinch of kosher salt

$\frac{1}{4}$ teaspoon pure vanilla extract

3 ounces raw almonds,
coarsely chopped

$\frac{1}{3}$ cup sweetened shredded coconut

$\frac{1}{2}$ cup high-quality semisweet
chocolate chips

Combine 1 cup of the cream and cream of coconut in a saucepan. Cook over medium heat, stirring frequently, until the mixture begins to steam; watch it carefully and make sure it does not come to a boil.

While the mixture heats, combine the remaining cream, milk powder, cornstarch, salt, and vanilla in a small bowl, and stir until smooth and both of the powders have dissolved.

Add the cornstarch mixture to the pan, and bring to a boil over low heat, stirring constantly. Whisk the mixture until smooth, and simmer the mixture over very low heat, stirring constantly, for 2 minutes, or until thickened. If the mixture is lumpy, strain it through a sieve.

Transfer the hot liquid to a storage container and press a sheet of plastic wrap directly onto the surface of the mixture to prevent a skin from forming. Refrigerate the mixture uncovered until it is completely chilled (below 40°F), or quick-cool it according to the method on page 14.

While the custard chills, preheat the oven to 350°F. Line a baking sheet with heavy-duty aluminum foil.

Toast the almonds for 5 to 7 minutes, or until browned and fragrant.

Freeze the chilled custard in an ice cream maker according to the manufacturer's instructions. Transfer the soft ice cream to a chilled mixing bowl and fold in the toasted almonds, coconut, and chocolate chips.

Serve immediately for a soft ice cream, or transfer the mixture to an airtight storage container and freeze until hard. Allow the ice cream to sit at room temperature for 15 minutes before serving if frozen solid.

ALMOND BUTTERCRUNCH ICE CREAM

ADAPTED FROM SWEET
REPUBLIC, SCOTTSDALE, AZ

*The crunchy bits are really
a buttery toffee, some of which is
ground to flavor the ice cream as
well. There's enough leftover
toffee from this recipe to
sprinkle over the servings, too.*

MAKES ABOUT 1 QUART

Toffee
$^1/_2$ cup whole raw almonds
Vegetable oil spray
4 ounces (1 stick) unsalted butter
1 cup granulated sugar
2 tablespoons light corn syrup
$^1/_4$ teaspoon kosher salt
$^3/_4$ teaspoon pure vanilla extract

Ice Cream
2 cups whole milk
1 cup heavy whipping cream
$^1/_4$ cup nonfat dry milk powder
$^1/_4$ teaspoon kosher salt
3 large egg yolks
2 tablespoons granulated sugar

For the toffee: Preheat the oven to 350°F. Line a 13 x 9-inch pan with heavy-duty aluminum foil. Toast the almonds for 5 to 7 minutes, or until fragrant and the nut meat is browned. Coarsely chop the almonds and set aside. Grease the foil with vegetable oil spray.

Combine the butter, sugar, corn syrup, salt, and $^1/_4$ cup water in a saucepan. Cook over medium heat until the butter is melted and the sugar is dissolved, stirring occasionally. Increase the heat to medium-high, and cook the mixture, stirring occasionally, until it is a deep golden brown and registers 300°F on a candy thermometer; this will take about 10 minutes.

Remove the pan from the heat, and stir in the toasted almonds and vanilla. Immediately pour the liquid into the greased pan, and spread it evenly.

Allow the toffee to cool for at least 1 hour, or until it has set up and is very brittle.

Break the toffee into bite-sized pieces with your hands, and then place the pieces in a heavy resealable plastic bag. Crush the toffee with the bottom of a small skillet. Set aside.

For the ice cream: Combine the milk, cream, milk powder, and salt in a medium saucepan, and stir well to dissolve the milk powder. Bring the mixture just to a simmer over medium heat, stirring occasionally.

Beat the egg yolks and sugar in a mixing bowl with a whisk until thick and light yellow in color. Slowly beat about one-third of the hot cream mixture into the eggs so they are gradually warmed up, and then return the contents of the mixing bowl to the saucepan. Place the pan over medium-low heat and stir constantly, reaching all parts of the bottom of the pan, until the mixture reaches about 170°F on an instant-read thermometer; at this point

(continued)

it begins to emit steam, thickens slightly, and coats the back of a spoon. This takes 3 to 6 minutes. Do not allow the mixture to boil or the eggs will scramble. Strain the custard through a fine sieve, if desired.

Combine ¹/₂ cup of the toffee with ¹/₂ cup of the hot custard, and purée it in a food processor fitted with the steel blade or in a blender. Stir the purée back into the custard.

Transfer the hot liquid to a storage container and press a sheet of plastic wrap directly onto the surface of the mixture to prevent a skin from forming. Refrigerate the mixture uncovered until it is completely chilled (below 40°F), or quick-cool it according to the method on page 14.

Freeze the mixture in an ice cream maker according to the manufacturer's instructions. When the ice cream is churned to a soft consistency, add ¹/₂ cup crushed toffee to the ice cream maker as the ice cream is churning.

Serve immediately for a soft ice cream, or transfer the mixture to an airtight storage container and freeze until hard. Allow the ice cream to sit at room temperature for 15 minutes before serving if frozen solid.

CASHEW CARAMEL ICE CREAM with CHOCOLATE SWIRL

ADAPTED FROM THE DAILY SCOOP, BARRINGTON, RI

The Saunderses, who own The Daily Scoop, are fond of transforming favorite candies into ice creams, and this one is based on the concept of the chocolate turtle. Buttery rich cashews are indeed an underutilized nut.

Combine the sugar and 2 tablespoons of water in a small saucepan, and bring it to a boil over medium-high heat. Swirl the pan by the handle but do not stir. Raise the heat to high, and allow syrup to cook until it reaches a walnut brown color, swirling the pot by the handle frequently.

Remove the pan from the heat, and stir in 1 cup of the cream with a long-handled spoon; the mixture will bubble furiously at first. Return the pan to low heat and stir until any lumps melt and the mixture is smooth.

Add the milk and corn syrup to the saucepan. Cook over medium heat, stirring frequently, until the mixture begins to steam; watch it carefully and make sure it does not come to a boil.

While the mixture heats, combine the remaining cream, milk powder, cornstarch, salt, and vanilla extract

$^1/_2$ cup granulated sugar

$1^1/_2$ cups heavy whipping cream, divided

$^3/_4$ cup whole milk

$^1/_4$ cup light corn syrup

2 tablespoons nonfat milk powder

2 tablespoons cornstarch

Pinch of kosher salt

$^1/_4$ teaspoon pure vanilla extract

3 ounces cashew halves, very coarsely chopped

2 ounces high-quality bittersweet chocolate, chopped

2 tablespoons unsalted butter

in a small bowl, and stir until smooth and both of the powders have dissolved.

Add the cornstarch mixture to the pan, and bring to a boil over low heat, stirring constantly. Whisk the mixture until smooth, and simmer the mixture over very low heat, stirring constantly, for 2 minutes, or until thickened. If the mixture is lumpy, strain it through a sieve.

Transfer the hot liquid to a storage container and press a sheet of plastic wrap directly onto the surface of the mixture to prevent a skin from forming. Refrigerate the mixture uncovered until it is completely chilled (below 40°F), or quick-cool it according to the method on page 14.

While the custard chills, preheat the oven to 350°F. Line a baking pan with heavy-duty aluminum foil. Toast the cashews for 5 to 7 minutes, or until browned and fragrant.

Combine the chocolate and butter in a small microwave-safe bowl. Heat in the microwave on medium (50 percent) power for 20 seconds. Stir, and repeat as necessary until the chocolate is melted and the mixture is smooth. Set aside at room temperature.

Freeze the chilled custard in an ice cream maker according to the manufacturer's instructions. Transfer the soft ice cream to a chilled mixing bowl and fold in the toasted cashews.

To make the swirl, transfer one-sixth of the ice cream to an airtight container. Top it will a few spoonfuls of the melted chocolate, and then repeat until all the ice cream and chocolate are layered. When serving the ice cream, dig into the container vertically so each serving contains some of the swirl.

Serve immediately for a soft ice cream, or freeze until hard. Allow the ice cream to sit at room temperature for 15 minutes before serving if frozen solid.

SESAME BRITTLE CINNAMON ICE CREAM

ADAPTED FROM KEFI,
NEW YORK, NY

Sesame seed candy is the chocolate kiss of Greece. If you have a Greek market around, you can buy the brittle instead of making it, and this recipe can be put together in a matter of minutes.

MAKES ABOUT 1 QUART

Brittle
Vegetable oil spray
$1/2$ cup sesame seeds
$3/4$ cup granulated sugar
2 tablespoons light corn syrup

Ice Cream
$2\,1/2$ cups whole milk, divided
$3/4$ cup heavy whipping cream
$1/2$ cup granulated sugar
$1/4$ cup light corn syrup
$1/2$ teaspoon ground cinnamon
$1/8$ teaspoon kosher salt
2 tablespoons nonfat
dry milk powder
2 tablespoons cornstarch
$1/4$ teaspoon pure vanilla extract

For the brittle: Grease an 8 x 8-inch baking pan with vegetable oil spray. Place the sesame seeds in a small dry skillet and toast for 2 to 3 minutes over medium heat, or until lightly brown. Set aside.

Combine the sugar, corn syrup, and $3/4$ cup water in a small saucepan. Cook over medium heat, swirling the pan by the handle, until the sugar dissolves. Raise the heat to high and boil the syrup until it reaches 240°F on a candy thermometer, or until the bubbles are large and thick. Stir in the toasted sesame seeds, and continue to boil over high heat until the syrup reaches 270°F on a candy thermometer, or when the syrup forms a brittle thread when dropped into a cup of ice water.

Immediately scrape the mixture into the prepared pan, and spread it evenly with an oiled rubber spatula. Allow the brittle to cool completely, and then break it into small pieces. Crush enough brittle to make $2/3$ cup of crumbs, and reserve the remainder for topping.

For the ice cream: Combine 2 cups of the milk, cream, sugar, corn syrup, cinnamon, and salt in a saucepan. Cook over medium heat, stirring frequently, until the mixture begins to steam; watch it carefully and make sure it does not come to a boil.

While the mixture heats, combine the remaining milk, milk powder, cornstarch, and vanilla extract in a small bowl, and stir until smooth and both of the powders have dissolved.

Add the cornstarch mixture to the pan, and bring to a boil over low heat, stirring constantly. Whisk the mixture until smooth, and simmer the mixture over very low heat, stirring constantly, for 2 minutes, or until thickened. If the mixture is lumpy, strain it through a sieve.

Transfer the hot liquid to a storage container, and press

a sheet of plastic wrap directly onto the surface of the mixture to prevent a skin from forming. Refrigerate the mixture uncovered until it is completely chilled (below 40°F), or quick-cool it according to the method on page 14.

Freeze the mixture in an ice cream maker according to the manufacturer's instructions. Transfer the soft ice cream to a chilled mixing bowl and fold in the crushed sesame brittle.

Serve immediately for a soft ice cream, or transfer the mixture to an airtight storage container and freeze until hard. Allow the ice cream to sit at room temperature for 15 minutes before serving if frozen solid. Sprinkle remaining crushed brittle on top, if desired.

TOASTED SESAME SEED and HONEY GELATO

ADAPTED FROM COLD FUSION
GELATO, NEWPORT, RI

With a bit of aromatic toasted sesame oil to emphasize the subtle flavor of the sesame seeds, this is a wonderfully sophisticated ending for any meal, especially if it features Mediterranean cuisines.

MAKES ABOUT 1 QUART

2 tablespoons sesame seeds

$2^3/_4$ cups whole milk, divided

$^3/_4$ cup heavy whipping cream

$^1/_2$ cup honey

$^1/_4$ cup light corn syrup

1 teaspoon toasted Asian
sesame oil

$^1/_8$ teaspoon kosher salt

2 tablespoons nonfat
dry milk powder

2 tablespoons cornstarch

Place the sesame seeds in a small dry skillet and toast for 2 to 3 minutes over medium heat, or until lightly brown. Set aside.

Combine $2^1/_4$ cups of the milk, cream, honey, corn syrup, sesame oil, and salt in a saucepan. Cook over medium heat, stirring frequently, until the mixture begins to steam; watch it carefully and make sure it does not come to a boil.

While the mixture heats, combine the remaining milk, milk powder, and cornstarch in a small bowl, and stir until smooth and both of the powders have dissolved.

Add the cornstarch mixture to the pan, and bring to a boil over low heat, stirring constantly. Whisk the mixture until smooth, and simmer the mixture over very low heat, stirring constantly, for 2 minutes, or until thickened. If the mixture is lumpy, strain it through a sieve.

Transfer the hot liquid to a storage container, and press a sheet of plastic wrap directly onto the surface of the mixture to prevent a skin from forming. Refrigerate the mixture uncovered until it is completely chilled (below 40°F), or quick-cool it according to the method on page 14.

Stir the toasted sesame seeds into the chilled custard and freeze in an ice cream maker according to the manufacturer's instructions. Serve immediately for a soft gelato, or transfer the mixture to an airtight storage container and freeze until hard. Allow the gelato to sit at room temperature for 15 minutes before serving if frozen solid.

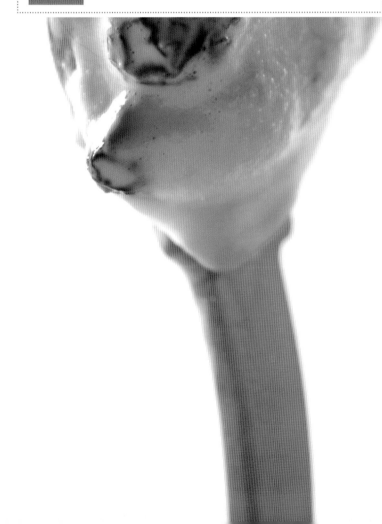

8 Laced with Liquor

American humorist Ogden Nash was famous for saying that "candy is dandy but liquor is quicker" as a way for a suitor to reach a lady's boudoir. If that's true, then these are the recipes he should be making to lure her. There's some type of wine or spirits included in each one, and as a true ingredient more than as a subtle note of flavor. But except for toddlers and those adults who must avoid any alcohol, I really don't think that a serving of one of these heady creations would bring on a "buzz."

And there's a great benefit that the inclusion of alcohol brings to any frozen dessert; it keeps it softer. In fact, fans of soft ice creams frequently add a few tablespoons of vodka, which cannot be tasted in the finished product, to all custard mixtures to prevent them from turning rock solid once frozen.

AN EDUCATION IN ALCOHOL

The type of alcohol included in beverages for human consumption is ethanol, which does freeze—at –174°F. That's a temperature never reached in the home freezer, which only reaches about –20°F, only in a chemistry lab. In contrast, water freezes at 32°F, and the freezing point of an alcoholic beverage is determined by the percentage of alcohol when compared to the percentage of water.

This is where the word *proof* enters the picture. The proof number listed on a bottle is twice the percentage of alcohol. For example, wine and beer are about twelve to twenty-four proof, which means they contain six to twelve percent alcohol, respectively. Anyone who has created a "wine–sicle" by forgetting about the bottle of white wine placed in the freezer to chill can verify that the home freezer is certainly cold enough to freeze the contents of a wine bottle!

But a bottle of 140–proof rum turns syrupy but never freezes solid because its alcohol content is high enough that the home freezer can't do the trick.

You'll find recipes in this chapter for light sorbets and luscious ice creams. And you'll find some containing chocolate, because while "liquor is quicker" it's also true that "candy is dandy."

CHAMPAGNE SORBET

ADAPTED FROM BASSETTS,
PHILADELPHIA, PA

You can't find an easier way to elevate a bowl of simple fruit salad to an elegant dessert fit for company than by topping it with this sorbet.

MAKES ABOUT 1 QUART

1 tablespoon unflavored gelatin
or powdered agar

$^1/_2$ cup sugar

$^1/_4$ cup light corn syrup

2 teaspoons freshly squeezed
lemon juice

$^1/_8$ teaspoon kosher salt

1 cup Champagne
or sparkling wine

Sprinkle the gelatin over $^1/_2$ cup cold water to soften.

Combine 2 cups of water with the sugar, corn syrup, lemon juice, and salt in a saucepan, and bring to a boil over medium heat, stirring occasionally. Cook for 1 minute over low heat, and then stir in softened gelatin. Cook for 1 minute, or until the gelatin dissolves. Remove the pan from the heat, and stir in the Champagne.

Transfer the hot liquid to a storage container. Refrigerate the mixture uncovered until it is completely chilled (below 40°F), or quick-cool it according to the method on page 14.

Freeze the mixture in an ice cream maker according to the manufacturer's instructions. Serve immediately for a soft sorbet, or transfer the mixture to an airtight storage container and freeze until hard. Allow the sorbet to sit at room temperature for 15 minutes before serving if frozen solid.

MANGO MIMOSA SORBET

ADAPTED FROM SILVER MOON,
LOS GATOS, CA

While mimosa drinks are usually combinations of orange juice with Champagne, I much prefer this combo with puréed mango, which adds a more complex flavor.

MAKES ABOUT 1 QUART

2 teaspoons unflavored gelatin
or powdered agar

2 cups diced fresh mango
(from 2 to 3 mangoes,
depending on size)

$^2/_3$ cup Champagne or
sparkling wine

$^1/_4$ cup light corn syrup

1 tablespoon freshly
squeezed lemon juice

Sprinkle the gelatin over $^1/_2$ cup cold water to soften.

Purée the mango with the Champagne in a food processor fitted with the steel blade or in a blender. Set aside.

Combine the corn syrup and lemon juice with $^3/_4$ cup cold water in a saucepan, and bring to a boil over medium-high heat, stirring occasionally. Stir the softened gelatin into the pan. Cook for 1 minute, or until the gelatin dissolves. Remove the pan from the heat, and stir in the mango and Champagne mixture.

Transfer the hot liquid to a storage container, and refrigerate uncovered until it is completely chilled (below 40°F), or quick-cool it according to the method on page 14.

Freeze the mixture in an ice cream maker according to the manufacturer's instructions. Serve immediately for a soft sorbet, or transfer the mixture to an airtight storage container and freeze until hard. Allow the sorbet to sit at room temperature for 15 minutes before serving if frozen solid.

APRICOT and WHITE WINE SORBET

ADAPTED FROM GIOVANNA GELATO, NEWTON, MA

A combination of apricot nectar and intensely flavored dried apricots add depth to this refreshing sorbet. You could also substitute sparkling wine in the recipe.

MAKES ABOUT 1 QUART

$1/2$ cup granulated sugar

2 tablespoons cornstarch

Pinch of kosher salt

$2 1/2$ cups apricot nectar

$1/2$ cup chopped dried apricots

$1/2$ cup dry white wine

2 teaspoons freshly squeezed lemon juice

Combine the sugar and $1/3$ cup water in a small saucepan. Bring to a boil over medium heat, swirling the pan to dissolve the sugar but not stirring the mixture. Increase the heat to high, and cook the syrup until the firm-ball stage and the temperature registers 245°F to 250°F on a candy thermometer; the bubbles will be very large and the mixture will be very thick.

While the syrup is cooking combine the cornstarch and salt with $1/4$ cup cold water in a small cup, and stir well to dissolve the cornstarch.

Remove the syrup from the heat, and stir the cornstarch mixture into the sugar syrup. Cook the mixture on low for 1 minute, or until it becomes translucent and very thick. Set aside.

In another saucepan, combine the apricot nectar and dried apricots, and bring to a boil over medium-high heat, stirring occasionally. Cook for 5 minutes, or until the liquid is reduced by one-fourth. Strain out the dried apricots and purée them with $1/2$ cup of the nectar in a food processor fitted with the steel blade or in a blender.

Add the apricot mixture and the purée apricots to the saucepan with the sugar syrup-cornstarch mixture, and cook over low heat, stirring constantly, until the mixture is smooth. Stir in the wine and lemon juice.

Transfer the hot liquid to a storage container, and refrigerate uncovered until it is completely chilled (below 40°F), or quick-cool it according to the method on page 14.

Freeze the mixture in an ice cream maker according to the manufacturer's instructions. Serve immediately for a soft sorbet, or transfer the mixture to an airtight storage container and freeze until hard. Allow the sorbet to sit at room temperature for 15 minutes before serving if frozen solid.

PIÑA COLADA SORBET

ADAPTED FROM BOULDER
ICE CREAM, BOULDER, CO

*Here's a quick trip to the islands!
And it has enough rum in it to taste
like a real drink, too. Serve it in a
fruit smoothie made with tropical
fruits like mango and papaya, or
in a island-inspired sundae.*

MAKES ABOUT 1 QUART

2 teaspoons unflavored gelatin
or powdered agar

1 cup cream of coconut, such as
Coco Lopez, well-stirred

$1/4$ cup corn syrup

1 (8-ounce) can crushed pineapple
packed in pineapple juice

$1/8$ teaspoon kosher salt

$1/3$ cup light rum

2 tablespoons freshly
squeezed lime juice

Sprinkle the gelatin over $1/2$ cup of cold water to soften.

Combine the cream of coconut, corn syrup, pineapple with the juice from the can, salt, and $1^1/3$ cups water in a saucepan. Stir well, and heat to almost simmering over medium heat. Stir in the softened gelatin and cook for 1 minute, or until the gelatin dissolves.

Stir in the rum and lime juice.

Transfer the hot liquid to a storage container, and refrigerate uncovered until it is completely chilled (below 40°F), or quick-cool it according to the method on page 14.

Freeze the mixture in an ice cream maker according to the manufacturer's instructions. Serve immediately for a soft sorbet, or transfer the mixture to an airtight storage container and freeze until hard. Allow the sorbet to sit at room temperature for 15 minutes before serving if frozen solid.

GRAPEFRUIT CAMPARI SORBET

ADAPTED FROM BLUE MOON
SORBET, QUECHEE, VT

This vivid pink sorbet is the dessert version of a cool summer brunch drink. The slight bitterness of the Campari is a foil to the refreshing grapefruit.

MAKES ABOUT 1 QUART

2 teaspoons unflavored gelatin
or powdered agar

$3/4$ cup granulated sugar

$2^1/2$ cups freshly squeezed
grapefruit juice

$1/3$ cup Campari

Sprinkle the gelatin over $1/2$ cup of cold water to soften.

Combine the sugar and $1/2$ cup water in a saucepan, and stir well. Cook over medium heat, swirling the pan occasionally, until the sugar dissolves. Stir in the softened gelatin and cook for 1 minute, or until the gelatin dissolves.

Stir the grapefruit juice and Campari into the sugar syrup.

Transfer the hot liquid to a storage container, and refrigerate uncovered until it is completely chilled (below 40°F), or quick-cool it according to the method on page 14.

Freeze the mixture in an ice cream maker according to the manufacturer's instructions. Serve immediately for a soft sorbet, or transfer the mixture to an airtight storage container and freeze until hard. Allow the sorbet to sit at room temperature for 15 minutes before serving if frozen solid.

Blue Moon Sorbet, Quechee, VT

WHILE IT'S SAID THAT SOMETHING RARE COMES ALONG ONLY ONCE IN A BLUE moon, John Donaldson and Pamela Frantz want to make their artisan sorbets an exception to that rule. Their Blue Moon Sorbet line, available in many New England states at specialty stores, is intended to fill a market niche so that consumers can enjoy what has been a rarity on the market—restaurant-quality fruit sorbets—as often as they want.

John, an Illinois native, graduated from the Culinary Institute of America in Hyde Park, New York, in the late 1970s, and became pastry chef at highly acclaimed Prince and Pauper Restaurant in Woodstock, Vermont. He and Pamela met there when she came to work as the bar manager.

"One day I was looking in the supermarket for a sorbet as interesting as the ones I did for the restaurant and there was nothing there," John recalls. "My wife told me I was nuts to think about a sorbet company, but about a year later we made our first batch."

Blue Moon sorbets are all made with fruits, and about half of the line has some liquor or liqueur added. John's favorite is the Pear Ginger Sorbet (page 125) while Pamela's is Grapefruit Campari (page 163). "They both represent what we're trying to do," he says. "They are complex flavors that you don't find everywhere." Except once in a "blue moon."

RASPBERRY CASSIS SORBET

ADAPTED FROM BLUE MOON
SORBET, QUECHEE, VT

*There are some really intense
yet delicate berry flavors going
on in this sorbet: fresh raspberries
and black currants are blended
with crème de cassis, a European
black currant liqueur.*

MAKES ABOUT 1 QUART

2 teaspoons unflavored gelatin
or powdered agar

2 cups fresh raspberries or
frozen raspberries, thawed

$1/2$ cup black currants

$1/2$ cup granulated sugar

$1/8$ teaspoon kosher salt

$1/3$ cup crème de cassis

1 tablespoon freshly
squeezed lemon juice

Sprinkle the gelatin over $1/2$ cup of cold water to soften.

Combine the raspberries, black currants, sugar, salt, and 1 cup water in a saucepan, and stir well. Bring to a boil over medium-high heat, stirring often. Stir in the softened gelatin and cook for 1 minute, or until the gelatin dissolves. Set aside to cool for 5 minutes.

Purée the mixture in a food processor fitted with the steel blade or in a blender. Stir in the crème de cassis and lemon juice.

Transfer the hot liquid to a storage container, and refrigerate uncovered until it is completely chilled (below 40°F), or quick-cool it according to the method on page 14.

Freeze the mixture in an ice cream maker according to the manufacturer's instructions. Serve immediately for a soft sorbet, or transfer the mixture to an airtight storage container and freeze until hard. Allow the sorbet to sit at room temperature for 15 minutes before serving if frozen solid.

CITRUS COINTREAU SORBET with CHOCOLATE

ADAPTED FROM
MORA ICED CREAMERY,
BAINBRIDGE ISLAND, WA

This refreshing yet decadent sorbet is called Tango on Mora's menu, reflecting the owners' Argentinean heritage. There's a combination of orange and lemon, some heady orange liqueur, and then a good dose of chocolate. You'll want to dance, too.

MAKES ABOUT 1 QUART

2 teaspoons unflavored gelatin

$2^1/_2$ cups freshly squeezed orange juice

$^1/_4$ cup freshly squeezed lemon juice

$^1/_2$ cup granulated sugar

$^1/_8$ teaspoon kosher salt

$^1/_3$ cup Cointreau or other orange-flavored liqueur

2 ounces bittersweet chocolate, chopped

Sprinkle the gelatin over $^1/_2$ cup of cold water to soften.

Combine the orange juice, lemon juice, sugar, salt, and $^3/_4$ cup water in a saucepan. Heat the mixture over medium heat to dissolve the sugar. Stir in the softened gelatin and cook for 1 minute, or until the gelatin dissolves. Stir in the Cointreau.

Transfer the hot liquid to a storage container, and refrigerate uncovered until it is completely chilled (below 40°F), or quick-cool it according to the method on page 14.

Freeze the mixture in an ice cream maker according to the manufacturer's instructions. Transfer the soft sorbet to a chilled mixing bowl and fold in the chopped chocolate. Serve immediately for a soft sorbet, or transfer the mixture to an airtight storage container and freeze until hard. Allow the sorbet to sit at room temperature for 15 minutes before serving if frozen solid.

Mora Iced Creamery, Bainbridge Island, WA

MANY ITALIAN GELATO-MAKERS LIVE A LIFE OF ENDLESS SUMMER BY SPLIT-ting their time between the northern and southern hemispheres. Just when it's getting to be fall in Bologna, it's becoming spring in Buenos Aires. So they commute between Europe and South America to maximize their market.

It was in Argentina that both Ana Orselli, who was of Italian heritage, and her husband Jerry Perez, whose family was solidly Argentine, were introduced to gelato as well as each other. The word *mora* means blackberry in both Spanish and Italian, and it is grows wild on this island that is a short ferry ride from Seattle. That was the rationale for choosing it as the name when they opened Mora Iced Creamery in 2004.

The flavors at the firm's three stores range from the traditional to the avant garde. In the former category are customers' favorites like Swiss Chocolate (page 50), while the more modern include a concoction like Citrus Cointreau Sorbet with Chocolate (page 166), which is called "Tango" on the menu in honor of their native country's famous dance.

Jerry, who holds an MBA, is general manager of the company, while Ana, who was trained in the visual arts, manages the stores. She recalls her own childhood when she sees families come into Mora, because it was trips to a gelato shop that marked the arrival of spring.

MOJITO
ICE

*Everything you need is right here—
there's mint, lime, and rum. This
could easily be served as an intermezzo as well as a dessert, especially
for a meal with a Cuban menu.*

MAKES ABOUT 1 QUART

2 teaspoons unflavored gelatin
or powdered agar

$^1/_2$ cup granulated sugar

$^1/_3$ cup light corn syrup

$^1/_3$ cup chopped fresh mint

$^1/_3$ cup freshly squeezed lime juice

2 teaspoons grated lime zest

$^1/_3$ cup light rum

2 tablespoons Triple Sec

Sprinkle the gelatin over $^1/_2$ cup cold water to soften.

Combine the sugar and corn syrup with 2 cups water in a saucepan and bring to a boil over medium-high heat, stirring occasionally. Stir in the softened gelatin and cook for 1 minute, or until the gelatin dissolves. Stir in the mint. Cover the pan and remove the pan from the heat. Allow the mixture to steep for 30 minutes, then strain the mixture through a fine sieve, pressing with the back of a spoon to extract as much liquid as possible.

Stir the lime juice, lime zest, rum, and Triple Sec into the strained liquid.

Transfer the hot liquid to a storage container, and refrigerate uncovered until it is completely chilled (below 40°F), or quick-cool it according to the method on page 14.

Freeze the mixture in an ice cream maker according to the manufacturer's instructions. Serve immediately for a soft sorbet, or transfer the mixture to an airtight storage container and freeze until hard. Allow the sorbet to sit at room temperature for 15 minutes before serving if frozen solid.

CINNAMON BOURBON ICE CREAM

ADAPTED FROM MOOMERS,
TRAVERSE CITY, MI

*Aromatic cinnamon is given
a more complex flavor with
a few shots of bourbon in this
ice cream. It's sensational
served with pecan pie.*

MAKES ABOUT 1 QUART

8 to 10 (3-inch) cinnamon sticks

$1^{1}/_{2}$ cups whole milk, divided

1 cup heavy whipping cream

$^{1}/_{4}$ cup granulated sugar

$^{1}/_{4}$ cup light corn syrup

$^{1}/_{8}$ teaspoon kosher salt

3 tablespoons nonfat
dry milk powder

2 tablespoons cornstarch

3 tablespoons bourbon

$^{1}/_{4}$ teaspoon pure vanilla extract

Place the cinnamon sticks in a heavy plastic bag, and hit them with the bottom of a small saucepan to crush them.

Combine 1 cup of the milk, cream, sugar, corn syrup, and salt in a saucepan. Cook over medium heat, stirring frequently, until the mixture reaches a simmer. Add the crushed cinnamon sticks, and stir well. Cover the pan and remove the pan from the heat. Allow the mixture to steep for 30 minutes, then strain the mixture through a fine sieve, pressing with the back of a spoon to extract as much liquid as possible. Return the mixture to the pan.

While the mixture steeps, combine the remaining milk, milk powder, cornstarch, bourbon, and vanilla extract in a small bowl, and stir until smooth and both of the powders have dissolved.

Add the cornstarch mixture to the pan, and bring to a boil over low heat, stirring constantly. Whisk until smooth, and simmer the mixture for 2 minutes, or until thickened. If the mixture is lumpy, strain it through a sieve.

Transfer the hot liquid to a storage container and press a sheet of plastic wrap directly onto the surface of the mixture to prevent a skin from forming. Refrigerate the mixture uncovered until it is completely chilled (below 40°F), or quick-cool it according to the method on page 14.

Freeze the mixture in an ice cream maker according to the manufacturer's instructions. Serve immediately for a soft ice cream, or transfer the mixture to an airtight storage container and freeze until hard. Allow the ice cream to sit at room temperature for 15 minutes before serving if frozen solid.

IRISH COFFEE ICE CREAM

ADAPTED FROM BASSETTS,
PHILADELPHIA, PA

This ice cream spiked with real Jamison Irish Whiskey was added to the flavor list about two generations ago as a way to end a family squabble. While delicious on its own, it's even more mouth-watering with Hot Fudge Sauce (page 210).

MAKES ABOUT 1 QUART

1 $^1/_2$ cups heavy whipping cream

1 $^1/_4$ cups whole milk, divided

$^1/_2$ cup granulated sugar

$^1/_4$ cup light corn syrup

2 to 3 tablespoons instant coffee powder

$^1/_8$ teaspoon kosher salt

3 tablespoons nonfat dry milk powder

2 tablespoons cornstarch

$^1/_4$ teaspoon pure vanilla extract

$^1/_4$ cup Irish whiskey

Combine the cream, $^1/_2$ cup milk, sugar, corn syrup, instant coffee powder, and salt in a saucepan. Cook over medium heat, stirring frequently, until the mixture begins to steam; watch it carefully and make sure it does not come to a boil.

While the mixture heats, combine the remaining milk, milk powder, cornstarch, and vanilla extract in a small bowl, and stir until smooth and both of the powders have dissolved.

Add the cornstarch mixture to the pan, and bring to a boil over low heat, stirring constantly. Whisk the mixture until smooth, and simmer the mixture over very low heat, stirring constantly, for 2 minutes, or until thickened. If the mixture is lumpy, strain it through a sieve. Stir in the Irish whiskey.

Transfer the hot liquid to a storage container and press a sheet of plastic wrap directly onto the surface of the mixture to prevent a skin from forming. Refrigerate the mixture uncovered until it is completely chilled (below 40°F), or quick-cool it according to the method on page 14.

Freeze the mixture in an ice cream maker according to the manufacturer's instructions. Serve immediately for a soft ice cream, or transfer the mixture to an airtight storage container and freeze until hard. Allow the ice cream to sit at room temperature for 15 minutes before serving if frozen solid.

Tip: Evaporating Alcohol from Foods

The recipes in this chapter all contain some sort of alcohol, but you can tame them by adding the spirits to the custard along with the cornstarch mixture. While not all of the alcohol will boil away, a portion of it will.

AMARETTO GELATO

ADAPTED FROM COLD FUSION
GELATO, NEWPORT, RI

Amaretto holds a special place in Italian cuisine, and this light yet creamy gelato gains its flavor from a combination of nuts, liqueur, and almond extract. It's an elegant way to end an Italian dinner.

MAKES ABOUT 1 QUART

1 ounce blanched slivered almonds

$2^1/_2$ cups whole milk, divided

$^3/_4$ cup heavy whipping cream

$^1/_2$ cup amaretto liqueur

$^1/_4$ cup granulated sugar

$^1/_4$ cup light corn syrup

$^1/_8$ teaspoon kosher salt

2 tablespoons nonfat dry milk powder

2 tablespoons cornstarch

$^1/_2$ teaspoon pure almond extract

Combine the almonds and $^1/_2$ cup milk in a food processor fitted with the steel blade or in a blender, and purée until smooth. Transfer the mixture to a saucepan.

Add $1^1/_2$ cups of the milk, cream, amaretto, sugar, corn syrup, and salt to the pan. Cook over medium heat, stirring frequently, until the mixture begins to steam; watch it carefully and make sure it does not come to a boil.

While the mixture heats, combine the remaining milk, milk powder, cornstarch, and almond extract in a small bowl, and stir until smooth and both of the powders have dissolved.

Add the cornstarch mixture to the pan, and bring to a boil over low heat, stirring constantly. Whisk the mixture until smooth, and simmer the mixture over very low heat, stirring constantly, for 2 minutes, or until thickened. If the mixture is lumpy, strain it through a sieve.

Transfer the hot liquid to a storage container, and press a sheet of plastic wrap directly onto the surface of the mixture to prevent a skin from forming. Refrigerate the mixture uncovered until it is completely chilled (below 40°F), or quick-cool it according to the method on page 14.

Freeze the mixture in an ice cream maker according to the manufacturer's instructions. Serve immediately for a soft gelato, or transfer the mixture to an airtight storage container and freeze until hard. Allow the gelato to sit at room temperature for 15 minutes before serving if frozen solid.

Variation: Substitute skinned hazelnuts for the almonds and a hazelnut liqueur, such as Frangelico, for the amaretto.

AMARETTO PEACH ICE CREAM

ADAPTED FROM BONNIE BRAE, DENVER, CO

Once you taste how the almond flavor from the amaretto liqueur enhances the sweetness of the peaches you'll add it to all peach desserts.

MAKES ABOUT 1 QUART

3 ripe peaches or 1 (12-ounce) bag frozen peach slices, thawed

1 cup heavy whipping cream

$^3/_4$ cup whole milk, divided

$^1/_4$ cup granulated sugar

$^1/_4$ cup light corn syrup

2 tablespoons amaretto liqueur

$^1/_8$ teaspoon kosher salt

2 tablespoons nonfat dry milk powder

2 tablespoons cornstarch

$^1/_4$ teaspoon pure vanilla extract

$^1/_4$ teaspoon pure almond extract

If using fresh peaches, bring a saucepan of water to a boil over high heat. Add the peaches and blanch them for 40 seconds. Remove the peaches from the pan with a slotted spoon, and run them under cold water. When cool enough to handle, slip off the skins, discard the pits, and cut the peaches into 1-inch cubes. Using either fresh or frozen peaches, purée them in a food processor fitted with the steel blade or in a blender.

Combine the peach purée, cream, $^1/_4$ cup milk, sugar, corn syrup, amaretto, and salt in a saucepan. Cook over medium heat, stirring frequently, until the mixture begins to steam; watch it carefully and make sure it does not come to a boil.

While the mixture heats, combine the remaining milk, milk powder, cornstarch, vanilla extract, and almond extract in a small bowl, and stir until smooth and both of the powders have dissolved.

Add the cornstarch mixture to the pan, and bring to a boil over low heat, stirring constantly. Whisk the mixture until smooth, and simmer the mixture over very low heat, stirring constantly, for 2 minutes, or until thickened. If the mixture is lumpy, strain it through a sieve.

Transfer the hot liquid to a storage container and press a sheet of plastic wrap directly onto the surface of the mixture to prevent a skin from forming. Refrigerate the mixture uncovered until it is completely chilled (below 40°F), or quick-cool it according to the method on page 14.

Freeze the mixture in an ice cream maker according to the manufacturer's instructions. Serve immediately for a soft ice cream, or transfer the mixture to an airtight storage container and freeze until hard. Allow the ice cream to sit at room temperature for 15 minutes before serving if frozen solid.

BANANAS FOSTER ICE CREAM

ADAPTED FROM SWEET REPUBLIC, SCOTTSDALE, AZ

Here's the ice cream version of the legendary dessert invented at Brennan's in New Orleans. The bananas are caramelized, which accentuates their sweetness.

MAKES ABOUT 1 QUART

2 very ripe bananas,
cut into $^3/_4$-inch slices

$^1/_2$ cup firmly packed
light brown sugar

2 tablespoons unsalted
butter, melted

$1^1/_2$ cups whole milk

$^1/_2$ cup heavy whipping cream

3 tablespoons nonfat
dry milk powder

$^1/_4$ teaspoon kosher salt

3 large egg yolks

2 tablespoons granulated sugar

$^1/_4$ teaspoon pure vanilla extract

2 tablespoons dark rum

2 tablespoons crème de
banana or additional dark rum

Preheat the oven to 375°F. Line a 13 x 9-inch pan with heavy-duty aluminum foil.

Toss the bananas with the brown sugar and butter in the baking pan. Bake the bananas for 30 minutes, stirring occasionally, or until they are very tender. Set aside.

Combine the milk, cream, milk powder, and salt in a medium saucepan, and stir well to dissolve the milk powder. Bring the mixture just to a simmer, stirring occasionally.

Beat the eggs yolks, sugar, and vanilla in a mixing bowl with a whisk until thick and light yellow in color. Slowly beat about one-third of the hot cream mixture into the eggs so they are gradually warmed up, and then return the contents of the mixing bowl to the saucepan. Place the pan over medium-low heat and stir constantly, reaching all parts of the bottom of the pan, until the mixture reaches about 170°F on an instant-read thermometer; at this point it begins to emit steam, thickens slightly, and coats the back of a spoon. This takes 3 to 6 minutes. Do not allow the mixture to boil or the eggs will scramble. Strain the custard through a fine sieve, if desired.

Combine the bananas and any juices from the pan and 1 cup of the custard in a food processor fitted with the steel blade or in a blender. Purée until smooth, and then stir the purée, rum, and crème de banana into the custard.

Transfer the hot liquid to a storage container and press a sheet of plastic wrap directly onto the surface of the mixture to prevent a skin from forming. Refrigerate the mixture uncovered until it is completely chilled (below 40°F), or quick-cool it according to the method on page 14.

Freeze the mixture in an ice cream maker according to the manufacturer's instructions. Serve immediately for a soft ice cream, or transfer the mixture to an airtight storage container and freeze until hard. Allow the ice cream to sit at room temperature for 15 minutes before serving.

RUM RAISIN ICE CREAM

ADAPTED FROM THE DAILY
SCOOP, BARRINGTON, RI

*I think that rum raisin was
the only liquor-laced ice cream on
the market until very recently, and
it's a classic worthy of being
included in everyone's repertoire.*

MAKES ABOUT 1 QUART

$^2/_3$ cup raisins

$^1/_2$ cup light rum

2 cups heavy whipping
cream, divided

$^3/_4$ cup whole milk

$^1/_2$ cup granulated sugar

$^1/_4$ cup light corn syrup

2 tablespoons nonfat
dry milk powder

2 tablespoons cornstarch

Pinch of kosher salt

$^1/_4$ teaspoon pure vanilla extract

Combine the raisins and rum in a small saucepan, and heat until just simmering. Cover the pan, remove the pan from the heat, and allow the raisins to macerate for at least 30 minutes and up to 1 day.

Combine $1^1/_2$ cups of the cream, milk, sugar, and corn syrup in a saucepan. Cook over medium heat, stirring frequently, until the mixture begins to steam; watch it carefully and make sure it does not come to a boil.

While the mixture heats, combine the remaining cream, milk powder, cornstarch, salt, and vanilla extract in a small bowl, and stir until smooth and both of the powders have dissolved.

Add the cornstarch mixture to the pan, and bring to a boil over low heat, stirring constantly. Whisk the mixture until smooth, and simmer the mixture over very low heat, stirring constantly, for 2 minutes, or until thickened. If the mixture is lumpy, strain it through a sieve. Stir the raisin rum mixture into the custard.

Transfer the hot liquid to a storage container and press a sheet of plastic wrap directly onto the surface of the mixture to prevent a skin from forming. Refrigerate the mixture uncovered until it is completely chilled (below 40°F), or quick-cool it according to the method on page 14.

Freeze the mixture in an ice cream maker according to the manufacturer's instructions. Serve immediately for a soft ice cream, or transfer the mixture to an airtight storage container and freeze until hard. Allow the ice cream to sit at room temperature for 15 minutes before serving if frozen solid.

COFFEE LIQUEUR ICE CREAM with BROWNIE BITS

ADAPTED FROM SILVER MOON, LOS GATOS, CA

Chocolate and coffee can't be beaten, especially when the coffee takes the form of sweet Kahlúa in a creamy ice cream.

MAKES ABOUT 1 QUART

$1^{1}/_{2}$ cups heavy whipping cream, divided

$^{3}/_{4}$ cup whole milk

$^{1}/_{2}$ cup granulated sugar

$^{1}/_{4}$ cup light corn syrup

2 tablespoons nonfat dry milk powder

2 tablespoons cornstarch

Pinch of kosher salt

$^{1}/_{4}$ teaspoon pure vanilla extract

$^{1}/_{2}$ cup coffee liqueur, such as Kahlúa

$^{3}/_{4}$ cup crumbled Fudge Brownies (page 234) or purchased chocolate brownies

Combine 1 cup of the cream, milk, sugar, and corn syrup in a saucepan. Cook over medium heat, stirring frequently, until the mixture begins to steam; watch it carefully and make sure it does not come to a boil.

While the mixture heats, combine the remaining cream, milk powder, cornstarch, salt, and vanilla extract in a small bowl, and stir until smooth and both of the powders have dissolved.

Add the cornstarch mixture to the pan, and bring to a boil over low heat, stirring constantly. Whisk the mixture until smooth, and simmer the mixture over very low heat, stirring constantly, for 2 minutes, or until thickened. If the mixture is lumpy, strain it through a sieve. Stir in the coffee liqueur.

Transfer the hot liquid to a storage container and press a sheet of plastic wrap directly onto the surface of the mixture to prevent a skin from forming. Refrigerate the mixture uncovered until it is completely chilled (below 40°F), or quick-cool it according to the method on page 14.

Freeze the mixture in an ice cream maker according to the manufacturer's instructions. Transfer the soft ice cream to a chilled mixing bowl and fold in the crumbled brownies.

Serve immediately for a soft ice cream, or transfer the mixture to an airtight storage container and freeze until hard. Allow the ice cream to sit at room temperature for 15 minutes before serving if frozen solid.

Silver Moon, Los Gatos, CA

IT'S A RARE ICE CREAM OR SORBET THAT COMES WITH A LABEL THAT SAYS IT cannot be sold to minors, but that's the case with the spirited frozen treats made by Sheri Tate, who describes herself as the "owner, founder, chief executive officer, product developer, and dish washer" of Silver Moon Desserts; she took on all these roles when she started the company in 2008. But it's also rare to find a product line based on the marriage of two traditional after-dinner favorites—ice cream and liqueurs.

In addition to classic after-dinner combinations, she also makes such flavors as Mojito Ice (page 168) and Mango Mimosa (page 159) that can do double duty and be served as an intermezzo as well.

A Michigan native, she recalls cranking an ice cream machine by hand to enjoy all the region's fresh summer fruits. Learning how to cook from her mother and grandmother, both of whom she calls "experienced gourmet cooks," Tate started experimenting and making ice cream for her own dinner parties. At the time she was working in marketing, and wondered why no company had introduced "an adult, upscale line of liqueur-infused ice creams and sorbets, so I decided to give it a go," she says.

In addition to selling flavors like Coffee Liqueur Ice Cream with Brownie Bits (opposite), with Bailey's Irish Cream as a key ingredient, to customers in California, she also supplies some of the Bay Area's finest restaurants with her creations.

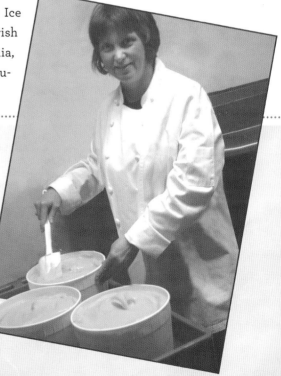

Sheri Tate, owner of Silver Moon

GRAND MARNIER CHOCOLATE CHIP ICE CREAM

ADAPTED FROM BONNIE BRAE,
DENVER, CO

*This also makes a great filling
for a Baked Alaska (page 228)
and Profiteroles (page 225).*

MAKES ABOUT 1 QUART

$1^1/_4$ cups heavy whipping cream

$^3/_4$ cup whole milk, divided

$^1/_4$ cup granulated sugar

$^1/_4$ cup unsweetened cocoa powder

$^1/_4$ cup light corn syrup

3 tablespoons Grand Marnier liqueur
or other orange-flavored liqueur

$^1/_8$ teaspoon kosher salt

2 tablespoons nonfat
dry milk powder

2 tablespoons cornstarch

1 ($3^1/_2$-ounce) bar semisweet
chocolate, chopped

$^1/_2$ cup high-quality semisweet
chocolate chips

Combine the cream, $^1/_2$ cup milk, sugar, cocoa powder, corn syrup, Grand Marnier, and salt in a saucepan. Cook over medium heat, stirring frequently, until the mixture begins to steam; watch it carefully and make sure it does not come to a boil.

While the mixture heats, combine the remaining milk, milk powder, and cornstarch in a small bowl, and stir until smooth and both of the powders have dissolved.

Add the cornstarch mixture to the pan, and bring to a boil over low heat, stirring constantly. Whisk the mixture until smooth, and simmer the mixture over very low heat, stirring constantly, for 2 minutes, or until thickened. Remove from the heat. If the mixture is lumpy, strain it through a sieve.

Add the chopped chocolate to the custard, and allow it to sit for 2 minutes, or until melted. Whisk to blend.

Transfer the hot liquid to a storage container and press a sheet of plastic wrap directly onto the surface of the mixture to prevent a skin from forming. Refrigerate the mixture uncovered until it is completely chilled (below 40°F), or quick-cool it according to the method on page 14.

Freeze the mixture in an ice cream maker according to the manufacturer's instructions. Transfer the soft ice cream to a chilled mixing bowl and fold in the chocolate chips.

Serve immediately for a soft ice cream, or transfer the mixture to an airtight storage container and freeze until hard. Allow the ice cream to sit at room temperature for 15 minutes before serving if frozen solid.

ORANGE LIQUEUR ICE CREAM with FIG SWIRL

ADAPTED FROM SILVER MOON,
LOS GATOS, CA

The orange brandy in the ice cream accentuates the sweetness of the fruit in the swirl. Try this in the Fried Ice Cream Balls (page 227); the additional crunchy crust is stellar.

MAKES ABOUT 1 QUART

Ice Cream

1 (3-ounce) package cream cheese, at room temperature

$3/4$ cup whole milk

$1 1/4$ cups heavy whipping cream, divided

$1/2$ cup granulated sugar

$1/4$ cup light corn syrup

2 tablespoons nonfat dry milk powder

2 tablespoons cornstarch

Pinch of kosher salt

$1/4$ teaspoon pure vanilla extract

$1/3$ cup Grand Marnier or other orange-flavored liqueur

Swirl

2 ounces dried Turkish figs, stemmed and chopped

2 tablespoons granulated sugar

For the ice cream: Combine the cream cheese and milk in a food processor fitted with the steel blade or in a blender. Purée until smooth; transfer the mixture to a saucepan.

Add $3/4$ cup of the cream, sugar, and corn syrup to the pan. Cook over medium heat, stirring frequently, until the mixture begins to steam; watch it carefully and make sure it does not come to a boil.

While the mixture heats, combine the remaining cream, milk powder, cornstarch, salt, and vanilla extract in a small bowl, and stir until smooth and both of the powders have dissolved.

Add the cornstarch mixture to the pan, and bring to a boil over low heat, stirring constantly. Whisk the mixture until smooth, and simmer the mixture over very low heat, stirring constantly, for 2 minutes, or until thickened. If the mixture is lumpy, strain it through a sieve. Stir in the orange liqueur.

Transfer the hot liquid to a storage container and press a sheet of plastic wrap directly onto the surface of the mixture to prevent a skin from forming. Refrigerate the mixture uncovered until it is completely chilled (below 40°F), or quick-cool it according to the method on page 14.

While the custard chills, make the fig swirl: Combine the chopped figs, sugar, and $1/4$ cup water in a small saucepan, and bring to a boil over medium-high heat, stirring occasionally. Reduce the heat to low, and simmer the figs for 10 to 12 minutes, or until soft. Purée the figs in a food processor fitted with a steel blade or in a blender, and transfer the purée to a small bowl. Keep the fig purée at room temperature.

Freeze the chilled custard in an ice cream maker according to the manufacturer's instructions.

(continued)

To make the fig swirl: Transfer one-sixth of the soft ice cream to an airtight container. Top it with a few spoonfuls of the fig purée, and then repeat until all the ice cream and fig purée are layered. When serving the ice cream, dig into the container vertically so each serving contains some of the swirl.

Serve immediately for a soft ice cream, or freeze until hard. Allow the ice cream to sit at room temperature for 15 minutes before serving if frozen solid.

CRÈME DE MENTHE CHOCOLATE CHIP ICE CREAM

ADAPTED FROM SILVER MOON, LOS GATOS, CA

Here's the grown-up version of chocolate-mint ice cream. Even though there's a lot of chocolate in it, add some Hot Fudge Sauce (page 210) to really pour on the decadence.

MAKES ABOUT 1 QUART

1 1/2 cups heavy whipping cream, divided

3/4 cup whole milk

1/2 cup granulated sugar

1/4 cup light corn syrup

2 tablespoons nonfat dry milk powder

2 tablespoons cornstarch

Pinch of kosher salt

1/4 teaspoon pure mint extract or mint oil

1/2 cup crème de menthe

3/4 cup high-quality bittersweet chocolate chips

Combine 1 cup of the cream, milk, sugar, and corn syrup in a saucepan. Cook over medium heat, stirring frequently, until the mixture begins to steam; watch it carefully and make sure it does not come to a boil.

While the mixture heats, combine the remaining cream, milk powder, cornstarch, salt, and mint extract in a small bowl, and stir until smooth and both of the powders have dissolved.

Add the cornstarch mixture to the pan, and bring to a boil over low heat, stirring constantly. Whisk the mixture until smooth, and simmer the mixture over very low heat, stirring constantly, for 2 minutes, or until thickened. If the mixture is lumpy, strain it through a sieve. Stir in the crème de menthe.

Transfer the hot liquid to a storage container and press a sheet of plastic wrap directly onto the surface of the mixture to prevent a skin from forming. Refrigerate the mixture uncovered until it is completely chilled (below 40°F), or quick-cool it according to the method on page 14.

Freeze the mixture in an ice cream maker according to the manufacturer's instructions. Transfer the soft ice cream to a chilled mixing bowl and fold in the chocolate chips.

Serve immediately for a soft ice cream, or transfer the mixture to an airtight storage container and freeze until hard. Allow the ice cream to sit at room temperature for 15 minutes before serving if frozen solid.

9 Other Great Flavors

Some of these ice creams represent the most exciting flavor combinations in the book, but they defy easy categorization. Some are made with herbs, while there's even one made with pungent Roquefort blue cheese. There are also ice cream and gelato versions of classic desserts like tiramisù and pumpkin pie. In all, this chapter is a true potpourri, and one you won't want miss.

LEMON THYME SORBET

ADAPTED FROM GIOVANNA
GELATO, NEWTON, MA

Combining tart lemon juice with herbs is commonplace in savory dishes, and it also works magically in this refreshing yet creamy sorbet.

MAKES ABOUT 1 QUART

1 cup granulated sugar
2 tablespoons cornstarch
Pinch of kosher salt
1 cup freshly squeezed lemon juice
2 tablespoons fresh thyme leaves
1 tablespoon grated lemon zest

Combine the sugar and $2/3$ cup water in a small saucepan. Bring to a boil over medium heat, swirling the pan to dissolve the sugar but not stirring the mixture. Increase the heat to high, and cook the syrup until the firm-ball stage and temperature registers 245°F to 250°F on a candy thermometer; the bubbles will be very large and the mixture will be very thick.

While the syrup is cooking combine the cornstarch and salt with $1/4$ cup cold water in a small cup, and stir well to dissolve the cornstarch.

Remove the syrup from the heat, and stir the cornstarch mixture into the sugar syrup. Cook the mixture on low for 1 minute, or until it becomes translucent and very thick. Remove from the heat.

Add the lemon juice, thyme leaves, lemon zest, and 2 cups of water to the pan with the cornstarch mixture, and whisk until smooth.

Transfer the hot liquid to a storage container, and refrigerate uncovered until it is completely chilled (below 40°F), or quick-cool it according to the method on page 14.

Freeze the mixture in an ice cream maker according to the manufacturer's instructions. Serve immediately for a soft sorbet, or transfer the mixture to an airtight storage container and freeze until hard. Allow the sorbet to sit at room temperature for 15 minutes before serving if frozen solid.

LAVENDER GELATO

ADAPTED FROM GIOVANNA
GELATO, NEWTON, MA

*A floral perfume and delicate
flavor characterize this gelato.
It's very subtle, and should follow
an elegant meal. Make sure the
lavender flowers you use come from
a specialty food store and not
a florist; not all lavender is
appropriate for cooking.*

MAKES ABOUT 1 QUART

3 cups whole milk, divided
$^1/_4$ cup dried lavender flowers
$^1/_2$ cup granulated sugar
$^1/_4$ cup light corn syrup
2 tablespoons nonfat
dry milk powder
2 tablespoons cornstarch
Pinch of kosher salt
$^1/_4$ teaspoon pure vanilla extract

Combine 2$^1/_2$ cups of the milk and the lavender flowers in a saucepan, and bring to a simmer over medium heat. Cover the pan and remove from the heat. Allow the mixture to steep for 30 minutes, then strain the mixture through a fine sieve, pressing with the back of a spoon to extract as much liquid as possible. Return the mixture to the pan.

Add the sugar and corn syrup to the pan. Cook over medium heat, stirring frequently, until the mixture begins to steam; watch it carefully and make sure it does not come to a boil.

While the mixture heats, combine the remaining milk, milk powder, cornstarch, salt, and vanilla extract in a small bowl, and stir until smooth and both of the powders have dissolved.

Add the cornstarch mixture to the pan, and bring to a boil over low heat, stirring constantly. Whisk the mixture until smooth, and simmer the mixture over very low heat, stirring constantly, for 2 minutes, or until thickened. If the mixture is lumpy, strain it through a sieve.

Transfer the hot liquid to a storage container and press a sheet of plastic wrap directly onto the surface of the mixture to prevent a skin from forming. Refrigerate the mixture uncovered until it is completely chilled (below 40°F), or quick-cool it according to the method on page 14.

Freeze the mixture in an ice cream maker according to the manufacturer's instructions. Serve immediately for a soft gelato, or transfer the mixture to an airtight storage container and freeze until hard. Allow the gelato to sit at room temperature for 15 minutes before serving if frozen solid.

BASIL LIME SORBET

ADAPTED FROM SWEET
REPUBLIC, SCOTTSDALE, AZ

This sorbet is sufficient reason to bring back the custom of serving a "palate cleanser" when switching from white to red wines at formal dinners.

MAKES ABOUT 1 QUART

2 teaspoons unflavored gelatin
or powdered agar
1 cup granulated sugar
Pinch of kosher salt
1 cup freshly squeezed lime juice
$^{1}/_{2}$ cup finely chopped fresh basil
1 tablespoon grated lime zest

Sprinkle the gelatin over $^{1}/_{2}$ cup cold water to soften.

Combine the sugar, salt, and 1 cup water in a saucepan, and bring to a boil over medium-high heat. Stir the softened gelatin into the pan. Cook for 1 minute, or until the gelatin dissolves.

Remove the pan from the heat, and stir in $1^{1}/_{2}$ cups cold water, along with the lime juice, basil, and lime zest.

Transfer the hot liquid to a storage container, and refrigerate uncovered until it is completely chilled (below 40°F), or quick-cool it according to the method on page 14.

Freeze the mixture in an ice cream maker according to the manufacturer's instructions. Serve immediately for a soft sorbet, or transfer the mixture to an airtight storage container and freeze until hard. Allow the sorbet to sit at room temperature for 15 minutes before serving if frozen solid.

ROSEMARY OLIVE OIL GELATO

ADAPTED FROM GS GELATO,
FORT WALTON BEACH, FL

The slightly woody aroma of rosemary is enhanced by similar qualities in the Mexican vanilla in this gelato. Using olive oil in gelato is a restaurant trend that is wending its way into shops, too.

MAKES ABOUT 1 QUART

$1/4$ cup chopped fresh rosemary

$1/2$ cup extra-virgin olive oil

2 cups whole milk, divided

$1/2$ cup heavy whipping cream

$1/3$ cup granulated sugar

$1/4$ cup light corn syrup

$3/4$ teaspoon kosher salt

3 tablespoons nonfat dry milk powder

2 tablespoons cornstarch

2 teaspoons pure Mexican vanilla extract

Combine the rosemary and olive oil in a small saucepan over low heat. Cook for 3 minutes, stirring occasionally. Remove the pan from the heat, and allow the mixture to sit at room temperature for 2 hours.

Combine $1^1/2$ cups of the milk, cream, sugar, corn syrup, and salt in a saucepan. Cook over medium heat, stirring frequently, until the mixture begins to steam; watch it carefully and make sure it does not come to a boil.

While the mixture heats, combine the remaining milk, milk powder, cornstarch, and vanilla extract in a small bowl, and stir until smooth and both of the powders have dissolved.

Add the cornstarch mixture to the pan, and bring to a boil over low heat, stirring constantly. Whisk the mixture until smooth, and simmer the mixture over very low heat, stirring constantly, for 2 minutes, or until thickened. If the mixture is lumpy, strain it through a sieve. Stir in the rosemary oil, and whisk well.

Transfer the hot liquid to a storage container and press a sheet of plastic wrap directly onto the surface of the mixture to prevent a skin from forming. Refrigerate the mixture uncovered until it is completely chilled (below 40°F), or quick-cool it according to the method on page 14.

Freeze the mixture in an ice cream maker according to the manufacturer's instructions. Serve immediately for a soft gelato, or transfer the mixture to an airtight storage container and freeze until hard. Allow the gelato to sit at room temperature for 15 minutes before serving if frozen solid.

MINT GOAT MILK ICE CREAM with CHOCOLATE CHIPS

ADAPTED FROM LÁLOO'S, PETALUMA, CA

There are large chips of imported Swiss milk chocolate in this robustly flavored mint ice cream that is perfect to serve around the holidays.

MAKES ABOUT 1 QUART

2$^1/_2$ cups goat milk

2 ounces fresh goat cheese, crumbled

$^1/_2$ cup granulated sugar, divided

$^1/_8$ teaspoon kosher salt

3 large egg yolks

$^3/_4$ to 1$^1/_4$ teaspoons pure mint oil

$^2/_3$ cup milk chocolate chips, preferably imported Swiss chips

Combine the goat milk, goat cheese, $^1/_4$ cup sugar, and salt in a medium saucepan, and stir well to dissolve the milk powder. Bring the mixture just to a simmer, stirring occasionally.

Beat the egg yolks, remaining $^1/_4$ cup sugar, and mint oil in a mixing bowl with a whisk until thick and light yellow in color. Slowly beat about one-third of the hot goat milk mixture into the eggs so they are gradually warmed up, and then return the contents of the mixing bowl to the saucepan. Place the pan over medium-low heat and stir constantly, reaching all parts of the bottom of the pan, until the mixture reaches about 170°F on an instant-read thermometer; at this point it begins to emit steam, thickens slightly, and coats the back of a spoon. This takes 3 to 6 minutes. Do not allow the mixture to boil or the eggs will scramble. Strain the custard through a fine sieve, if desired.

Transfer the hot liquid to a storage container and press a sheet of plastic wrap directly onto the surface of the mixture to prevent a skin from forming. Refrigerate the mixture uncovered until it is completely chilled (below 40°F), or quick-cool it according to the method on page 14.

Freeze the mixture in an ice cream maker according to the manufacturer's instructions. Transfer the soft ice cream to a chilled mixing bowl, and fold in the chocolate chips.

Serve immediately for a soft ice cream, or transfer the mixture to an airtight storage container and freeze until hard. Allow the ice cream to sit at room temperature for 15 minutes before serving if frozen solid.

REAL MINT ICE CREAM with CHOCOLATE CHIPS

ADAPTED FROM SWEET REPUBLIC, SCOTTSDALE, AZ

Because this recipe uses steeped fresh mint to create a very clean flavor, it is included with the herb recipes.

MAKES ABOUT 1 QUART

2 cups whole milk

1 cup heavy whipping cream

$1/2$ cup granulated sugar, divided

$1/4$ cup nonfat dry milk powder

$1/4$ teaspoon kosher salt

$1/2$ cup chopped fresh mint leaves

3 large egg yolks

$1/4$ to $1/2$ teaspoon pure mint extract or mint oil

$3/4$ cup finely chopped bittersweet chocolate

Combine the milk, cream, $1/4$ cup sugar, milk powder, and salt in a medium saucepan, and stir well to dissolve the milk powder. Bring the mixture just to a simmer over medium heat, stirring occasionally.

Stir in the chopped mint. Cover the pan and remove from the heat. Allow the mixture to steep for 30 minutes, then strain the mixture through a fine sieve, pressing with the back of a spoon to extract as much liquid as possible.

Beat the egg yolks, remaining $1/4$ cup sugar, and mint extract in a mixing bowl with a whisk until thick and light yellow in color. Slowly beat about one-third of the hot cream mixture into the eggs so they are gradually warmed up, and then return the contents of the mixing bowl to the saucepan. Place the pan over medium-low heat and stir constantly, reaching all parts of the bottom of the pan, until the mixture reaches about 170°F on an instant-read thermometer; at this point it begins to emit steam, thickens slightly, and coats the back of a spoon. This takes 3 to 6 minutes. Do not allow the mixture to boil or the eggs will scramble. Strain the custard through a fine sieve, if desired.

Transfer the hot liquid to a storage container and press a sheet of plastic wrap directly onto the surface of the mixture to prevent a skin from forming. Refrigerate the mixture uncovered until it is completely chilled (below 40°F), or quick-cool it according to the method on page 14.

Stir the chopped chocolate into the chilled custard and freeze in an ice cream maker according to the manufacturer's instructions. Serve immediately for a soft ice cream, or transfer the mixture to an airtight storage container and freeze until hard. Allow the ice cream to sit at room temperature for 15 minutes before serving if frozen solid.

DULCE DE LECHE GELATO

ADAPTED FROM GIOVANNA GELATO, NEWTON, MA

Dulce de leche means "sweet milk" in Spanish; this variation on caramel is popular throughout Latin America. Simmering a can of sweetened condensed milk in a saucepan of water makes it easy to make.

MAKES ABOUT 1 QUART

1 (14-ounce) can sweetened condensed whole milk

3 cups whole milk, divided

2 tablespoons nonfat dry milk powder

2 tablespoons cornstarch

Pinch of kosher salt

$3/4$ teaspoon pure vanilla extract

Take the label off the unopened can of sweetened condensed milk, and cover the can with water in a saucepan. Bring to a boil over high heat, then reduce the heat to medium and simmer the can for 2 hours. Make sure to add water to keep the can covered at all times. Remove the can from the water, and when cool enough to handle, open and scrape the contents into a saucepan.

Add $2\frac{1}{2}$ cups of the milk to the pan, and whisk well. Cook over medium heat, stirring frequently, until the mixture begins to steam; watch it carefully and make sure it does not come to a boil.

While the mixture heats, combine the remaining milk, milk powder, cornstarch, salt, and vanilla in a small bowl, and stir until smooth and both of the powders have dissolved.

Add the cornstarch mixture to the pan, and bring to a boil over low heat, stirring constantly. Whisk the mixture until smooth, and simmer the mixture over very low heat, stirring constantly, for 2 minutes, or until thickened. If the mixture is lumpy, strain it through a sieve.

Transfer the hot liquid to a storage container and press a sheet of plastic wrap directly onto the surface of the mixture to prevent a skin from forming. Refrigerate the mixture uncovered until it is completely chilled (below 40°F), or quick-cool it according to the method on page 14.

Freeze the mixture in an ice cream maker according to the manufacturer's instructions. Serve immediately for a soft gelato, or transfer the mixture to an airtight storage container and freeze until hard. Allow the gelato to sit at room temperature for 15 minutes before serving if frozen solid.

PINK PEPPERMINT ICE CREAM

ADAPTED FROM McCONNELL'S,
SANTA BARBARA, CA

Here's what Christmas should be about! It's bright pink with big pieces of crunchy peppermint candy. Top it with Hot Fudge Sauce (page 210) for a richer treat.

MAKES ABOUT 1 QUART

$1\frac{1}{4}$ cups heavy whipping cream

$\frac{3}{4}$ cup whole milk

1 cup crushed red and white peppermint hard candies or candy canes

$\frac{1}{2}$ cup granulated sugar, divided

$\frac{1}{4}$ cup nonfat dry milk powder

$\frac{1}{8}$ teaspoon kosher salt

3 large egg yolks

$\frac{1}{4}$ to $\frac{1}{2}$ teaspoon pure mint extract or mint oil

$\frac{1}{8}$ teaspoon pure vanilla extract

Combine the cream, milk, $\frac{1}{2}$ cup crushed candy, $\frac{1}{4}$ cup sugar, milk powder, and salt in a medium saucepan, and stir well to dissolve the milk powder. Bring the mixture just to a simmer, stirring occasionally.

Beat the egg yolks, remaining $\frac{1}{4}$ cup sugar, mint extract, and vanilla extract in a mixing bowl with a whisk until thick and light yellow in color. Slowly beat about one-third of the hot cream mixture into the eggs so they are gradually warmed up, and then return the contents of the mixing bowl to the saucepan. Place the pan over medium-low heat and stir constantly, reaching all parts of the bottom of the pan, until the mixture reaches about 170°F on an instant-read thermometer; at this point it begins to emit steam, thickens slightly, and coats the back of a spoon. This takes 3 to 6 minutes. Do not allow the mixture to boil or the eggs will scramble. Strain the custard through a fine sieve, if desired.

Transfer the hot liquid to a storage container and press a sheet of plastic wrap directly onto the surface of the mixture to prevent a skin from forming. Refrigerate the mixture uncovered until it is completely chilled (below 40°F), or quick-cool it according to the method on page 14.

Stir the remaining crushed candy into the chilled custard and freeze in an ice cream maker according to the manufacturer's instructions. Serve immediately for a soft ice cream, or transfer the mixture to an airtight storage container and freeze until hard. Allow the ice cream to sit at room temperature for 15 minutes before serving if frozen solid.

BLACK LICORICE ICE CREAM

ADAPTED FROM DOOR COUNTY
ICE CREAM FACTORY,
SISTER BAY, WI

Black licorice ice cream, with a decidedly anise flavor, is only made in the Midwest, and it's one of the favorites in Door County. It is, however, hard to match with a sauce. It's best on its own.

MAKES ABOUT 1 QUART

$2\frac{1}{2}$ cups heavy whipping cream, divided

10 (1-inch) black licorice candies

$\frac{1}{2}$ cup firmly granulated sugar

$\frac{1}{4}$ cup light corn syrup

2 tablespoons Pernod or other anise-flavored liqueur

$\frac{1}{8}$ teaspoon kosher salt

$\frac{1}{2}$ cup whole milk

$\frac{1}{4}$ cup nonfat dry milk powder

$\frac{1}{4}$ teaspoon pure vanilla extract

Combine $\frac{1}{2}$ cup of the cream and the candies in a food processor fitted with the steel blade or in a blender, and purée until smooth. Scrape the mixture into a saucepan.

Add the remaining cream, sugar, corn syrup, Pernod, and salt to the pan. Cook over medium heat, stirring frequently, until the mixture begins to steam; watch it carefully and make sure it does not come to a boil.

While the mixture heats, combine the milk, milk powder, and vanilla extract in a small bowl, and stir until smooth. Add the mixture to the pan, and bring to a boil over low heat, stirring constantly. Whisk the mixture until smooth, and simmer the mixture over very low heat, stirring constantly, for 2 minutes, or until thickened.

Transfer the hot liquid to a storage container and press a sheet of plastic wrap directly onto the surface of the mixture to prevent a skin from forming. Refrigerate the mixture uncovered until it is completely chilled (below 40°F), or quick-cool it according to the method on page 14.

Freeze the mixture in an ice cream maker according to the manufacturer's instructions. Serve immediately for a soft ice cream, or transfer the mixture to an airtight storage container and freeze until hard. Allow the ice cream to sit at room temperature for 15 minutes before serving if frozen solid.

Door County Ice Cream Factory, Sister Bay, WI

TODD FRISONI'S FAMILY BOUGHT A SUMMER HOME IN SISTER BAY, A VILLAGE IN Wisconsin's Door County, in 1988. The Illinois native was then only ten years old, and could have hardly imagined that in less than two decades it would be his home, and he would be owner of Door County Ice Cream.

Door County has been referred to many times as the "Cape Cod of the Midwest." This small peninsula sticking into the Great Lakes was a dangerous passage still dotted with old shipwrecks, and because of the hazards of the water French explorers called it *Portes des Morts Passage*, or "Door to the Way of Death." And like Cape Cod on the Atlantic coast, this is a vacation haven.

Frisoni began working at Door County Ice Cream Factory before his senior year at the University of Wisconsin at Madison in 1994. Six years later he bought the company, and is now raising his family in Door County year-round, although the shop is only open in the summer.

Door County Ice Cream is known to make one of the best versions of a Midwestern classic—Black Licorice Ice Cream (page 194). Frisoni recalls a gentleman from Kansas who was visiting Green Bay, far to the south of Sister Bay. He filled a cooler with black licorice ice cream only. But one of Frisoni's personal favorites is the Pumpkin Pie Ice Cream (page 205) because of its creamy consistency and use of aromatic spices.

DESERT HONEY FROZEN YOGURT

ADAPTED FROM SWEET REPUBLIC, SCOTTSDALE, AZ

There's a magical tartness to this yogurt that balances so well with the sweetness of the honey. This is a fantastic topping for fruit salad.

MAKES ABOUT 1 QUART

$^1/_2$ cup nonfat dry milk powder

$^1/_2$ cup skim milk

$^1/_2$ cup honey (Sweet Republic makes it with desert blossom)

$^1/_4$ cup granulated sugar

$^1/_4$ teaspoon kosher salt

3 cups plain Greek-style whole milk yogurt, such as Fage

$^1/_2$ teaspoon pure vanilla extract

Combine the milk powder, skim milk, honey, sugar, and salt in a small saucepan and whisk well to dissolve the milk powder. Place the pan over medium heat and cook, stirring frequently, until the sugar dissolves. Pour the mixture into a mixing bowl, and whisk in the yogurt and vanilla.

Transfer the mixture to a storage container and press a sheet of plastic wrap directly onto the surface of the mixture to prevent a skin from forming. Refrigerate the mixture uncovered until it is completely chilled (below 40°F), or quick-cool it according to the method on page 14.

Freeze the mixture in an ice cream maker according to the manufacturer's instructions. Serve immediately for a soft frozen yogurt, or transfer the mixture to an airtight storage container and freeze until hard. Allow the frozen yogurt to sit at room temperature for 15 minutes before serving if frozen solid.

ROQUEFORT CHEESE ICE CREAM with DATE SWIRL

ADAPTED FROM SWEET
REPUBLIC, SCOTTSDALE, AZ

Serving a sweet Sauternes wine with Roquefort blue cheese is a classic pairing because the sweetness of the wine balances the saltiness and pungency of the cheese. This sophisticated ice cream incorporates a similar pairing of flavors.

MAKES ABOUT 1 QUART

2 cups whole milk

1 cup heavy whipping cream

$1/2$ cup granulated sugar, divided

$1/4$ cup nonfat
dry milk powder

$1/4$ teaspoon kosher salt

3 large egg yolks

3 ounces Roquefort or other
blue-veined cheese, crumbled

6 to 8 dried dates,
pitted and chopped

Combine the milk, cream, $1/4$ cup sugar, milk powder, and salt in a medium saucepan, and stir well to dissolve the milk powder. Bring the mixture just to a simmer over medium heat, stirring occasionally.

Beat the eggs yolks and remaining $1/4$ cup sugar with a whisk until thick and light yellow in color. Slowly beat about one-third of the hot cream mixture into the eggs so they are gradually warmed up, and then return the contents of the mixing bowl to the saucepan. Place the pan over medium-low heat and stir constantly, reaching all parts of the bottom of the pan, until the mixture reaches about 170°F on an instant-read thermometer; at this point it begins to emit steam, thickens slightly, and coats the back of a spoon. This takes 3 to 6 minutes. Do not allow the mixture to boil. Remove from the heat and strain through a fine sieve.

Remove $1/2$ cup of the custard, and set aside. Add the cheese to the remaining custard and whisk well.

Transfer the hot liquid to a storage container and press a sheet of plastic wrap directly onto the surface of the mixture to prevent a skin from forming. Refrigerate the mixture uncovered until it is completely chilled (below 40°F), or quick-cool it according to the method on page 14.

Combine the dates and reserved custard in a food processor or a blender. Purée until smooth, and refrigerate.

Freeze the chilled custard in an ice cream maker according to the manufacturer's instructions. To make the swirl, transfer one-sixth of the soft ice cream to an airtight container. Top it with a few spoonfuls of the reserved date purée, and then repeat until all the ice cream and date purée are layered.

Serve immediately for a soft ice cream, or freeze until hard. Allow the ice cream to sit at room temperature for 15 minutes before serving if frozen solid.

GREEN TEA ICE CREAM

ADAPTED FROM BASSETT'S,
PHILADELPHIA, PA

*Powdered green tea gives
this subtly flavored ice cream a
brilliant green color. Made from
a very high-quality tea, matcha
is frequently too bitter for Western
palates, but in ice cream it's balanced by both sugar and dairy.
This is a wonderful way to
end an Asian meal.*

MAKES ABOUT 1 QUART

$1^1/_4$ cups heavy whipping cream

$1^1/_4$ cups whole milk, divided

$^1/_2$ cup granulated sugar

$^1/_4$ cup light corn syrup

3 tablespoons powdered
Japanese green tea (matcha)

$^1/_8$ teaspoon kosher salt

3 tablespoons nonfat
dry milk powder

2 tablespoons cornstarch

$^1/_2$ teaspoon pure vanilla extract

Combine the cream, $^1/_2$ cup milk, sugar, corn syrup, green tea, and salt in a saucepan. Cook over medium heat, stirring frequently, until the mixture begins to steam; watch it carefully and make sure it does not come to a boil.

While the mixture heats, combine the remaining milk, milk powder, cornstarch, and vanilla extract in a small bowl, and stir until smooth and both of the powders have dissolved.

Add the cornstarch mixture to the pan, and bring to a boil over low heat, stirring constantly. Whisk the mixture until smooth, and simmer the mixture over very low heat, stirring constantly, for 2 minutes, or until thickened. If the mixture is lumpy, strain it through a sieve.

Transfer the hot liquid to a storage container and press a sheet of plastic wrap directly onto the surface of the mixture to prevent a skin from forming. Refrigerate the mixture uncovered until it is completely chilled (below 40°F), or quick-cool it according to the method on page 14.

Freeze the mixture in an ice cream maker according to the manufacturer's instructions. Serve immediately for a soft ice cream, or transfer the mixture to an airtight storage container and freeze until hard. Allow the ice cream to sit at room temperature for 15 minutes before serving if frozen solid.

GINGER ICE CREAM

ADAPTED FROM MITCHELL'S,
SAN FRANCISCO, CA

Made with lots of fresh ginger steeped in the cream, this is a flavorful ice cream that serves as a wonderful finale to any spicy meal.

MAKES ABOUT 1 QUART

1 cup heavy whipping cream

$^3/_4$ cup whole milk, divided

$^1/_3$ cup grated fresh ginger

$^1/_4$ cup granulated sugar

$^1/_4$ cup light corn syrup

$^1/_2$ teaspoon ground ginger

$^1/_8$ teaspoon kosher salt

2 tablespoons cornstarch

2 tablespoons nonfat dry milk powder

$^1/_4$ teaspoon pure vanilla extract

Combine the cream, $^1/_2$ cup milk, ginger, sugar, corn syrup, ground ginger, and salt in a saucepan. Cook over medium heat, stirring frequently, until the mixture reaches a simmer. Cover the pan and remove from the heat. Allow the mixture to steep for 30 minutes, then strain the mixture through a fine sieve, pressing with the back of a spoon to extract as much liquid as possible. Return the mixture to the pan.

While the mixture steeps, combine the remaining milk, cornstarch, milk powder, and vanilla extract in a small bowl, and stir until smooth and both of the powders have dissolved.

Add the cornstarch mixture to the pan, and bring to a boil over low heat, stirring constantly. Whisk the mixture until smooth, and simmer the mixture over very low heat, stirring constantly, for 2 minutes, or until thickened. If the mixture is lumpy, strain it through a sieve.

Transfer the hot liquid to a storage container and press a sheet of plastic wrap directly onto the surface of the mixture to prevent a skin from forming. Refrigerate the mixture uncovered until it is completely chilled (below 40°F), or quick-cool it according to the method on page 14.

Freeze the mixture in an ice cream maker according to the manufacturer's instructions. Serve immediately for a soft ice cream, or transfer the mixture to an airtight storage container and freeze until hard. Allow the ice cream to sit at room temperature for 15 minutes before serving if frozen solid.

GINGER CREAM ICE CREAM

ADAPTED FROM BOULDER ICE
CREAM COMPANY, BOULDER, CO

*The ginger flavor in this ice cream
is very subtle, and it's almost an
aftertaste. It makes this a wonderful
ice cream to top hearty desserts like
pumpkin pie, or any baked good
made with warm spices.*

MAKES ABOUT 1 QUART

1¾ cups heavy whipping cream

¾ cup whole milk

½ cup granulated sugar, divided

2 tablespoons nonfat
dry milk powder

2 tablespoons grated fresh ginger

⅛ teaspoon kosher salt

2 large eggs

1 large egg yolk

2 teaspoons freshly
squeezed lemon juice

¼ teaspoon pure vanilla extract

Combine the cream, milk, ¼ cup sugar, milk powder, ginger, and salt in a medium saucepan, and stir well to dissolve the milk powder. Bring the mixture just to a simmer, stirring occasionally.

Cover the pan and remove from the heat. Allow the mixture to steep for 30 minutes, then strain the mixture through a fine sieve, pressing with the back of a spoon to extract as much liquid as possible. Return the mixture to the pan.

Beat the eggs, egg yolk, remaining ¼ cup sugar, lemon juice, and vanilla extract in a mixing bowl with a whisk until thick and light yellow in color. Slowly beat about one-third of the hot cream mixture into the eggs so they are gradually warmed up, and then return the contents of the mixing bowl to the saucepan. Place the pan over medium-low heat, and stir constantly, reaching all parts of the bottom of the pan, until the mixture reaches about 170°F on an instant-read thermometer; at this point it begins to emit steam, thickens slightly, and coats the back of a spoon. This takes 3 to 6 minutes. Do not allow the mixture to boil or the eggs will scramble. Strain the custard through a fine sieve, if desired.

Transfer the hot liquid to a storage container and press a sheet of plastic wrap directly onto the surface of the mixture to prevent a skin from forming. Refrigerate the mixture uncovered until it is completely chilled (below 40°F), or quick-cool it according to the method on page 14.

Freeze the mixture in an ice cream maker according to the manufacturer's instructions. Serve immediately for a soft ice cream, or transfer the mixture to an airtight storage container and freeze until hard. Allow the ice cream to sit at room temperature for 15 minutes before serving if frozen solid.

VIETNAMESE CINNAMON GELATO

ADAPTED FROM COLD FUSION
GELATO, NEWPORT, RI

Vietnamese cinnamon, available by mail order if not at your supermarket, is the spiciest and most aromatic of the species, and it creates a magical flavor when juxtaposed with the creaminess of this gelato.

MAKES ABOUT 1 QUART

2$\frac{1}{2}$ cups whole milk, divided

$\frac{3}{4}$ cup heavy whipping cream

$\frac{1}{2}$ cup granulated sugar

$\frac{1}{4}$ cup light corn syrup

1 to 1$\frac{1}{2}$ teaspoons ground Vietnamese cinnamon

$\frac{1}{8}$ teaspoon kosher salt

2 tablespoons nonfat dry milk powder

2 tablespoons cornstarch

$\frac{1}{4}$ teaspoon pure vanilla extract

Combine 2 cups of the milk, cream, sugar, corn syrup, cinnamon, and salt in a saucepan. Cook over medium heat, stirring frequently, until the mixture begins to steam; watch it carefully and make sure it does not come to a boil.

While the mixture heats, combine the remaining milk, milk powder, cornstarch, and vanilla extract in a small bowl, and stir until smooth and both of the powders have dissolved.

Add the cornstarch mixture to the pan, and bring to a boil over low heat, stirring constantly. Whisk the mixture until smooth, and simmer the mixture over very low heat, stirring constantly, for 2 minutes, or until thickened. If the mixture is lumpy, strain it through a sieve.

Transfer the hot liquid to a storage container and press a sheet of plastic wrap directly onto the surface of the mixture to prevent a skin from forming. Refrigerate the mixture uncovered until it is completely chilled (below 40°F), or quick-cool it according to the method on page 14.

Freeze the mixture in an ice cream maker according to the manufacturer's instructions. Serve immediately for a soft gelato, or transfer the mixture to an airtight storage container and freeze until hard. Allow the gelato to sit at room temperature for 15 minutes before serving if frozen solid.

AVOCADO JALAPEÑO ICE CREAM

ADAPTED FROM SWEET REPUBLIC, SCOTTSDALE, AZ

Avocados are so inherently creamy that churning them into ice cream is a natural! This slightly sweet frosty treat delivers some heat from the peppers as a finish. Serve a dollop in a bowl of chilled gazpacho.

MAKES ABOUT 1 QUART

1 cup whole milk

$^1/_2$ cup heavy whipping cream

2 tablespoons nonfat
dry milk powder

1 teaspoon kosher salt

3 large egg yolks

3 tablespoons granulated sugar

2 ripe avocados, peeled and diced

$^1/_3$ cup plain whole
milk yogurt, preferably
Greek-style, such as Fage

2 tablespoons freshly
squeezed lime juice

1 to 2 jalapeño peppers, seeds
and ribs removed, finely chopped

Combine the milk, cream, milk powder, and salt in a medium saucepan, and stir well to dissolve the milk powder. Bring the mixture just to a simmer, stirring occasionally.

Beat the eggs yolks and sugar in a mixing bowl with a whisk until thick and light yellow in color. Slowly beat about one-third of the hot cream mixture into the eggs so they are gradually warmed up, and then return the contents of the mixing bowl to the saucepan. Place the pan over medium-low heat and stir constantly, reaching all parts of the bottom of the pan, until the mixture reaches about 170°F on an instant-read thermometer; at this point it begins to emit steam, thickens slightly, and coats the back of a spoon. This takes 3 to 6 minutes. Do not allow the mixture to boil or the eggs will scramble. Strain the custard through a fine sieve, if desired.

Transfer the hot liquid to a storage container and press a sheet of plastic wrap directly onto the surface of the mixture to prevent a skin from forming. Refrigerate the mixture uncovered until it is completely chilled (below 40°F), or quick-cool it according to the method on page 14.

Combine 1 cup of the chilled custard with the avocados, yogurt, and lime juice in a food processor fitted with the steel blade or in a blender. Purée until smooth; transfer to a mixing bowl. Stir the remaining custard and chopped jalapeño into the avocado purée.

Freeze the mixture in an ice cream maker according to the manufacturer's instructions. Serve immediately for a soft ice cream, or transfer the mixture to an airtight storage container and freeze until hard. Allow the ice cream to sit at room temperature for 15 minutes before serving if frozen solid.

CARROT CAKE ICE CREAM with CREAM CHEESE SWIRL

ADAPTED FROM MOOMERS,
TRAVERSE CITY, MI

It's clearly too much trouble to make a whole carrot cake to have a bit left to fold into a creamy ice cream with subtle spicing, but if you have a carrot cake or can buy a slice, this is a really great treat.

MAKES ABOUT 1 QUART

Ice Cream
$1^1/_2$ cups whole milk, divided
$3/_4$ cup heavy whipping cream
$1/_4$ cup granulated sugar
$1/_4$ cup light corn syrup
$1/_4$ teaspoon ground cinnamon
$1/_8$ teaspoon freshly grated nutmeg
$1/_8$ teaspoon kosher salt
3 tablespoons nonfat
dry milk powder
$1^1/_2$ tablespoons cornstarch
$1/_4$ teaspoon pure vanilla extract
$2/_3$ cup chopped carrot cake

Swirl
1 (3-ounce) package cream
cheese, at room temperature
$2/_3$ cup confectioners' sugar
$1/_4$ teaspoon pure vanilla extract

For the ice cream: Combine $3/_4$ cup of the milk, cream, milk, sugar, corn syrup, cinnamon, nutmeg, and salt in a saucepan. Cook over medium heat, stirring frequently, until the mixture begins to steam; watch it carefully and make sure it does not come to a boil.

While the mixture heats, combine the remaining milk, milk powder, cornstarch, and vanilla extract in a small bowl, and stir until smooth.

Add the cornstarch mixture to the pan, and bring to a boil over low heat, stirring constantly. Whisk until smooth, and simmer the mixture for 2 minutes, or until thickened. If the mixture is lumpy, strain it through a sieve.

Transfer the hot liquid to a storage container and press a sheet of plastic wrap directly onto the surface of the mixture to prevent a skin from forming. Refrigerate the mixture uncovered until it is completely chilled (below 40°F), or quick-cool it according to the method on page 14.

While the custard chills, prepare the swirl: Combine the cream cheese, confectioners' sugar, and vanilla extract in a mixing bowl. Beat at low speed with an electric mixer to combine. Increase the speed to medium and beat for 2 minutes, or until light and fluffy. Set aside.

Freeze the custard in an ice cream maker according to the manufacturer's instructions. Fold in the carrot cake pieces.

To make the swirl, transfer one-sixth of the ice cream to an airtight container. Top it with a few spoonfuls of the cream cheese mixture, and then repeat until all the ice cream and cream cheese mixture is layered. When serving the ice cream, dig into the container vertically so each serving contains some of the swirl.

Serve immediately for a soft ice cream, or freeze until hard. Allow the ice cream to sit at room temperature for 15 minutes before serving if frozen solid.

PUMPKIN PIE ICE CREAM

ADAPTED FROM DOOR
COUNTY ICE CREAM FACTORY,
SISTER BAY, WI

*Here's a natural for a fall
or winter dinner, and it can
successfully be made with canned
pumpkin, which speeds up its
preparation. Try it topped with
Marshmallow Sauce (page 215).*

MAKES ABOUT 1 QUART

2 1/2 cups heavy whipping cream

3/4 cup canned pure pumpkin
(not pumpkin pie filling)

1/2 cup firmly packed dark
brown sugar

1/4 cup light corn syrup

1/2 teaspoon ground cinnamon

1/4 teaspoon ground ginger

1/8 teaspoon kosher salt

1/2 cup whole milk

1/4 cup nonfat
dry milk powder

1/4 teaspoon pure vanilla extract

Combine the cream, pumpkin, brown sugar, corn syrup, cinnamon, ginger, and salt in a saucepan. Whisk until smooth.

Cook over medium heat, stirring frequently, until the mixture begins to steam; watch it carefully and make sure it does not come to a boil.

While the mixture heats, combine the milk, milk powder, and vanilla extract in a small bowl, and stir until smooth. Add the mixture to the pan, and bring to a boil over low heat, stirring constantly. Whisk the mixture until smooth, and simmer the mixture over very low heat, stirring constantly, for 2 minutes, or until thickened.

Transfer the hot liquid to a storage container and press a sheet of plastic wrap directly into the surface of the mixture to prevent a skin from forming. Refrigerate the mixture uncovered until it is completely chilled (below 40°F), or quick-cool it according to the method on page 14.

Freeze the mixture in an ice cream maker according to the manufacturer's instructions. Serve immediately for a soft ice cream, or transfer the mixture to an airtight storage container and freeze until hard. Allow the ice cream to sit at room temperature for 15 minutes before serving if frozen solid.

Variations: Add 2 to 3 tablespoons of rum or bourbon to the custard, and fold 1/2 to 3/4 cup chopped toasted walnuts into the churned ice cream.

SABAYON GELATO

ADAPTED FROM
MORA ICED CREAMERY,
BAINBRIDGE ISLAND, WA

Sabayon is an egg-thickened custard that fits with both French and Italian food. This subtle gelato is an elegant way to top fresh fruit, or it can be topped with some Strawberry Sauce (page 216).

MAKES ABOUT 1 QUART

$1/2$ cup Marsala wine

$1/2$ cup granulated sugar, divided

$1^3/_4$ cups heavy whipping cream

1 cup whole milk

$1/4$ cup light corn syrup

2 tablespoons nonfat
dry milk powder

Pinch of kosher salt

6 large egg yolks

$1/2$ teaspoon pure vanilla extract

Combine the Marsala and $1/4$ cup sugar in a saucepan, and bring to a boil over medium heat, stirring occasionally. Simmer the mixture until reduced by half.

Add the cream, milk, corn syrup, and nonfat milk powder, and salt to the saucepan. Cook over medium heat, stirring frequently, until the mixture begins to steam; watch it carefully and make sure it does not come to a boil.

Beat the egg yolks, remaining $1/4$ cup sugar, and vanilla extract in a mixing bowl with a whisk until thick and light yellow in color. Slowly beat about one-third of the hot cream mixture into the eggs so they are gradually warmed up, and then return the contents of the mixing bowl to the saucepan. Place the pan over medium-low heat and stir constantly, reaching all parts of the bottom of the pan, until the mixture reaches about 170°F on an instant-read thermometer; at this point it begins to emit steam, thickens slightly, and coats the back of a spoon. This takes 3 to 6 minutes. Do not allow the mixture to boil or the eggs will scramble. Strain the custard through a fine sieve, if desired.

Transfer the hot liquid to a storage container and press a sheet of plastic wrap directly onto the surface of the mixture to prevent a skin from forming. Refrigerate the mixture uncovered until it is completely chilled (below 40°F), or quick-cool it according to the method on page 14.

Freeze the mixture in an ice cream maker according to the manufacturer's instructions. Serve immediately for a soft gelato, or transfer the mixture to an airtight storage container and freeze until hard. Allow the gelato to sit at room temperature for 15 minutes before serving if frozen solid.

TIRAMISÙ ICE CREAM

ADAPTED FROM BONNIE BRAE,
DENVER, CO

*All the necessary components
of this legendary dessert
are represented—from the
cocoa and coffee to bits of
ladyfinger cookies.*

MAKES ABOUT 1 QUART

$^3/_4$ cup whole milk, divided

1 (3-ounce) package cream cheese,
at room temperature

$^1/_4$ cup light corn syrup

1 cup heavy whipping cream

$^1/_3$ cup granulated sugar

3 tablespoons Marsala wine

2 teaspoons unsweetened
cocoa powder

1 teaspoon instant
espresso powder

$^1/_8$ teaspoon kosher salt

$^1/_8$ teaspoon ground cinnamon

2 tablespoons nonfat
dry milk powder

2 tablespoons cornstarch

$^1/_4$ teaspoon pure vanilla extract

6 to 8 ladyfingers

$^1/_4$ cup strong brewed
coffee, chilled

Combine $^1/_2$ cup of the milk, cream cheese, and corn syrup in a food processor fitted with the steel blade or in a blender, and purée until smooth. Transfer the purée to a saucepan.

Add the cream, sugar, Marsala, cocoa, espresso powder, salt, and cinnamon to the saucepan, and stir well. Cook over medium heat, stirring frequently, until the mixture begins to steam; watch it carefully and make sure it does not come to a boil.

While the mixture heats, combine the remaining milk, milk powder, cornstarch, and vanilla extract in a small bowl, and stir until smooth and both of the powders have dissolved.

Add the cornstarch mixture to the pan, and bring to a boil over low heat, stirring constantly. Whisk the mixture until smooth, and simmer the mixture over very low heat, stirring constantly, for 2 minutes, or until thickened. If the mixture is lumpy, strain it through a sieve.

Transfer the hot liquid to a storage container and press a sheet of plastic wrap directly onto the surface of the mixture to prevent a skin from forming. Refrigerate the mixture uncovered until it is completely chilled (below 40°F), or quick-cool it according to the method on page 14.

While the custard chills, break the ladyfingers into $^3/_4$-inch pieces, and sprinkle with the coffee. Set aside.

Freeze the chilled custard in an ice cream maker according to the manufacturer's instructions. Transfer the soft ice cream to a chilled mixing bowl and fold in the cookie pieces. Serve immediately for a soft ice cream, or transfer the mixture to an airtight storage container and freeze until hard. Allow the ice cream to sit at room temperature for 15 minutes before serving if frozen solid.

10 Sauces and Celebrations

It's hard to improve on a bowl of ice cream or sorbet and a spoon as the perfect treat. But there are times when you may want to dress it up a little—for company or just for the fun of it. That's where the recipes in this chapter come in.

Once you discover how easy it is to make your own sauces, and how the quality is so far superior to those you can buy, you'll never reach for a jar from the supermarket shelves again. Also included are edible ice cream cups—including chocolate bowls—and cones, as well as ways to delight children of all ages with homemade ice cream sandwiches.

Rounding out the recipes are some airy angel food cakes that are wonderful to serve with sorbets for a light dessert, and use up lots of the leftover egg whites that you may be left with if making ice creams that call for only egg yolks.

HOT FUDGE SAUCE

Everyone should know how to make a great hot fudge sauce; it's so much better than anything you can buy and it's easy enough to make that you can always have it around. This is very intensely flavored from the combination of chocolate and cocoa.

MAKES ABOUT 2$\frac{1}{2}$ CUPS

10 ounces high-quality
bittersweet chocolate
1 cup heavy whipping cream
$\frac{1}{4}$ cup unsweetened cocoa powder
$\frac{1}{2}$ teaspoon pure vanilla extract
Pinch of kosher salt

Chop the chocolate into pieces no larger than a lima bean, and set aside.

Pour the cream into a saucepan, and place it over medium heat. Whisk in the cocoa powder, vanilla, and salt. Bring to a simmer, whisking frequently, until the mixture is smooth.

When the cream begins to simmer, remove the pan from the heat. Add the chocolate, cover the pan, and allow it to sit for 5 minutes; uncover and wisk well until the sauce is smooth. If lumps remain, place the sauce over low heat and continue to whisk until smooth.

Transfer the sauce to a container, and refrigerate for up to 1 week or freeze for up to 3 months. To serve, heat the sauce in the microwave on medium (50 percent) power for 30 second intervals, or until liquid and warm, stirring well between microwave times.

Variations: Add 2 tablespoons instant coffee powder to the pan along with the cocoa for a mocha sauce, or add 2 tablespoons of your favorite liquor or liqueur to the sauce.

HARD CHOCOLATE ICE CREAM COATING

This is a personal favorite because I love the contrast of the soft, creamy ice cream and crunchy, hard chocolate. While it's easy to spoon it over bowls of ice cream, for cones, try using a squeeze bottle to coat so that the ice cream scoops don't fall off.

MAKES 1 1/2 CUPS

1 (6-ounce) package high-quality chocolate chips
4 tablespoons (1/2 stick) unsalted butter, cut into small pieces
1/4 cup vegetable oil
Pinch of kosher salt

Combine the chocolate, butter, oil, and salt in a small saucepan, and cook over low heat, stirring frequently, until the chocolate and butter melt and the mixture is smooth.

Spoon while hot over ice cream, and reheat to a liquid consistency if the coating has cooled.

MAPLE WALNUT SAUCE

Maybe it's because I've lived a good part of my life in New England, but this combination of crunchy nuts with flavorful maple syrup never ceases to please me. It's wonderful over just about any ice cream or sorbet not flavored with fruit, and can be refrigerated for up to one week.

MAKES 1 1/2 CUPS

3 ounces walnuts, coarsely chopped
2/3 cup light corn syrup
2/3 cup pure maple syrup
1/4 cup granulated sugar
Pinch of kosher salt
1 teaspoon freshly squeezed lemon juice

Preheat the oven to 350°F. Line a baking sheet with heavy-duty aluminum foil.

Toast the nuts for 5 to 7 minutes, or until browned. Remove the nuts from the oven, and set aside.

Combine the corn syrup, maple syrup, sugar, salt, and 1/4 cup water in a saucepan, and bring to a boil over medium-high heat, stirring occasionally. Reduce the heat to medium-low, and simmer the sauce for 3 minutes.

Allow the sauce to reach room temperature, and then stir in the lemon juice and walnuts.

Variation: Add 1/4 teaspoon ground cinnamon or 1/4 teaspoon ground ginger to the sauce as it simmers.

CARAMEL SAUCE

Caramel is simply sugar and water cooked to a high temperature, and once that's done just add some butter and cream: then you've got caramel sauce.

MAKES ABOUT $1^1/_2$ CUPS

$1^1/_2$ cups granulated sugar
$^1/_4$ teaspoon kosher salt
4 tablespoons ($^1/_2$ stick) unsalted butter, cut into small pieces
1 cup heavy whipping cream
1 teaspoon pure vanilla extract

Combine the sugar, salt, and 1 cup of water in a saucepan, and bring to a boil over medium-high heat. Swirl the pan by the handle but do not stir. Raise the heat to high, and allow syrup to cook until it reaches a walnut brown color, swirling the pot by the handle frequently.

Remove the pan from the heat, and stir in the butter and cream with a long-handled spoon; the mixture will bubble furiously at first. Return the pan to low heat and stir until any lumps are melted and the sauce is smooth. Stir in the vanilla. Serve hot, room temperature, or cold.

Variation: Reduce the vanilla to $^1/_2$ teaspoon and add 2 tablespoons of brandy, rum, or a liqueur to the sauce.

Tip: Cleaning the Pan

The easiest way to clean a pan in which you've caramelized sugar is to fill the pan with water and place it on the stove. Stir as the water comes to a boil and the pan will be virtually clean.

BUTTERSCOTCH SAUCE

The real difference between butterscotch and caramel is the type of sugar that's cooked; it's light brown sugar for butterscotch.

MAKES $1^1/_2$ CUPS

1 cup firmly packed light brown sugar
$^1/_4$ cup light corn syrup
4 tablespoons ($^1/_2$ stick) unsalted butter, cut into small pieces
$^1/_4$ teaspoon kosher salt
$^1/_2$ cup heavy whipping cream
$1^1/_2$ teaspoons pure vanilla extract

Combine the brown sugar, corn syrup, butter, and salt in a small saucepan. Bring to a boil over medium heat, stirring occasionally. Raise the heat to high, and boil the syrup for 4 to 5 minutes, or until it reaches the hard-ball stage and the temperature registers 280°F on a candy thermometer.

Remove the pan from the heat and stir in the cream and vanilla with a long-handled spoon; the mixture will bubble furiously at first. Return the pan to low heat and stir until any lumps are melted and the sauce is smooth. Serve the sauce warm or at room temperature.

Variation: Reduce the vanilla to $^1/_2$ teaspoon and add 2 to 3 tablespoons Scotch whiskey to the sauce.

MARSHMALLOW SAUCE

Here's a soda fountain favorite that goes back more than a century. It's similar to an Italian meringue frosting for cakes, and is to die for on any chocolate ice cream.

MAKES 1½ CUPS

¾ cup light corn syrup
½ cup granulated sugar
¾ teaspoon pure vanilla extract
2 large egg whites,
at room temperature
¼ teaspoon cream of tartar
Pinch of kosher salt
½ teaspoon pure vanilla extract

Combine the corn syrup, sugar, vanilla, and ¼ cup water in a saucepan and stir well. Cook over high heat, swirling the pan by its handle, until the mixture comes to a boil. Cook for 4 to 5 minutes, or until the syrup reaches the soft-ball stage and the temperature registers 240°F on a candy thermometer.

While the syrup boils, place the egg whites in a grease-free mixing bowl and beat at medium speed with an electric mixer until frothy. Add cream of tartar and salt, increase the speed to high, and beat until stiff peaks form.

Pour the hot syrup into the meringue very slowly with the mixer set on medium speed, and continue beating several minutes until mixture holds it shape. Beat in the vanilla. Transfer the sauce to a container and refrigerate until cold.

Note: The egg whites in this recipe may not be fully cooked. If salmonella is a problem in your area, you can use powdered egg whites.

LEMON CURD

Lemon curd is a classic English sauce that dates to the nineteenth century, and it's very special on frozen fruit treats such as Raspberry Sherbet (page 127) or Blood Orange Sorbet (page 114). You can refrigerate it for up to five days.

MAKES 1^1/$_2$ CUPS

2 large eggs
^{2}/$_3$ cup granulated sugar
^{1}/$_2$ cup freshly squeezed lemon juice
1 tablespoon grated lemon zest
^{1}/$_4$ teaspoon kosher salt
6 tablespoons (^{3}/$_4$ stick) unsalted butter, cut into small pieces

Combine the eggs and sugar in a saucepan, and whisk well until thick and lemon colored. Whisk in the lemon juice, lemon zest, and salt. Stir in the butter.

Place the saucepan over medium-low heat, and cook, stirring frequently, for 10 minutes, or until the curd is thick and small bubbles begin to appear on the surface.

Transfer the curd to a container and press a sheet of plastic wrap directly onto the surface to keep a skin from forming. Cool to room temperature and then refrigerate, tightly covered.

Variation: Substitute lime juice and lime zest for the lemon juice and lemon zest.

STRAWBERRY SAUCE

While a strawberry sauce can be as simple as fresh strawberries tossed with sugar, I like this slightly cooked sauce as an ice cream topping. The sauce is best eaten the day it's made, but it can be refrigerated for up to two days.

MAKES 2 CUPS

^{1}/$_4$ to ^{1}/$_2$ cup granulated sugar, depending on the sweetness of the berries
2 tablespoons cornstarch
Pinch of kosher salt
^{1}/$_4$ cup freshly squeezed orange juice
1 pound fresh strawberries, rinsed, hulled, and sliced if large

Combine the sugar, cornstarch, salt, and orange juice in a small cup, and stir well to dissolve the cornstarch.

Place the strawberries in a saucepan along with ^{1}/$_2$ cup water, and bring to a boil over medium-high heat, stirring occasionally. Add the cornstarch mixture and cook, stirring frequently, for 3 minutes, or until the mixture thickens. Remove the sauce from the heat, and cool to room temperature.

Variations: You can substitute fresh blueberries, raspberries, or any other berry for the strawberries. You can also substitute a few tablespoons of a fruit liqueur such as Chambord or Grand Marnier for some of the water.

ALMOND MACAROON ICE CREAM SANDWICHES

Chewy meringue cookies go exceptionally well with traditional gelato flavors like Chocolate Hazelnut (page 52) and Amaretto (page 171). They're studded with pine nuts that toast as they bake. You can keep the cookies for up to 4 days at room temperature in an airtight container.

MAKES 8 TO 12 SANDWICHES

1 (8-ounce) can almond paste

$1^{1}/_{4}$ cups granulated sugar

2 large egg whites

$^{3}/_{4}$ cup pine nuts

1 pint ice cream, softened

Preheat the oven to 325°F. Grease 2 baking sheets.

Break the almond paste into small pieces and place in a mixing bowl along with the sugar. Beat at medium speed with an electric mixer until combined. Increase the speed to high, add the egg whites, and beat until mixture is light and fluffy.

Drop heaping tablespoon portions of the batter onto the prepared baking sheets, spacing them 2 inches apart. Pat the pine nuts into the tops of the cookies.

Bake the cookies for 18 to 20 minutes, or until lightly browned. Place the baking sheets on wire racks, and cool the cookies completely.

Match up the cookies into pairs, and fill them with a few tablespoons of the ice cream. Wrap the sandwiches individually in plastic wrap, and freeze until firm.

BROWN SUGAR ICE CREAM SANDWICHES

The cookie part is similar to the matrix of chocolate chip cookies. They can be filled with just about any ice cream, and kids of all ages love them.

MAKES 8 TO 12 SANDWICHES

4 ounces (1 stick) unsalted butter, at room temperature

$^2/_3$ cup firmly packed dark brown sugar

1 large egg

$^1/_2$ teaspoon pure vanilla extract

$^1/_2$ teaspoon baking soda

$^1/_4$ teaspoon kosher salt

$1^1/_4$ cups all-purpose flour

$1^1/_2$ pints ice cream, softened

Preheat the oven to 375°F. Grease 2 baking sheets.

Combine the butter and brown sugar in a mixing bowl, and beat at medium speed with an electric mixer until blended. Increase the speed to high, and beat for 2 minutes, or until light and fluffy.

Add the egg and vanilla, and beat again for 1 minute, or until light and fluffy. Beat in the baking soda and salt. Beat in the flour until just blended.

Form the dough into 16 to 24 balls and arrange them on the baking sheets, at least $1^1/_2$ inches apart. Bake the cookies for 9 to 12 minutes for chewy cookies and 13 to 15 minutes for crispy cookies; the baking time will depend on the number of cookies made.

Allow the cookies to cool for 5 minutes on the baking sheets, and then transfer them to a wire rack to cool completely.

To form the sandwiches, place a dollop of ice cream on the flat side of 1 cookie and top it with the flat side of a second cookie. Wrap the sandwiches individually in plastic wrap, and freeze for at least 1 hour to chill. The sandwiches can be frozen for up to 4 days.

Variations: Add $^1/_2$ cup finely chopped nuts or steel-cuts oats to the dough.

CHOCOLATE LACE COOKIE ICE CREAM SANDWICHES

Called florentines in classic French cooking, these crispy, lacy cookies swirled with chocolate are a wonderful textural contrast to the creamy ice cream they enclose.

MAKES 12 TO 16 SANDWICHES

5 ounces slivered blanched almonds (about 1 cup)

$1/2$ cup granulated sugar

3 tablespoons unsalted butter

2 tablespoons light corn syrup

2 tablespoons heavy whipping cream

$1/2$ teaspoon pure vanilla extract

$1/4$ teaspoon kosher salt

1 tablespoon all-purpose flour

$1/4$ pound high-quality bittersweet chocolate, finely chopped

1 pint ice cream, softened

Combine the almonds and sugar in a food processor fitted with the steel blade, and pulse until finely ground.

Combine the almond mixture, butter, corn syrup, cream, vanilla, and salt in small saucepan and cook over medium heat for 2 minutes, or until the butter is melted and the sugar is dissolved.

Remove the pan from the heat and stir in the flour. Transfer the batter to a shallow bowl, and refrigerate until cold.

Preheat the oven to 350°F. Line 2 baking sheets with parchment paper.

Roll heaping 1 teaspoon portions of the batter into balls and arrange them 3 inches apart on the prepared baking sheets. Gently flatten the balls with the bottom of a glass or your fingertips.

Bake the cookies for 7 to 9 minutes, or until golden. Transfer the cookies with the parchment to a wire rack to cool completely.

Place the chocolate in a microwave-safe bowl and heat in the microwave on medium (50 percent) power for 45 seconds. Stir and repeat at 15 second intervals until the chocolate is melted and smooth.

Lightly brush the undersides of the cookies with chocolate and refrigerate them, chocolate-side up, for 3 to 5 minutes or until the chocolate is hard. Place some ice cream on the chocolate side of a cookie and top it with another cookie, chocolate-side down. Wrap the cookies in plastic wrap and freeze for 20 to 30 minutes.

CRÊPE CUPS

These delicate cups are baked in muffin tins to crisp them enough to hold the ice cream. While they should be baked on the day they're served, the crêpes themselves can be made up to three months in advance and frozen, with the pancakes separated by sheets of waxed paper.

MAKES 12 TO 16 CUPS

2 large eggs
$3/4$ cup whole milk
1 cup all-purpose flour
3 tablespoons unsalted butter, melted, plus additional for frying the crêpes
Pinch of kosher salt

Combine the eggs, milk, flour, butter, salt, and $1/2$ cup water in a blender. Blend at medium speed for 10 seconds. Refrigerate the batter for at least 1 hour, and up to 24 hours.

Preheat the oven to 350°F. Grease 12-cup muffin pans. Place a long sheet of plastic wrap on the counter near the stove.

Heat a small skillet or 8-inch crêpe pan over medium heat. Wipe the inside of the pan with a paper towel dipped in melted butter.

Pour $1/4$ cup of the batter into the center of the pan, and swirl the pan by its handle to spread the batter evenly. Cook the pancake for 30 seconds, and flip the pancake. Cook for 10 to 12 seconds, or until the pancake is browned on the second side.

Transfer the pancake to the plastic wrap, and repeat until all the crêpe batter is used, or you've made the number of pancakes you want.

Fold the crêpes in half, and form them into cups in the prepared muffin pan. Bake the cups for 10 to 12 minutes, or until slightly crispy. Allow to cool to room temperature before filling with ice cream.

Variation: Rather than turning the crêpes into cups, just place a portion of ice cream in the center, fold over the sides and roll it like an eggroll.

Tip: Letting Batters "Rest"

When making a crêpe, a step you really don't want to skip is allowing the batter to rest in the refrigerator. What this time accomplishes is to let the bubbles created by the blending to escape from the batter, which makes your crêpes far less likely to tear while you're cooking them.

TUILE COOKIE CUPS

These are delicately flavored crispy cookies that mold very easily when they emerge from the oven; they've been used for almost origami-like shapes by French pastry chefs for decades. Once cooled, they can be kept at room temperature for up to 2 days.

MAKES 6 TO 8

$\frac{1}{2}$ cup all-purpose flour

$\frac{1}{2}$ cup confectioners' sugar

$\frac{1}{4}$ teaspoon kosher salt

5 large egg whites

4 tablespoons ($\frac{1}{2}$ stick) unsalted butter, melted

$\frac{1}{2}$ teaspoon pure vanilla extract

Combine the flour, sugar, and salt in a mixing bowl, and stir well. Add the egg whites, butter, and vanilla extract, and whisk until smooth. Allow the batter to rest for 1 hour.

Preheat the oven to 350°F. Line 2 baking sheets with parchment paper and draw 5-inch circles on the parchment paper. Invert 6 to 8 (4-ounce) glass or plastic bowls onto the counter.

Drop heaping tablespoons of the batter into the center of the drawn circles, and spread the batter with the back of a spoon to fill the circles. Bake the cookies for 5 to 8 minutes, or until golden brown.

Remove the cookies one at a time from the baking sheet, and drape each one over a glass or bowl to make a cup shape. Work quickly, and if the cookies become too brittle to drape, place the baking sheet back in the oven for 10 to 15 seconds to soften them again. Cool the cups completely on the glasses or bowls.

Variation: To make tuile cones, create and bake the cookies as detailed above, but when they come out of the oven roll them into a cone shape, holding the bottom of the point together for a few seconds. Stand the cones in narrow-necked glasses to cool completely.

CHOCOLATE CUPS

We've all seen these in stores and they're outrageously expensive! These bowls made from pure chocolate hold ice cream, and can then be eaten as a finale. They're really easy to make if you follow these directions carefully. However, I don't suggest this as an activity to do with children because if the balloons pop—which is easy to do—you could have chocolate all over the kitchen. The cups can be refrigerated for up to a week.

MAKES 8 TO 10 CUPS

10 ounces high-quality bittersweet chocolate, finely chopped

8 or 10 small balloons

Vegetable oil spray

Line a baking sheet with parchment paper.

Place the chocolate in a metal mixing bowl, and set it over a pan of simmering water (do not allow the water to touch the bowl). Allow the chocolate to melt slowly, and stir it until smooth.

While the chocolate melts, blow up the balloons to the size you want your cups to be. You will only be dipping the bottom of the balloon into the chocolate, so use a bowl as your guide. Spray the bottoms of the balloons with vegetable oil spray.

Remove the bowl of melted chocolate from the pan, and dip the greased bottoms of the balloons in the chocolate. Stand the balloons on the prepared baking sheet, chocolate side down.

Refrigerate the dipped balloons for 30 minutes, or until totally set.

Pinch the top of the balloon between your fingers just under the knot, and cut a small hole between where your fingers are holding the balloon and the knot.

Release the air *very gradually*; if the air is released too quickly, the bowls can break. Carefully peel the balloons out of the chocolate bowls.

PROFITEROLES

Profiteroles are just baby cream puffs that can be filled with ice cream and then topped with a sauce or a glaze of chocolate: the Hard Chocolate Ice Cream Coating works best (page 212). The dough is called pâte à choux in classic French cooking, and it's a useful dough to learn how to bake. These freeze very well; reheat them in a 350°F oven for 5 to 7 minutes, or until crisp.

MAKES ABOUT 3 DOZEN

6 tablespoons ($^3/_4$ stick)
unsalted butter

2 teaspoons granulated sugar

$^1/_2$ teaspoon kosher salt

$^1/_4$ teaspoon pure vanilla extract

$^3/_4$ cup all-purpose flour

5 large eggs, divided

1 to 1$^1/_2$ pints ice cream, softened

Hard Chocolate Ice Cream
Coating, page 212, warmed to
a spreadable consistency

Preheat the oven to 375°F. Grease two cookie sheets.

Combine the butter, sugar, salt, vanilla, and 1 cup of water in a saucepan, and bring to a boil over medium-high heat, stirring occasionally. Remove the pan from the heat, and add flour all at once. Using a wooden paddle or wide wooden spoon, beat the flour into the liquid until it is smooth.

Place the saucepan over high heat and beat mixture constantly for 1 to 2 minutes, or until it forms a mass that leaves the sides of the pan and begins to coat the bottom of the pan.

Transfer the mixture to a food processor fitted with the steel blade. Add 4 of the eggs, 1 at a time, beating well between each addition and scraping the sides of the work bowl between each addition; the egg should be totally incorporated into the dough before another one is added. (This can also be done by hand, but it takes a long time to beat it until the eggs are incorporated.)

Scrape the dough into a pastry bag fitted with a $^1/_2$-inch round nozzle. Pipe mounds 1-inch in diameter and $^1/_2$-inch high onto the baking sheets, allowing 2 inches between the puffs.

Beat the remaining egg with a pinch of salt, and brush only the tops of the dough mounds with a small pastry brush or rub gently with a finger dipped in the egg wash. (Be careful not to drip the egg wash onto the baking sheet or egg may prevent dough from puffing.)

Bake the puffs for 20 to 25 minutes, or until the puffs are golden brown and crusty to the touch. Remove the pans from the oven.

(continued)

Use the tip of a paring knife to cut a slit in the side of each puff to allow steam to escape. Turn off the oven, and place baked puffs back into the oven with the oven door ajar for 5 minutes. Remove the puffs, and transfer to a wire rack to cool.

To serve, split puffs with a serrated knife, and fill with ice cream. Brush each profiterole with some of the Hard Chocolate coating and allow to set for a few minutes in the freezer.

Note: The puffs can be made up to 1 day in advance and kept at room temperature in an airtight container. Fill with ice cream just before serving.

Variations: To make 12 large cream puffs: Make the mounds of dough 2$\frac{1}{2}$ inches wide and 1 inch high. Or pipe the dough into lines of the same dimensions for éclair shape. Bake at 425°F for 20 minutes, and then reduce the heat to 375°F and bake for an additional 10 to 15 minutes. Remove the pans from the oven, and split puffs using a serrated knife. Turn off the oven, and place baked puffs back into the oven with the oven door ajar for 10 minutes to finish crisping. Cool puffs in halves rather than whole, and pull out any dough from the center of the puffs that might be soggy.

To make 1 large cream puff ring (called a *Paris Breast* in classic French cooking): Flour the greased baking sheet, and draw a 10-inch circle on the baking sheet, using a pot lid or platter as a guide. Pipe two thick lines side by side, using the drawn , circle as a guide, and then nestle one line into the crevice between the two. Bake for 20 minutes at 425°F, and then 25 minutes at 350°F. Split the ring in half using a serrated knife, pull out the damp dough, and crisp as described above.

FRIED ICE CREAM BALLS

This isn't a spur of the moment dessert; the ice cream balls spend many hours freezing between steps, so it's best to start this recipe the day before you plan to fry the balls and serve them. However, they are always a hit, and are quite easy to make. The contrast between the crispy coating and chilly ice cream is fantastic. You can try them with the Caramel Sauce (page 213), or topped with any sauce in this chapter.

MAKES 4 TO 6 SERVINGS

1 quart ice cream, softened
3 large eggs
2 tablespoons granulated sugar
1 teaspoon pure vanilla extract
6 cups cornflakes (about 7 ounces)
4 cups vegetable oil for frying

Line a baking sheet with plastic wrap, and freeze the sheet for 10 minutes. Using an ice cream scoop, scoop out balls of the ice cream onto the chilled baking sheet; you should have 12 balls. Freeze the balls, covered with plastic wrap, for at least 3 hours, or until very hard.

Combine the eggs, sugar, and vanilla extract in a mixing bowl, and whisk well. Place the cornflakes in a food processor fitted with the steel blade, and chop very finely using on-and-off pulsing; this can also be done by placing cornflakes in a heavy resealable plastic bag and hitting the bag with the bottom of a heavy skillet. Place the crushed cornflakes in a shallow bowl.

One at a time, dip the ice cream balls into the egg mixture, allowing any excess to drip off, and roll them in the cornflake crumbs to coat well. Return the balls to the freezer, covered, and freeze for at least 1 hour and up to 4 hours. Reserve the remaining cornflakes, and refrigerate the remaining egg mixture. Repeat coating process, and freeze for a minimum of 4 hours after the second coating.

Heat the oil in a deep-sided saucepan or deep-fryer to a temperature of 375°F. Working in batches of 2 or 3 balls, fry the balls for 30 seconds or until golden. Remove the balls from the pan with a slotted spoon, and drain them on paper towels. Repeat with remaining balls, and serve immediately.

Variations: You can substitute crushed puffed rice cereal, cookie crumbs, or graham cracker crumbs for the cornflakes, and you can also add $1/2$ cup finely chopped nuts or shredded sweetened coconut to any of the crumb options.

BAKED ALASKA

No ice cream book would be complete without giving you the method—although it hardly counts as a complex recipe—for this classic meringue-covered dish of ice cream and cake. If you pack the freshly churned ice cream into the loaf pan as soon as it's made it saves a step in the recipe. The dish supposedly dates to the late nineteenth century, and was created at famed Delmonico's restaurant in New York to celebrate the purchase of the Alaska territory.

MAKES 8 TO 10 SERVINGS

$1^1/_2$ quarts ice cream or sorbet (either one flavor or a combination), softened

1 (1-pound) frozen pound cake, thawed, or homemade pound cake baked in a loaf pan

10 large egg whites

$^3/_4$ teaspoon cream of tartar

$^1/_4$ teaspoon kosher salt

$1^1/_4$ cups granulated sugar, preferably superfine

$^3/_4$ teaspoon pure vanilla extract

$^3/_4$ cup confectioners' sugar

Line a loaf pan with plastic wrap, and pack the loaf pan with the ice cream. Cover the top of the loaf pan with plastic wrap, and freeze for at least 4 hours, or until very firm.

While the ice cream chills, cut the pound cake into $^1/_2$-inch slices, and arrange the cake slices in rectangle measuring 11 inches long and 7 inches wide on an ovenproof platter or baking sheet lined with parchment paper.

Unmold the ice cream onto the center of the cake rectangle, and return it to the freezer. This can be done up to 1 day in advance.

Place the egg whites in a grease-free bowl and beat at medium speed with an electric mixer until frothy. Add the cream of tartar and salt, and continue beating, increasing the speed to high, until soft peaks form. Continue beating, adding the sugar 1 tablespoon at a time, until the meringue is glossy and stiff peaks form. With the mixer at the lowest speed, beat in the vanilla.

Cover the ice cream and cake layer completely with the meringue; it should be about $1^1/_2$ inches thick all around. Form swirls in the meringue with a thin spatula or the back of a spoon. Return the Baked Alaska to the freezer for 2 to 3 hours.

Preheat the oven to 500°F.

Sift the confectioners' sugar over the top of the meringue. Bake the dish for 3 to 4 minutes, or until the peaks are golden brown. Remove the cake from the oven, and allow it to soften for 5 minutes at room temperature before slicing.

Tip: Creating an Ice Cream Mosaic

Baked Alaska is stunning in and of itself, but if you want to add even more visual interest, use a pint of each of three ice creams which have different colors. Use an ice cream scoop, and pack the loaf pan with alternating balls of the three.

MERINGUE LAYER TORTE

When you're making ice cream, chances are you're going to have some egg whites around because so many of the recipes call for the yolks only. That's why creating a "cake" with meringue layers filled with ice cream is a great idea. It looks stunning when presented at the table, and the meringue creates a crispy contrast with the creamy ice cream.

MAKES 3 (9-INCH) LAYERS

4 large egg whites,
at room temperature

$1/4$ teaspoon cream of tartar

Pinch of kosher salt

1 cup granulated sugar

$1/2$ teaspoon pure vanilla extract

1 pint ice cream
(your favorite flavor), softened

Preheat the oven to 250°F. Line 2 baking sheets with parchment paper, and using a plate or cake pan as a guide, draw 3 (9-inch) circles on the sheets of parchment paper—two on one sheet and one on the other.

Place the egg whites in a grease-free mixing bowl and beat at medium speed with an electric mixer until frothy. Add the cream of tartar and salt, increase the speed to high, and beat until soft peaks form.

Add the sugar, 1 tablespoon at a time, and continue to beat until stiff peaks form and meringue is glossy.

Place equal portions of the meringue in the center of each circle, and spread the meringue evenly to fill the circles. Bake the layers for 1 hour, switching the position of the baking sheets in the oven after 30 minutes. The layers should be crisp and firm.

Turn off the oven, and cool the layers completely on the baking sheets in the oven. Remove the layers from the oven, and peel off the parchment paper.

To serve, line a cake plate with 2 overlapping sheets of waxed paper or plastic wrap. Place on layer on the plate, and gently spread with $1/2$ of the softened ice cream. Repeat with another layer and ice cream, ending with the third layer. Place the torte in the freezer for at least 1 hour to firm before serving.

Variation: Substitute firmly packed dark brown sugar for the granulated sugar and you'll have a more flavorful torte that is excellent with nut ice creams.

CITRUS ANGEL FOOD CAKE

The tangy flavors of orange and lemon complement the light, airy quality of angel food cake. You can make this cake a few days in advance and keep it at room temperature, lightly covered with plastic wrap.

MAKES 10 TO 12 SERVINGS

$^3/_4$ cup freshly squeezed orange juice

2 tablespoons grated orange zest

2 tablespoons grated lemon zest

$^3/_4$ cup cake flour

$^3/_4$ cup granulated sugar, divided

10 large egg whites, at room temperature

1 teaspoon cream of tartar

Pinch of kosher salt

Preheat the oven to 350°F. Rinse a tube pan and shake it over the sink to remove excess moisture, but do not wipe it dry. Set aside.

Combine the orange juice, orange zest, and lemon zest in a small heavy saucepan, and bring to a boil over medium heat. Reduce the heat to low, and cook until the mixture is reduced by three-fourths. Pour the reduction into a bowl, and refrigerate until cool.

Sift the flour with $^1/_4$ cup of the sugar, and set aside.

Place the egg whites in a grease-free mixing bowl and beat at medium speed with an electric mixer until frothy. Add the cream of tartar and salt, increase the speed to high, and beat until soft peaks form. Add the remaining sugar, 1 tablespoon at a time, and continue to beat until stiff peaks form and meringue is glossy.

Reduce the speed to low and beat in cooled orange juice mixture. Gently fold flour mixture into the meringue and scrape the batter into the tube pan.

Bake the cake in the center of the oven for 40 to 55 minutes, or until a cake tester or skewer comes out clean. Remove the cake from the oven and invert the cake onto the neck of a tall bottle for at least $1^1/_2$ hours, or until cool. Run a knife or spatula around the outside of the pan to loosen cake and invert cake onto a serving plate.

Variation: Substitute lime zest for the lemon zest.

Tips: Beating Egg Whites

Eggs should always be at room temperature when baking, because the whites will not increase in volume properly if they are chilled. A quick way to bring the temperature up is to place the eggs in a bowl of very hot tap water for 5 minutes before separating them.

CHOCOLATE ANGEL FOOD CAKE

Light and airy angel food cake takes very well to being flavored with cocoa powder; it delivers a lot of chocolate flavor with very few calories, too. You can make this cake a few days in advance and keep it at room temperature, lightly covered with plastic wrap.

MAKES 10 TO 12 SERVINGS

5 tablespoons unsweetened cocoa powder

$3/4$ cup cake flour

$3/4$ cup granulated sugar, divided

10 large egg whites, at room temperature

$3/4$ teaspoon cream of tartar

$1/4$ teaspoon kosher salt

1 teaspoon pure vanilla extract

Preheat the oven to 350°F. Rinse out a tube pan and shake it over the sink to remove excess moisture, but do not wipe it dry. Set aside.

Sift together the cocoa, flour, and $1/4$ cup of sugar. Set aside.

Place the egg whites in a grease-free bowl and beat at medium speed with an electric mixer until frothy. Add the cream of tartar and salt, and continue beating, increasing the speed to high, until soft peaks form. Continue beating, adding remaining sugar, 1 tablespoon at a time, until the meringue is glossy and forms stiff peaks. With the mixer at the lowest speed, beat in the vanilla. Gently fold the cocoa mixture into the meringue, being careful to avoid streaks of white meringue. Scrape the batter into the tube pan.

Bake the cake in the center of the oven for 40 to 55 minutes, or until a cake tester or skewer comes out clean. Remove the cake from the oven and invert the cake onto the neck of a tall bottle for at least $1\frac{1}{2}$ hours, or until cool. Run a knife or spatula around the outside of the pan to loosen cake and invert cake onto a serving plate.

Variation: For a mocha-flavored angel food cake, dissolve 1 tablespoon instant espresso powder in 2 tablespoons boiling water, and allow the mixture to cool to room temperature. Add it to the batter along with the vanilla.

FUDGE BROWNIES

Not only are these rich brownies delicious topped with ice cream but they are perfect for fold-ins. They also keep very well for up to 5 days in an airtight container.

MAKES ABOUT 1 DOZEN

4 ounces high-quality bittersweet chocolate, chopped

1 ounce unsweetened chocolate, chopped

6 tablespoons ($^3/_4$ stick) unsalted butter

$^2/_3$ cup granulated sugar

$^3/_4$ teaspoon pure vanilla extract

$^1/_4$ teaspoon kosher salt

2 large eggs

$^1/_2$ cup all-purpose flour plus extra for flouring the baking pan

$^1/_2$ cup semisweet chocolate chips

Preheat the oven to 350°F. Grease and flour an 8 x 8-inch baking pan.

Combine the bittersweet chocolate, unsweetened chocolate, butter, sugar, vanilla, and salt in a saucepan. Cook over low heat, stirring occasionally, until the chocolates are melted and the mixture is smooth. Set aside to cool for 15 minutes, or until the mixture is room temperature.

Whisk the eggs into the chocolate mixture, 1 at a time, beating well between the additions. Then fold in the flour and chocolate chips until just blended.

Spread the batter evenly in the prepared pan. Bake in the center of the oven for 25 to 30 minutes, or until a toothpick inserted in the center comes out with crumbs but not wet batter. Cool the pan completely on a wire rack before cutting and removing the brownies from the pan.

Variations: Substitute pure almond extract for the pure vanilla extract or add $^1/_2$ teaspoon ground cinnamon to the brownie batter.

Contributing Creameries

SCOOP WOULD NOT BE A BOOK WITHOUT THE COOPERATION OF THE PARTICI-
pating shops and creameries. Most of them ship their products, if you'd rather order them
than make them, or you can bring this list with you if you're traveling and make a visit to their
shops a vacation destination.

Those participants listed without an address sell their products through a variety of retail
outlets; go to their web sites for more information on an outlet nearest you.

Bassetts
45 North 12th Street
Reading Terminal Market
Philadelphia, PA 19107
215-925-4315
www.bassettsicecream.com

Blue Moon Sorbet
P.O. Box 874
Quechee, VT 05059
802-295-1165
www.bluemoonsorbet.com

Bonnie Brae Ice Cream
799 South University Boulevard
Denver, CO 80209
303-777-0808
www.bonniebraeicecream.com

Boulder Ice Cream
Boulder, CO
303-720-1105
www.bouldericecream.com

Ciao Bella
Florham Park, NJ
Eugene, OR
800-GELATO3
www.ciaobellagelato.com

Cold Fusion Gelato
389 Thames Street
Newport, RI 02840
401-849-6777
www.coldfusiongelato.com

Daily Scoop
230 County Road
Barrington, RI 02806
401-245-0100
446B Thames Street
Bristol, RI 02809
401-254-2223
www.dailyscoopicecream.com

**Door County
Ice Cream Factory**
11051 State Highway 42
Sister Bay, WI 54234
920-854-9693
www.doorcountyicecream.com

GaGa's
P.O. Box 6909
Warwick, RI 02887
401-921-1377
www.gonegaga.net

Giovanna Gelato
Newton, MA
617-320-4647
www.giovannigelato.com

Graeter's
Cincinnati, OH
513-721-3323
www.graeters.com

GS Gelato
1785 Fim Boulevard
Fort Walton Beach, FL 32547
850-243-5455
www.gsgelato.com

Herrell's Ice Cream
8 Old South Street
Northampton, MA 01060
413-586-9700
46L Gerard Street
Huntington, NY 11743
631-673-1100
1010 Mass MoCA Way
North Adams, MA 01247
413-346-3859
www.herrells.com

LáLoo's
Petaluma, CA 94952
707-763-1491
www.laloos.com

Lappert's
869 Bridgeway
Sausalito, CA 94804
415-331-3035

130 North Palm Canyon Drive
Palm Springs, CA 92262
760-778-3700
223 Ohio Avenue
Richmond, CA 94804
510-231-2340
12265 Scripps Poway Parkway
San Diego, CA 92064
858-577-0015
www.lapperts.com

McConnell's
201 West Mission Street
Santa Barbara, CA 93105
805-569 2323
3241 East Main Street
Ventura, CA 93003
805-650-6410
www.mcconnells.com

Mitchell's
688 San Jose Avenue
San Francisco, CA 94110
415-648-2300
www.mitchellsicecream.com

Moomers Ice Cream
7263 North Long Lake Road
Traverse City, MI 49684
231-941-4122
www.moomers.com

Mora Iced Creamery
139 Madrone Lane
Bainbridge Island, WA 98110
206-855-8822
www.moraicecream.com

Silver Moon Desserts
PO Box 320614
Los Gatos, CA 95032
877-778-8009
www.silvermoondesserts.com

Sweet Republic
9160 East Shea Boulevard
Scottsdale, AZ 85260
480-248-6979
www.sweetrepublic.com

Index